WHERE THE SOUTH WINDS BLOW
Ancient Evidence of Paleo South Americans

Where the South Winds Blow

Ancient Evidence of Paleo South Americans

Edited by Laura Miotti, Mónica Salemme, and Nora Flegenheimer

A Peopling of the Americas Publication
Robson Bonnichsen, General Editor
Ruth Gruhn, Series Editor

WHERE THE SOUTH WINDS BLOW
Ancient Evidence of Paleo South Americans

©2003 Center for the Study of the First Americans. All rights reserved. No part of this book may be reproduced, projected, stored in a retrieval system, or transmitted, for whatever purpose, in any form or by any means, whether electronic, mechanical, magnetic, photographic, laser, or otherwise, without the prior written permission of the Center for the Study of the First Americans, Department of Anthropology, Texas A&M University, College Station, TX 77843-4352.

Design and typesetting by C & C Wordsmiths, Blue Hill, Maine.
Printed in the United States of America by Thomson-Shore, Inc., Dexter, MI.

Distributed by the Texas A&M University Press, College Station, TX.
This book is printed on 100% acid-free paper.

ISBN: 1-55889-455-1

COVER

Left, Selk'nam (hunter-gatherer natives from northern Tierra del Fuego), dressed in guanaco leather, looking to the Atlantic Ocean.

Below, a group of Selk'nam (most of them women), gathering molluscs along the Atlantic coast in northern Tierra del Fuego.

Photos from Charles Furlong Wellington, 1907. Permission to reprint photos granted by the Archives of Museo del Fin del Mundo, Ushuaia, Tierra del Fuego, Argentina.

THE CENTER FOR THE STUDY OF THE FIRST AMERICANS

The Center for the Study of the First Americans (CSFA) is a unit of the Department of Anthropology, College of Liberal Arts, Texas A&M University, College Station, TX. The CSFA was established in July 1981 by a seed grant from Mr. William Bingham's Trust for Charity (renamed Bingham Trust). The mission of the Center is the promotion of interdisciplinary scholarly dialogue and the stimulation of public interest on the subject of the peopling of the Americas through research, education, and outreach. Toward these goals:

- CSFA designs and implements programs of study and research involving the physical, biological, and cultural sciences;
- CSFA provides leadership and coordination to scholars world wide on the subject of the First Americans;
- CSFA promotes an open dialogue between government, business, avocation archaeologists, and the Native American community on the preservation of cultural and biological resources, and other issues relating to the study of the First Americans.
- CSFA disseminates the product of this synergism through education programs reaching a broad range of groups, including school children, the general public, and international scholars.

The mission of the Center's staff and Advisory Board is to further the goals and programs of the CSFA, which has a membership of over 1400 individuals. The Center's office and research laboratories are located in the Anthropology Building on the TAMU campus. The Center's faculty and associates include:

Robson Bonnichsen	Director and General Editor e-mail: rbonnichsen@tamu.edu
Michael R. Waters	Associate Director and Editor, *CRP* e-mail: mwaters@tamu.edu
Laurie Lind	Office Manager e-mail: csfa@tamu.edu
James M. Chandler	Editor, Mammoth Trumpet e-mail: wordsmiths@acadia.net
Ruth Gruhn	Series Editor of CSFA books

The Center's Peopling of the Americas publication program focuses on the earliest Americans and their environments. The Center solicits high-quality original manuscripts in English. For information write to: Robson Bonnichsen, Center for the Study of the First Americans, Department of Anthropology, Texas A&M University, 4352 TAMU, College Station, TX 77843-4352. *Current Research in the Pleistocene* presents note-length articles about current research in the interdisciplinary field of Quaternary studies as it relates to the peopling of the Americas. The submission deadline is February 15 of each calendar year. In addition, the Center publishes a quarterly newsmagazine, the *Mammoth Trumpet,* written for both general and professional audiences. Subscription to the *Mammoth Trumpet* is by membership in the Center. Contact Laurie Lind, CSFA, Department of Anthropology, Texas A&M University, 4352 TAMU, College Station, TX 77843-4352; phone (979) 845-4046, fax (979) 845-4070 for more information about the CSFA, its programs, and membership in the Center. The CSFA is a non-profit organization that depends on gifts and grants for its support. To learn about America's earliest cultural and biological heritage, join the Center today. For more information check our Web site:

www.CenterFirstAmericans.com to become **www.CenterFirstAmericans.org**

Contents

From the Guest Editors of *Where the South Winds Blow*

Laura Miotti[1], Mónica Salemme[2], and Nora Flegenheimer[3]

This volume focuses on South American archaeological evidence during the late-Pleistocene/ early-Holocene transition and is dedicated to the First Americans. The subject was addressed just a few times in academic publications of several authors, such as *Estudios Atacameños 8* (Núñez and Meggers 1987); *Quaternary International* in volumes 49/50 (Eriksen and Straus 1998), and 53/54 (Zárate 1999), or of a single author (Dillehay 2000). Recently it has received attention in other media, such as the *Mammoth Trumpet* from the Center for the Study of the First Americans (Miotti and Salemme 2001). This is an excellent opportunity to present both new and previous findings and their impact in constructing alternative models about the peopling of the Americas. Solid arguments about South American archaeological evidence are useful in rethinking how and when the Americas were peopled.

South America is a continent of archaeological and paleoenvironmental particularities. It is marked by enormous contrasts—great regions covered by rain forest, wide and long rivers, high cordilleras, ample plains, and plateaus. This great environmental mosaic and the immediacy of the sea would have offered the first colonizers multiple migration routes, not all of them necessarily terrestrial. Such characteristics of the Southern Cone as the prevalence of maritime rather than continental conditions, smaller areas occupied by glaciers during the LGM (ca. 18,000 yr B.P.) compared with North America, and archaeological evidence persuade us that some previous models are simplistic and mechanical. Nowadays

We detect a happy shift, an emphasis on First Americans studies. The past 50 years have seen a

[1] Departmento de Arqueología, Facultad de Ciencias Naturales y Museo, Universidad Nacional de La Plata–CONICET. e-mail: miotti@netverk.com.ar

[2] Laboratorio de Geología del Cuaternario, CADIC–CONICET, and Universidad Nacional de la Patagonia, Ushuaia, Argentina. e-mail: labcuat@satlink.com

[3] CONICET—Area Arqueol. y Antrop., Museo Municipal de Ciencias Naturales de Necochea, C.C. 275, 7630 Necochea, Argentina. e-mail: noraf@necocheanet.com.ar

> disarray of information and scant of communication among groups of South American models. . . . Today more and more groups of archaeologists working in South America are demonstrating that the Clovis-First model does not seem to be the only way to explain the peopling of the Americas. Regional models presented by South American colleagues are a challenge for the near future (Miotti and Salemme, 2001: 18).

Greater complexity and variability of the early archaeological record than previously thought and the usefulness of testing a variety of possible interpretations have been evident for some time in South American studies (Miotti and Flegenheimer 1994:11). Recent interpretations about early peopling are not as monolithic as they used to be, and a trend is emerging towards a more open-minded approach to the subject (Miotti 1999; 2000; Politis 1999).

Most of the articles contained in this volume were presented at the international workshop of the International Union for Quaternary Research (INQUA), "The colonization of South America during Pleistocene/Holocene transition," held December 2000 at the National University of La Plata, Argentina; colleagues who were not able to attend that meeting were invited to present results of their investigations in this special issue. It is a unique opportunity to compile basic data (new sites, radiocarbon dating, stratigraphic profiles, artifacts, etc.) of research about early peopling all over South America. An additional consideration is that North American scientists find it hard to access much of the research carried out by South American scholars. Many of the available publications are written in Spanish or Portuguese and therefore are difficult for many North American colleagues to read. Moreover, the lack of first-hand knowledge of artifacts, sites, and of the archaeologists themselves makes it difficult to assess the importance and validity of the information. We believe the INQUA meeting and this publication are of great value in bringing together from both continents archaeologists working on the same subject.

The contributors come from almost all countries of South America, as well as from North America and France. All are currently involved in different research projects in the Southern Cone. Other colleagues, notably Robson Bonnichsen, Alan Bryan, Ruth Gruhn, Robert Kelly, and Augusto Cardich, although they have not contributed to this volume, nevertheless have supported this initiative in various ways, and at the INQUA meeting they shared with us their ideas on the peopling of South America during the Pleistocene/Holocene transition.

Figure 1 shows the location of sites discussed in this volume, as well as those mentioned in Miotti et al. (2000). Table 1 lists sites, countries, approximate chronologies, and authors.

Acknowledgment

We are deeply indebted to Ruth Gruhn and Robson Bonnichsen for encouraging us to prepare articles for this volume as a way to vouch for research carried out in South America.

References Cited

Dillehay, T. D.
2000 *The Settlement of the Americas. A New Prehistory*. Basic Books, New York.

Eriksen, B. V., and L. G. Straus (editors)
1998 As the World Warmed: Human Adaptations across the Pleistocene/Holocene Boundary. *Quaternary International* 49/50.

Miotti, L. L.
1999 Quandary: The Clovis Phenomenon, the First Americans, and the View from the Patagonia

Region. Paper presented at Clovis and Beyond Conference, Santa Fe, NM. In *Clovis and Beyond: New Perspectives in First Americans Studies*, The Center for the Study of the First Americans, in press.

2000 Migrar, Poblar, Colonizar: Tres Conceptos que Evocan las Imágenes de la Apropiación Humana del Nuevo Mundo. Presentación en 2da Reunión Internacional de Teoría Arqueológica en América del Sur. *Libro de Resúmenes*:120–122, Olavarría, Argentina.

Miotti, L., and N. Flegenheimer
1994 El Paleoindio y los Primeros Americanos: Introducción del Simposio. *Actas y Memorias del XI Congreso Nacional de Arqueología Argentina.* (Resúmenes expandidos) *Revista del Museo de Historia Natural de San Rafael.* T XIII (1–4):11-12.

Miotti, L., and M. Salemme
2001 Pleistocene Winds Blow from South America about the First Americans. *Mammoth Trumpet* 16 (2). Center for the Study of First Americans.

Miotti, L., M. Salemme, G. R. Cattáneo, and R. Paunero (editors)
2000 Book of Abstracts. *International Workshop "The Colonization of South America, during Pleistocene/Holocene Transition."* La Plata, Argentina.

Núñez, L., and B. Meggers (editors)
1987 *El Paleoindio al Sur de la Línea Ecuatorial.* Estudios Atacameños, 8. Special Volume. Universidad del Norte, San Pedro de Atacama, Chile.

Politis, G. G.
1999 La Estructura del Debate sobre el Poblamiento de América. *Boletín de Arqueología*, 14(2):25–51. Fundación de Investigaciones Arqueológicas Nacionales, Santa Fe de Bogotá, D.C., Colombia.

Zárate, M. A. (editor)
1999 The Pleistocene/Holocene Transition and Human Occupation in South America. *Quaternary International* 53/54.

Table 1. Site locations in Figure 1, radiocarbon ages, and authors of papers. Sites marked ● are discussed in this volume; sites marked △ were only presented at the December 2000 INQUA meeting at La Plata (Miotti et al. 2000).

Site in Figure 1	Country	Site, locality, or area	^{14}C dating (ka B.P.)	Author(s)
1 ●	Colombia	San Isidro and Peña Colorada	10–9	C. Gnecco
2 ●	Perú	Paiján	10.8–8.5	T. Dillehay, J. Rossen, P. Netherly, G. Maggard, and K. Stackelbeck
3 ●	Perú	Quebrada de los Burros	10–9	D. Lavallée
4 ●	Chile	Quereo—Los Vilos	12–11.7	D. Jackson S.
5 ●	Brazil	Santa Elina Cave	27–10.1	A. Vialou
6 ●	Uruguay	Pay Paso site 1	10–9.5	R. Suárez
7 △	Uruguay	Valisas, Cabo Polonio, and El Chuy	13–7	J. L. Mass
8 ●	Argentina	Cerro El Sombrero	10.7–10.2	N. Flegenheimer
9 ●	Argentina	Paso Otero 5	10.4–10.2	V. Holliday, G. Martínez, E. Johnson, and B. Buchanan
10 ●	Argentina	La Moderna	12.3–6.7	G. Politis, E. Johnson, M. Gutiérrez, and W. Hartwell
11 ●	Argentina	Tixi, El Abra, Burucuyá, and La Brava caves; Los Pinos Rockshelter; and Amalia 2 site	10.5–9.8	D. Mazzanti
12 ●	Argentina	Geoarchaeology Tandilia Range	10.5–9.8	G. Martínez and M. Osterrieth
13 ●	Argentina	Arroyo Malo 3	9.4	G. Neme and S. Diéguez
14 ●	Argentina	Agua de la Cueva	11–7.5	A. García
15 ●	Argentina	Cerro Tres Tetas and La María localities	11.5–10.2	R. Paunero
16 ●	Argentina	Piedra Museo	13–9.3	L. Miotti, M. Salemme, and J. Rabassa
16 △	Argentina	Piedra Museo—microfauna	10–9	U. Pardiñas
17 ●	Argentina	Piedra Museo	12.9–9.3	L. Miotti and R. Cattáneo
18 ●	Argentina	Cerro Casa de Piedra 7	9.7	T. Civalero and C. Aschero
19 ●	Argentina	Chorrillo Malo 2	9.7	N. Franco and L. Borrero
20 ●	Chile	Tres Arroyos	12.3–8.7	M. Massone
21 ●	Argentina-Brazil	Arroyo Seco and Lagoa Santa	12–8.5	G. Barrientos, H. Pucciarelli, G. Politis, I. Pérez, and M. Sardi
21 △	Argentina	Arroyo Seco 2		M. Salemme
22 ●	Argentina	Pollen analyses: PM y Los Toldos	12.9–7.4	A. Borromei
23 ●	Argentina	Pollen analyses: Agua de la Cueva, Co. La China and Los Toldos	12.6–8.5	M. Páez, M. Zárate, V. Mancini, and A. Prieto
24 ●	Chile	Monte Verde	12.5	M. Pino
25 △	Uruguay	Lithic quarries		N. Flegenheimer, C. Bayón, M. Valente, J. Baeza, and J. Femenías
26 △	Chile	Cueva Lago Sofía 1	11	A. Prieto
27 △	Chile	Baño Nuevo	9.2	F. Mena
28 △	Argentina	Alto Río Pinturas (north of Santa Cruz)	9.4–8	A. Aguerre
29 △	Argentina	Epullán Grande and Traful I caves	9.9–7.9	U. Pardiñas
30 △	Chile	Tagua Tagua	11.4	L. Núñez A.
31 △	Argentina	Gruta del Indio	11–8	H. Lagiglia
32 △	Argentina	Humaitá tradition sites	9–5	A. Rizzo
33 △	Brazil	Southern Brazil	14–11.5	A. Schmidz and A. Jacobus
34 △	Brazil	Pedra Furada	50–5	M. Faure, C. Guérin, and F. Parenti
35 △	Colombia	Middle Magdalena River	10.4–10	C. López, M. Cano, and J. Realpe
36 △	Venezuela	Taima Taima and Coro area	14–12	P. Moretti

Figure 1. Location of sites.

Agrilocalities during the Pleistocene/Holocene Transition in Northern South America

Cristóbal Gnecco

The undeniable existence of agriculture and village life in many parts of the Americas by 5000 yr B.P. obscures the fact that it was preceded by human management of vegetable and animal resources. However, recent research has produced a substantial body of information about the incidence of past human activity in neotropical forests and its significant impact on the relative abundance of resources; the effects of forest clearing and induced fire are especially relevant in this regard (e.g., Piperno 1990; Piperno et al. 1991). Evidence from tropical forests from southern Colombia suggests that human intervention and manipulation began during the late Pleistocene. Data obtained at San Isidro, a single-component preceramic site located in the valley of Popayán (Gnecco and Mora 1997), indicate anthropogenic disturbance of the surrounding forests by 10,000 yr B.P.; two standard ^{14}C determinations on charcoal from the archaeological deposit rendered the following dates: 9530 ± 100 yr B.P. (B-65877) and 10,050 ± 100 yr B.P. (B-65878). An additional AMS determination on a charred seed rendered 10,030 ± 60 yr B.P. (B-93275). A pollen sample associated with the preceramic deposit includes secondary vegetation, such as trees and herbaceous plants (Gramineae, Cyperaceae, and two pioneer species of open environments, *Plantago* and *Trema*), amidst a majority of mature, primary forest species. This indicates the existence at the site or in its surroundings of an open or partially open forest clearing during the time of human occupation. The prevalence of primary forest species, however, shows that the phenomenon recorded was not a complete clearing or deforestation but the creation of a space open enough to admit the growth of pioneer species. Although it is not possible to determine if this clearing was deliberately or accidentally produced, the existence of this space near an archaeological site is not coincidental. A circumstantial fact worth mentioning is the finding of a polished, beveled artifact in San Isidro (Figure 1A), although this particular tool lacks use-wear patterns or organic residues of any kind.

Universidad del Cauca, Colombia. e-mail: cgnecco@unicauca.edu.co

The analysis of pollen from San Isidro highlights another important issue, the association of current allopatric species. Although this can be explained by arguing that the vegetation surrounding the site at the time of its occupation around the Pleistocene/Holocene boundary has no modern analogs, it is also possible to say that the useful species from the lowlands represented in the pollen sample, especially *Virola,* may have been transported from their original habitat, and perhaps also cultivated. The nonnatural association of certain species, not necessarily cultigens, could indicate human manipulation of the environment.

We also have indirect evidence of anthropogenic impact on the ecosystems from San Isidro and Peña Roja (Gnecco and Mora 1997), a site in the middle Caquetá River with a preceramic component dated to about 10,000 calendar years ago: 9125 ± 250 yr B.P. (GX-17395); 9160 ± 90 yr B.P. (B-52963); and 9250 ± 140 yr B.P. (B-52964) (Cavelier et al. 1995; Gnecco and Mora 1997:687). The dominance (92 percent) of a still unidentified spherical fruit from San Isidro and of palm fruits from Peña Roja (more than 99 percent) could simply represent dietary preferences or natural abundance, as in the "islands of resources" reported for the Amazon by Posey (1984:117); but it may also indicate humanly induced concentration of palms and other edible plants and their seasonal exploitation by mobile parties. The contemporary ethnographical record of Amazonian groups (from hunter-gatherers to farmers) is helpful in this regard. Politis (1996), for instance, has shown that the mobility strategy of the Nukak promotes the concentration in and around abandoned camps of useful species, especially palms; these places, which Politis (1996) has called "wild orchards," are periodically visited and exploited. Likewise, Amazonian farmers plant and tend forest clearings that are apparently abandoned afterwards; however, they are not abandoned but left unattended to encourage colonization by useful species such as medicinal plants and perennial herbs with large roots and edible trunks, and for planting other economically useful plants (Piperno 1989:541; Posey 1983:244–246; 1984:114–117); Posey (1984, 1993) has called them forest fields and coined the term "nomad agriculture" (Posey 1983) to describe this particular efficient form of resource management and maximization. Creating forest clearings in tropical forests, episodic owing to natural phenomena and continuous owing to human agents, favored the proliferation of useful vegetable species and also of animals (cf. Cooke and Piperno 1993:30; Posey 1983, 1984); the exploitation of the additional animal biomass resulting from the human intervention of tropical forests has been called "garden hunting" by Linares (1976).

Although ethnobotanical research, especially in the Amazon, has shown that the difference between wild, semidomesticated, and fully domesticated plants and between natural and intervened forests is tenuous (cf. Harris 1989), it is still possible to determine the existence of cultigens by genetic changes fixed through cultural selection. In this regard the only probable evidence of cultigens in the Colombian tropical forests at the Pleistocene/Holocene boundary is (a) six charred seeds of the genus *Persea* found in San Isidro, the largest of which is 6 cm long (Figure 1C); although it may well be a wild specimen, it is more likely a cultivar of the species *Persea americana* given its size, larger than the average for wild populations (Smith 1966, 1969); (b) two charred seeds of the genus *Erythrina* from San Isidro, likely of the species *Erythrina edulis,* a cultivar extensively cultivated and eaten in the mountain forests and rain forests of northern South America (Figure 1D); (c) phytoliths of *Lagenaria siceraria* found in the preceramic component of Peña Roja; in this component, phytoliths of

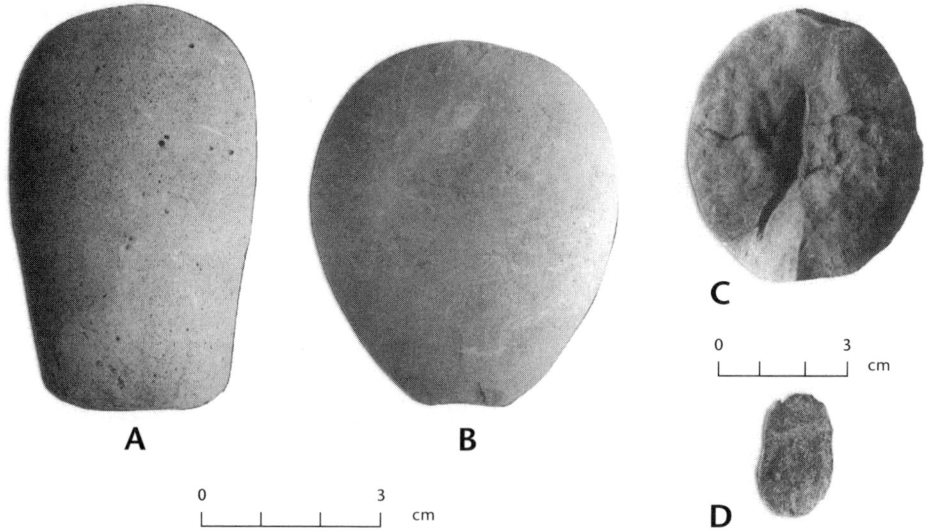

Figure 1. **A,** Polished, beveled artifact from San Isidro; **B,** phytoliths of the family *Marantacea* found in one of the edge-ground cobbles from San Isidro; **C,** charred seed of the genus *Persea* found in San Isidro; **D,** two charred seeds of the genus *Erythrina* from San Isidro.

an unidentified Cucurbitacea have also been found, although its status as a probable cultivar still has to be determined (I. Cavelier pers. comm.); (d) phytoliths of the family Marantacea found in one of the edge-ground cobbles from San Isidro (Figure 1B); it is likely they belong to the cultivar *Maranta arundinacea,* resulting from grinding the rhizomes of that plant with that tool (D. R. Piperno pers. comm.).

Thus, the hunter-gatherers of the Pleistocene/Holocene boundary were not only using but also managing and improving the productivity of forest resources. Hunter-gatherers from San Isidro were already impacting and altering the ecosystem with practices such as forest clearing, selective planting, and domestication. Rindos (1984:176) coined the concept "agrilocality" to describe specialized domestication and regular spatiotemporal patterns that anticipate the emergence and development of agroecology. These patterns, linked to territoriality, indicate restricted mobility and specialization of resource use; both factors are responsible for transforming the structure of most ecosystems. Recent archaeological and paleoethnobotanical evidence indicates those agrilocalities may have started as early as the late Pleistocene. This conjecture departs from the traditional view of early hunter-gatherers as simply users of resources, especially animal resources, whose impact on ecosystems was negligible. Yet, from the point of view of territoriality the emergence of agrilocalities appears alternatively as its consequence and as its cause: as its consequence because restricted mobility and intensified territoriality would have forced its adoption as a result of pressure on the resource base; as its cause because certain social practices, such as sectional competition, may have demanded strategies to exploit resources beyond their natural productivity, resulting in zonal settlements that made previous mobility patterns obsolete.

The stereotype of the mobile hunter argues against territoriality and its associated aspects (e.g., social competition and the emergence of alternative strategies of occupation) and against the suggestion that exploiting focal resources, as in the southern coast of Peru (Keefer et al. 1998; Sandweiss et al. 1998), and altering and manipulating vegetable and animal resources (as in San Isidro) may have occurred from the very beginning of colonization and occupation and not as an incidental result of the crisis of previous patterns. The possible existence of territoriality since the late Pleistocene is precluded by the model of the "nomadic" hunter-gatherer espoused by most archaeologists for about 30 years; a principal characteristic of such nomadism is the absence of territoriality, for if one of the best ways of dealing with variations in temporal and spatial distribution of resources is through mobility, then territoriality militates against survival (cf. Kelly 1995:14–15).

All these considerations suggest that the early peopling of northern South America can be conceived more as a slow process of colonization and occupation than as a rapid and directional migration. This interpretation resolves three problematic areas involved in nomadic, directional, and demic theories of early peopling: the stylistic diversity of late-Pleistocene assemblages from northern South America, the existence of territoriality and agrilocality, and the existence of pre-Clovis occupations.

References Cited

Cavelier, I., C. Rodriguez, S. Mora, L. F. Herrera, and G. Morcote
1995 No Sólo de Caza Vive el Hombre: Ocupación del Bosque Amazónico, Holoceno Temprano. In *Ambito y Ocupaciones Tempranas de la America Tropical,* edited by I. Cavelier and S. Mora, pp 27–44. Instituto Colombiano de Antropología-Fundación Erigaie, Bogotá, Colombia.

Cooke, R., and D. R. Piperno
1993 Native American Adaptations to the Tropical Forests of Central and South America before the European Colonization. In *Tropical Forests, People and Food,* edited by C. M. Hladik, A. Hladik, O. Linares, H. Pagezy, A. Semple, and M. Hadley, pp. 25–36. UNESCO-Parthenon, Paris.

Gnecco, C., and S. Mora
1997 Late Pleistocene/Early Holocene Tropical Forest Occupations at San Isidro and Peña Roja, Colombia. *Antiquity* 71:683–690.

Harris, D. H.
1989 An Evolutionary Continuum of People-plant Interaction. In *Foraging and Farming: The Evolution of Plant Exploitation,* edited by D. H. Harris and G. Hillman, pp. 11–24. Unwin Hyman, London.

Keefer, D. K., S. D. de France, M. E. Moseley, J. B. Richardson, D. R. Satterlee, and A. Day-Lewis
1998 Early Maritime Economy and El Niño Events at Quebrada Tacahuay. *Science* 281:1833–1835.

Kelly, R. L.
1995 *The Foraging Spectrum: Diversity in Hunter-Gatherer Lifeways.* Smithsonian Institution Press, Washington, D.C.

Linares, O. F.
1976 Garden Hunting in the American Tropics. *Human Ecology* 4:331–349.

Piperno, D. R.
1989 Non-affluent Foragers: Resource Availability, Seasonal Shortages, and the Emergence of Agriculture in Panamanian Tropical Forests. In *Foraging and Farming: The Evolution of Plant Exploitation*, edited by D. R. Harris and G. C. Hillman, pp. 538–554. Unwin Hyman, London.

1990 Aboriginal Agriculture and Land Usage in the Amazon Basin. *Journal of Archaeological Science* 17:665–677.

Piperno, D. R., M. B. Bush, and P. A. Colinvaux
1991 Paleoecological Perspectives on Human Adaptation in Central Panama. I. The Pleistocene. *Geoarchaeology* 6:202–226.

Politis, G.
1996 Moving to Produce: Nukak Mobility and Settlement Patterns in Amazonia. *World Archaeology* 27:492–511.

Posey, D. A.
1983 Indigenous Ecological Knowledge and Development of the Amazon. In *The Dilemma of Amazonian Development,* edited by E. Moran, pp. 225–257. Westview Press, Boulder, CO.
1984 A Preliminary Report on Diversified Management of Tropical Forests by the Kayapó Indians of the Brazilian Amazon. *Advances in Economic Botany* 1:112–126.
1993 The Importance of Semi-domesticated Species in Post-contact Amazonia: Effects of the Kayapó Indians on the Dispersal of Flora and Fauna. In *Tropical Forests, People and Food,* edited by C. M. Hladik, A. Hladik, O. Linares, H. Pagezy, A. Semple, and M. Hadley, pp. 63–71. UNESCO-Parthenon, Paris.

Rindos, D.
1984 *The Origins of Agriculture: An Evolutionary Perspective.* Academic Press, San Diego, CA.

Sandweiss, D. H., H. McInnis, R. L. Burger, A. Cano, B. Ojeda, R. Paredes, M. C. Sandweiss, and M. D. Glascock
1998 Quebrada Jaguay: Early South American Maritime Adaptations. *Science* 281:1830–1832.

Smith, C. E.
1966 Archaeological Evidence for Selection in Avocado. *Economic Botany* 20:169–175.
1969 Additional Notes on Pre-conquest Avocados in Mexico. *Economic Botany* 23:135–140.

New Archaeological Evidence of the Paiján Culture on the North Coast of Peru and Its Importance in Early Andean Prehistory

Tom D. Dillehay[1], Jack Rossen[2], Patricia J. Netherly[3], Greg Maggard[4], and Kary Lynn Stackelbeck[5]

We consider the development of increasingly localized, but not necessarily larger, social groups a critical aspect of the late-Pleistocene/early-Holocene transition on the north coast of Peru and especially of the development of early signatures of Andean civilization during the mid-Holocene period (ca. 7500–5000 yr B.P.). Most hunter-gatherer models of advanced cultural development propose linkages among demographic factors, subsistence strategies, and integrative mechanisms that seasonally aggregate larger groups of people in more permanent localities, a form of territorialism, and lead to institutionalized social and economic foundations of more complex hunters and gatherers, such as alliance and exchange networks (Dillehay 2000; Quilter 1991). Yet highly localized territorial circumscription in widely diverse and spatially compressed resource-rich habitats also may have stimulated the development of more stable and formalized ties between local aggregated groups. We believe these kinds of developments are suggested on the north coast of Peru for the hunter-gatherer Paiján culture (ca. 10,800–8500 yr B.P.) by the exploitation of a wide range of highly local resources, an increase of plant gathering, increased aggregation and permanency of groups, and the construction of permanent domestic structures. Claude Chauchat (1975), who has worked extensively on the Paiján culture in the Cupisnique Valley, believes the Paiján culture is associ-

[1] Dept. of Anthropology, University of Kentucky, Lexington, Kentucky. e-mail: dilleha@uky.edu

[2] Dept. of Anthropology, Ithaca College, New York. e-mail: jrossen@ithaca.edu

[3] Dept. of Anthropology, University of Kentucky, Lexington, Kentucky. e-mail: tahuin1@aol.com

[4] Dept. of Anthropology, University of Kentucky, Lexington, Kentucky. e-mail: GMaggard@aol.com

[5] Dept. of Anthropology, University of Kentucky, Lexington, Kentucky. e-mail: kstacke@aol.com

ated with a littoral and coastal-plain adaptation after the disappearance of megafauna in the period between 13,000 and 11,000 yr B.P.

In particular, the north coast valleys of Zaña, Jequetepeque, Cupisnique, Chicama, and Moche are rich in sites of both the unifacial (e.g., Richardson 1978) and the needle-nosed and stemmed Paiján cultures. Numerous early Paiján sites are located in or near several resource-rich habitats, including the vegetated lower hills of the Andes and the coastline, both usually within a 2-hour walk. Most sites yield a wide range of lithic artifacts, which suggests they were the camping places of small groups (Chauchat et al. 1998). The Paiján industry shows wide variation in the lithic types found at different sites, including points, various unifaces and limaces, debris, and occasionally grinding stones. These different tools reflect the varied activities carried out by the population, who fished, hunted wild game, and made use of wild plants. This last food source is indicated by the presence of macro-plant remains, milling stones, and sheen polish on the edges of some unifacial tools. There are also a number of much larger stone tool quarry sites and a few sites containing small stone residential structures.

The best-known Paiján area is the Cupisnique and Zaña valleys. More than 300 Paiján sites have been found stretching from 10–35 km inland from the sea to elevations of 1,000 m in these valleys. The early Paiján sites we have discovered and excavated in the Zana and Jequetepeque Valleys, radiocarbon dated between 10,800 and 10,000 yr B.P., suggest a seasonal pattern of movement, indicated by intermittent and thin micro-stratigraphic levels (1–3 cm thick) in sites. Many of these sites are situated along low-altitude passes cutting between the coastal plains and the vegetated Andean foothills. Seasonal occupation is also indicated by other findings: the remains of migratory birds and fish, and seasonally occurring plant species. To date, no architectural structures have been associated with these earlier sites. Instead, sites are lithic scatters ranging between 2000 and 5000 m^2 in size, often with overlapping clusters suggestive of reuse of the site by the same group or by multigroups over time. There are occasional hearths scattered randomly across site surfaces.

There is growing evidence that late Paiján groups were beginning to decrease their mobility, aggregate and establish more permanent camps, radiocarbon-dated between 10,000 and 8500 yr B.P. We find the aggregation of several small sites at the edge of the hilly ecotone near active springs and equidistant from the coast and vegetated hillsides. These sites were highly localized, indicated by the presence of very localized lithic raw material, grinding stones, and food remains. The degree of localization is inferred from the appearance of permanent stone structures and the presence of thicker and continuous habitational floors (0.5–20 cm) in those structures. These data collectively suggest people were occupying very specific habitats over a longer period. Several of these later sites are smaller, defined by 2- to 8-house structures made of stone and perishable side walls. The total site areas average between 200 and 1200 m^2. The shift from an early settlement pattern of larger bands based on movement between coastal desert plains and the western slopes of the Andes, probably on a seasonal basis, to a later circumscribed pattern of smaller groups in highly localized and diverse habitats like the ecotone edges of the valleys appears to have been rather rapid, occurring within a period of a few hundred years or shorter. It appears that some later sites may have provided a stable place for people to engage in prolonged social contact and exchange, and enhanced conditions for eventual population growth. These may have been some of the first pulses of institutional forms that later developed into Andean civilization, including social fusion, ecological complementariness, and corporate unity.

How do these sites link to later cultural developments? Beginning in the late 8th and 7th millennia coastal sites, many with attendant shell mounds, started to become common. Continuity in unifacial and bifacial forms lasted to about 8000 to 7000 yr B.P., at which time the technology shifted to more grinding stones. On the western slopes of the Andes in the nearby middle Zaña Valley is the Las Pircas culture, dated between 8500 and 6500 yr B.P., characterized by low earthen mounds possibly used for public ritual, possibly semi-domesticated cultigens, and exotic nonfood items (Dillehay et al. 1997). Similar developments were taking place elsewhere in the Andes and probably in various parts of South America. Between 5500 and 4500 yr B.P. several fully developed agricultural and maritime-based economies, some with large monumental architecture, had developed on the coast of southern Ecuador and Peru (Quilter 1991) and established the true beginnings of Andean civilization.

References Cited

Chauchat, C.
1975 The Paiján Complex, Pampa de Cupisnique, Perú. *Ñawpa Pacha* 17:143–146.

Chauchat, C., J. Briceno, and C. Galvez
1998 *Sitios Arqueológicos de la Zona de Cupisnique y Margen Derecha del Valle de Chicama.* Instituto Nacional de Cultura La Libertad-Instituto Francés de Estudios Andinos, Lima. Perú.

Dillehay, T. D.
2000 *The Settlement of the Americas: A New Prehistory.* Basic Books. New York.

Dillehay, T. D., J. Rossen, and P. Netherly
1997 The Nanchoc Tradition: The Beginnings of Andean Civilization. *American Scientist* 85:46–55.

Quilter, J.
1991 Late Preceramic Perú. *Journal of World Prehistory* 5(4):387–435.

Richardson III, J. B.
1978 Early Man on the Peruvian North Coast, Early Maritime Exploitation and the Pleistocene and Holocene Environment. In *Early Man in America from a Circum-Pacific Perspective,* edited by A. L. Bryan, pp. 274–289. Department of Anthropology, University of Alberta, Edmonton, AB.

The First Peopling of the South Pacific American Coast during the Pleistocene/Holocene Transition—A Case Study: The Prehistoric Campsite of Quebrada de los Burros (Tacna, Peru)

Danièle Lavallée

In the still valid context of the initial arrival of people in America via the far north of Asia and the Beringian isthmus, the peopling of the southern part of South America represents the end of the process. Therefore, in accordance with the traditional but debated Clovis-First hypothesis, the first human traces in this part of the continent ought to have appeared very late, in any case long after the fateful date of 11,500 yr B.P. (the medium age of the Clovis culture). However, recent discoveries demonstrate that the "uttermost part of the Earth," as far south as Tierra del Fuego, was settled around 12,000 yr B.P. Moreover, to investigate the peopling of America also implies studying possible ways of penetrating and advancing southward. In reply to the classical hypothesis of an advance through the interior of the land, an alternative theory by Knut Fladmark (1979) proposed that a maritime route could have been followed along the Pacific coast. We propose to contribute to this discussion with a synthetical summary of recent data obtained on the extreme south coast of Peru.

Quebrada de los Burros, located in the Tacna department (18° 00′ S, 70° 50′ W), is a narrow, short valley oriented roughly north-south. Although situated in a hyperarid natural context, springs occur at the base of the valley, creating small wetlands with a weak but permanent outflow. Moreover, very dense fog from the ocean during the southern winter blankets the western slopes of the desert hills and creates large expanses of *lomas*, spontane-

CNRS–UMR 8096 "Archéologie des Amériques,"Maison de l'Archéologie et de l'Ethnologie, 21 allée de l'université, 92023 NANTERRE Cedex, France. e-mail: lavallee@mae.u-paris10.fr

ous and intermittent plant formations at an altitude of 200–1000 m that accommodate a range of animals, from snails to rodents, large herbivorous cervids (*Hippocamelus antisensis*), camelids (*Lama guanicoe*), and birds. Among the plants, several edible rhizomes or tubers are encountered. In this quebrada were discovered and studied: 1) the remains of a campsite occupied by fishermen and shellfish collectors from 10,000 to 6000 yr B.P. (in fact, this appears to be one of the most ancient human settlements identified at the present time); and 2) a neighboring burial area that contains human remains of the cultural group "Chinchorro"; the skulls and often the large bones are coated with a homogeneous mixture of manganese oxide and fine clay. Vegetable charcoal and marine shells associated with the burials have been dated at 9790 ± 740 yr B.P. (Gif-10628 on charcoal, Cal B.C. 9717, 8529) and 11,030 ± 80 yr B.P. (Gif-11281 on marine shell).

Intensive excavations on a 76-m^2 continuous area yielded the remains of a large stratified settlement composed of 7 superimposed occupation levels over a depth of 2 m. The densest occupation, levels 6 to 2, is dated at 8730 ± 70 yr B.P. (Gif-10632 on charcoal, Cal B.C. 7908, 7547) and 6050 ± 80 yr B.P. (Gif-A99341 on charcoal, Cal B.C. 5209, 4780). Basal levels 7 and 8 excavated in 2000 have yet to be dated. Paleoclimatical analysis indicates a calm period of temperate climate between 8000 and 6000 yr B.P. and the existence of permanent ponds or bogs in the bottom of the valley (Fontugne et al. 1999). A permanent fresh water supply favored a human settlement about 2 km inland from the shoreline at the time of the occupation and at 180 m a.s.l.

Occupation levels consist of accumulations of faunal remains spatially associated with abundant lithic remains (more than 10,000 chipping products and bifacial and unifacial tools) and bone and shell tools related to fishing activities. Evidence of hearths, postholes, lithic chipping areas, and mollusk valves distributed in a spatially differentiated manner indicate the presence of human groups who carried out repeated domestic and technical activities (Lavallée et al. 1999).

The faunal assemblage consists mainly of fish remains—Sciaenidae, Carangidae, and Scombridae in decreasing order, and also Clupeidae (sardines) and Chondrichthyes (rays and sharks), two families whose presence has important implications concerning fishing techniques and mastery of the maritime environment. The identified species occupy different habitats, either near-shore waters, the epipelagic zone, or the open sea. This differentiated ethology implies a variety of fishing techniques, using hook and line or nets, either from the shore or from boats sturdy enough to get through the surf. Artifacts encountered even in the early levels include more than 300 bifacial lithic points (for darts or harpoons), harpoon foreshafts made of sea mammal bone, weights and barbs of compound fishhooks of bone or shell, and simple hooks of shell. Typologically these artifacts are identical to those found in some sites of the extreme northern Chilean coast, La Chimba-13, Acha-2 and Camarones-14 (Llagostera 1992; Muñoz O. et al. 1993 ; Schiappacasse and Niemeyer 1984). Material evidence of boats is lacking, but their use is suggested by the repeated captures of large fish of upper continental waters. On the other hand, mollusks, specifically the abundant *Concholepas concholepas* and *Mesodesma donacium*, could have been collected without using special techniques or tools. Finally, bones of a few specimens of terrestrial fauna—camelids, cervids, birds, and batrachians—found in all levels suggest that some land hunting took place during the whole occupation.

In conclusion, the Quebrada de los Burros inhabitants demonstrate from the earliest occupation a perfect control of maritime environment that implies a very long previous adaptation process. Other sites on the Pacific coast yield similar evidence and ages: Las Vegas-80 in Ecuador, with a "pre-Vegas" level dated between 10,800 and 10,000 yr B.P. (Stothert 1980), where remains of large fishes indicate seagoing skills; Amotape in north Peru, dated 11,200 ± 115 yr B.P. (on shell, SI-1415); farther north, Daisy Cave (ca. 10,300 yr B.P.) and Arlington Canyon (ca. 10,000 yr B.P.), located on two islands in the Santa Barbara Channel of California, which are situated 40 and 80 km from the modern shoreline at Santa Barbara and Santa Rosa and which apparently were not connected to the mainland during the Pleistocene (Erlandson 1994, 1998; Erlandson et al. 1996).

Nothing in the archaeological record of Quebrada de los Burros suggests the first coastal inhabitants were Andean highlands hunter-gatherers (the cordillera has been occupied by human groups since ca. 13,000 yr B.P.) who were forced to retreat to lower altitudes by the increasing cold of Younger Dryas (between 12,500 and 10,000 yr B.P.) and consequently adapted to a maritime environment. Indeed, the theory of a maritime migration route following the Pacific coast is a more credible alternative. Moreover, it better explains how human groups coming from the far north could have reached the far south between 15,000 and 10,000 yr B.P.

Future investigations carried out along the Pacific coast in areas where the continental shelf is narrow and at sites situated a distance from the shoreline, and therefore not affected by the postglacial rise of sea level, will produce more evidence of very ancient human groups who were already superbly adapted to living mainly from marine resources when the famous "Clovis" hunters reached the High Plains of North America.

References Cited

Erlandson, J. M.
1994 *Early Hunter-gatherers of the California Coast*, Plenum Press, New York.

Erlandson, J. M., D. J. Kennett, L. Ingram, D. A. Guthrie, D. P. Morris, M. A. Tveskov, G. J. West, and P. L. Walker
1996 An Archaeological and Paleontological Chronology for Daisy Cave (CA-SMI-261), San Miguel Island, California. *Radiocarbon* 38(2):355–373.

Erlandson, J. M., T. C. Rick, R. L. Vellanoweth, and D. J. Kennett
1999 Maritime Subsistence at a 9300 Year Old Shell Midden on Santa Rosa Island, California. *Journal of Field Archaeology* 26:255–265.

Fladmark, K. R.
1979 Routes: Alternative Migration Corridors for Early Man in North America. *American Antiquity* 44(1):55–69.

Fontugne, M., P. Usselmann, D. Lavallée, M. Julien, and C. Hatté
1999 El Niño Variability in the Coastal Desert of Southern Peru during the Mid-Holocene. *Quaternary Research* 52:171–179.

Lavallée, D., P. Béarez, A. Chevalier, M. Julien, P. Usselmann, and M. Fontugne
1999 Paleoambiente y Ocupación Prehistórica del Litoral Extremo-sur del Perú: Las Ocupaciones del Arcaico en la Quebrada de los Burros y Alrededores (Tacna, Perú). *Boletin de Arqueología* PUCP 3:393–416. Lima, Peru.

Llagostera, A. M.
1992 Early Occupations and the Emergence of Fishermen on the Pacific Coast of South America. In

Andean Past 3, edited by D. Sandweiss and Peter Kvietok, pp. 87–109. Cornell University Andean Studies Program, Ithaca, NY.

Muñoz Ovalle, I., B. Arriaza, and A. Aufderheide
1993 *Acha-2 y los Origenes del Poblamiento Humano en Arica.* Ediciones Universidad de Tarapacá, Arica, Chile.

Richardson, J. B. III
1978 Early Man in the Peruvian North Coast: Early Maritime Exploitation and Pleistocene and Holocene Environment. In *Early Man in America from a Circum-Pacific Perspective*, edited by A. L. Bryan, pp. 274–289. University of Alberta, Occasional Papers no. 1, Edmonton, AB.

Schiappacasse, V., and H. Niemeyer
1984 *Sitio Camarones 14. Descripción y Analisis Interpretativo de un Sitio Arcaico Temprano de la Quebrada de Camarones.* Museo Nacional de Historia Natural, Publicación Ocasional no. 41. Santiago, Chile.

Stothert, K. E.
1988 *La Prehistoria Temprana de la Peninsula de Santa Elena, Ecuador. Cultura Las Vegas.* Museo del Banco Central, Miscelanea Antropológica Ecuatoriana no. 10, Guayaquil and Quito, Ecuador.

Santa Elina Rockshelter, Brazil: Evidence of the Coexistence of Man and *Glossotherium*

Águeda Vilhena Vialou

The Santa Elina Rockshelter (15° 27′ 28″ S, 56° 46′ 93″ W) is located 100 km northwest of Cuiaba, at the geodesic center of South America on Serra das Araras, a Precambrian folding composed of limestone and dolomite of the Araras Formation and sandstone of the Raizama Formation (Alvarenga 1990; Ross 1987). This area lies in the Cuiaba-Paraguay catchment basin in central west Brazil.

A flat wall about 30 m high and inclined at 70°, with approximately 900 paintings of animals, human figures, and signs (Vialou 1994), forms a shelter 60 m long. Another low wall, in declivity and covered by sedimentation, is visible in part of the shelter; it lies 3–5 m distant from the painted wall, parallel to it and with the same inclination. The dwelling area is delimited by this gap.

At present, three units characterize the known stratigraphy because the shelter base has not yet been reached. They are labeled (Figure 1) from the most ancient to the most recent (Benadelhadi in Vilhena Vialou et al. 1995; Benabdelhadi in press).

In Unit III, the sediment is very sandy and rich in rubble. There is no charcoal. It is purely Pleistocene. Level III-4 is composed of compact, heterogeneous grayish pink sediment with some microlayers. In level III-3 and other places the sediment is brown, movable, and contains altered wood. Unit III is 60 cm thick.

Unit II consists of three thick homogeneous strata, with a total thickness of 120 cm. Vegetable remains are rare; burnt fruits occur with some leaves exclusively in the fireplaces,

Researcher USM 103, Muséum National d'Histoire Naturelle, Paris/FRE 2676 CNRS. Director of Prehistory and Paleo Environment Program in Mato Grosso a research program in collaboration between the Laboratory of Prehistory of the Muséum National d'Histoire Naturelle, Paris and the Museu de Arqueologia e Etnologia of the University of São Paulo. Institut de Paléontologie humaine, rue René Panhard, 75013 Paris, France. e-mail: avialou@mnhn.Fr

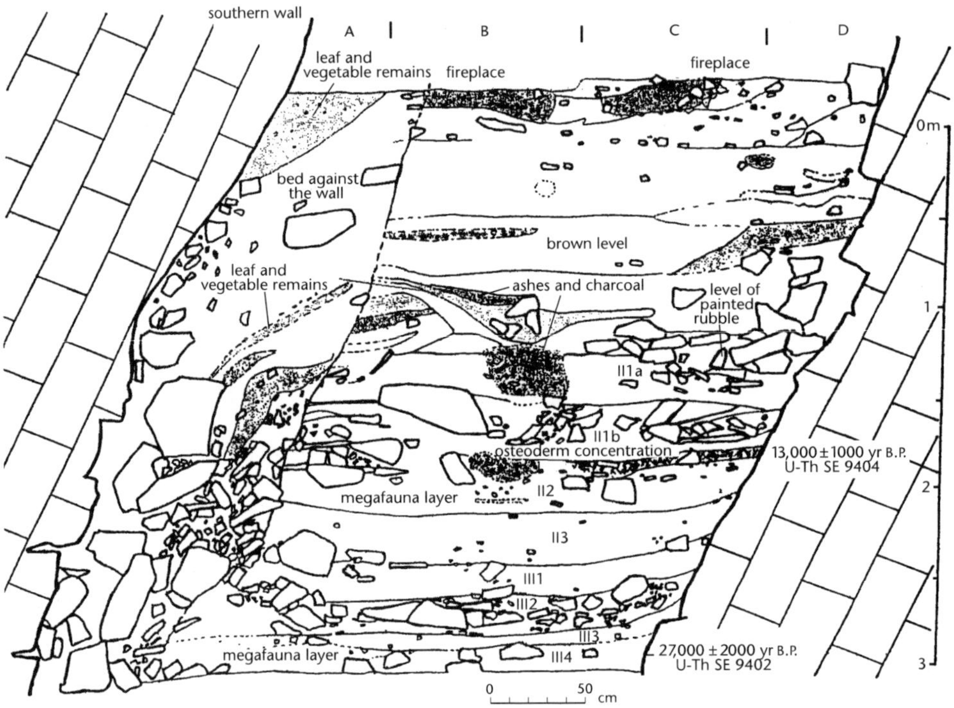

Figure 1. Santa Elina stratigraphic cross section 29/30 west. (M. Benabdelhadi, 2000).

without a big scattering of charcoal. The top of Unit II is in contact with the level of painted rubbles, distinguished from it by sandy silty sediment.

Unit I is formed of extremely thin pulverulent, silty sediment; strata are anthropogenic because of occupation remains such as combustion structures with very big charcoal pieces in vast amounts; several deposits of ash; stone arrangements; edible and worked vegetables; debitage of limestone, flint, and sandstone; and many hematite sticks used as a coloring agent. Occupations are continuous, starting from the level consisting of soil containing rubble spotted with red pigments dated 6000 yr B.P., up almost to present time (2000 to 400 years ago), characterized by absence of ceramics and the presence of approximately 80 wood stakes driven vertically in the soil. Unit I is 100–140 cm thick (Vilhena Vialou and Vialou 1989).

This report describes Units III and II. In Unit III, 3 m deep, an area of 18 m^2 was excavated; in Unit II, 2 m deep, the excavation was 40 m^2.

Remains

In Unit III the bone vestiges of *Glossotherium* aff. *G. lettsomi* (identified by C. Cartelle in Vilhena Vialou et al. 1995) occur in levels III-4 and III-3 at a depth of 3 m in soil characterized by the concentration of approximately 300 bone fragments; among them appear fragmented mandible, fragments of cranial bone with a molar, four vertebrae, and thousands of osteoderms in a limited area (ca. 8 m^2); over some meters around, few bone fragments and osteoderms appear. Because of the density of bone fragments, this level approaches 30 cm in thickness. Two osteoderms are pierced, and the faces of one of them have been abraded by man (Vilhena Vialou 1998).

Lithic material associated with the bones also appears in this sediment. Among 81 lithic artifacts, we count 27 tools—23 retouched tablets (19 of limestone and 4 of silica) and 4 retouched limestone flakes. They are abrupt and notched retouches, which reach the thickness of the tablet or flake edges. The types of tools are notched, denticulate, and include one lamellar microscraper in a silica tablet. Microwear and other signs of use are visible in some artifacts. Among the retouched and debitage products are 50 artifacts: 23 limestone flakes (measuring 1.8–4.5 cm) and 27 small flakes (1.2–2.2 cm), 25 of limestone and 2 of silica. These articles are formed mainly of cortical blanks or cortical remains. The butts are generally cortical; some are dihedral, filiform, or flat. The angle beside the impact point is equal to or greater than 110°. Among raw materials collected by man are three little rock crystals and one fragment of hematite (Figure 2).

The association of extinct faunal bone remains, *Glossotherium* aff. *G. lettsomi*, and lithic material is repeated 1 m above at level II-2, after a sandy layer lacking fauna and with scarce lithic artifacts. There are large fragments, including a flat bone (scapula), a thoracic vertebra, a tarsus, a lower molar M_2, as well as several bits of long bones and osteoderms spread over 10 m. However, hundreds of osteoderms are found in the western stratigraphic section at a depth of 180–200 cm depth; several detached bones in the same area also occur in level III-4 at a depth of 3 m, a new level. The lithic material, more than 200 artifacts, is characterized by limestone flakes, some retouched tablets, and flint debitage. The rock comes from sources as far as 2 km from the shelter.

Those data confer special distinction on Santa Elina because of the association of man and *Glossotherium*. The poor quality of over 400 bones of *Glossotherium* does not yet make it possible to detect cutting or butchering. The bone distribution is being studied (Figuti in press). Approximately 6,000 osteoderms and larger bones are spatially concentrated without significant shifting and with little scattering of millimetric pieces. We can dismiss the hypothesis of a paleontological site, an animal cemetery, or an area disturbed by animals. We notice indeed a coherent unity of data. Unit III contains a living floor where bones, instead of being widely scattered, are gathered within an area of 4 m^2.

Datings

Several ^{14}C datings correspond to the Holocene period, from 10,000 yr B.P. to recent periods (Fontugne in Vilhena Vialou et al. 1995). However, floated wood remains at Pleistocene levels (270 cm depth), dated by the standard radiocarbon method, gave ages of 22,500 ± 500 yr B.P. (Gif-9366) and 23,320 ± 1000 yr B.P. (Gif-9365). The wood remains were found at stratigraphic unit III-3/2, in a level just above the living floor of extinct fauna in III-4. The fauna was dated through its ossicles, the osteoderms, using the uranium-thorium method by the Laboratory of Prehistory of Muséum National d'Histoire Naturelle (Falguères in Vilhena Vialou et al. 1995; Falguères in press). Two ages were obtained, one for fauna situated in each of two different levels: in 26 C, z: 300 cm, in the level corresponding to the concentrated bones of *Glossotherium,* the osteoderms were dated at 27,000 ± 2000 yr B.P. (U-Th SE

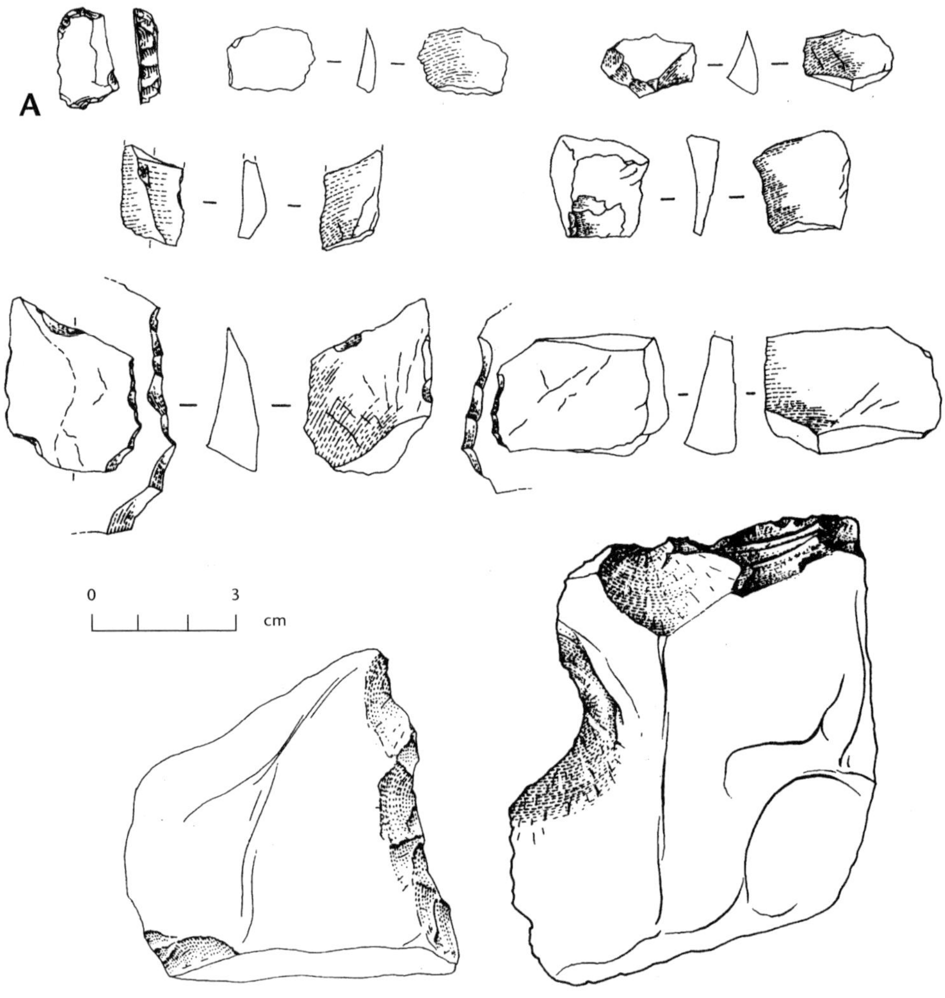

Figure 2. Santa Elina level III 4/3 products of debitage, retouched flakes, and retouched tablets of limestone. Notches and denticulates. **A**, abrupt retouches on microtablet of silica. From P. Paillet and L. Chiotti.

9402) within 1σ. Osteoderms collected beside the section at meter 29 C, z: 198 cm were dated at 13,000 ± 1000 yr B.P. (U-Th SE 9404) within 1σ. This latter date, skewed slightly toward older than actual by exogenous thorium in the sample, compares favorably with a result obtained by ^{14}C for a fireplace associated with the fauna, 10,120 ± 60 yr B.P. (Gif-8954), in 24 B at a depth of 205 cm.

Considering the rarity of the discoveries at the 300-cm level and the age given by the U-Th method, two new dating series on pieces of charcoal and on sandy sediment were performed using different methods, one by AMS (H.Valladas, Gif-sur-Yvette), the other by

OSL (J. Feathers, University of Washington); they report ages equivalent to those given by U-Th and ^{14}C, around 25,000 years ago.

Data Synthesis

Santa Elina is a special site because of the two deepest levels, which contain cultural vestiges and bone remains.

There are two distinct levels associated with fauna and cultural remains.

Fauna

- Fauna is represented by a single Pleistocene animal species, *Glossotherium* aff. *Glossotherium lettsomi*;
- specimens of the identified animal are incomplete carcasses;
- bone remains belong to one animal per level;
- fossil fauna exist only in two periods, and when man is present it is from 10,000 to more than 20,000 years ago.

Lithic Industry

- Debitage is limited to blocks and tablets of regional rock;
- retouches, created by notches in thin or thick edges, appear denticulate because they are continuous notches;
- steep micro retouches are found in small artifacts, flint, and micro tablets;
- large and small pieces show signs of use, wear, and polishing at the cutting edge.

It is important to note that in Santa Elina during the Holocene man diversified his choice of raw material, but in some cases he used regional rocks as the most productive source.

Some Outstanding Aspects of Other American Sites

There are few sites in South America where cultural vestiges and extinct fauna are associated. Sites dating from 13,000 to 11,000 yr B.P. with evidence of mastodon, like Monte Verde (Dillehay and Collins 1988) and Tagua Tagua (Montané 1968), and with other fossil animals, among them Mylodontidae as at Taima Taima (Gruhn and Bryan 1984) and Quereo (Nuñez et al. 1983), reveal interaction between hunting and domestic functions. In some sites in Patagonia dating to 11,000 yr B.P., *Mylodon* is linked to the production of fishtail projectile points, as at Fell (Bird 1938; Emperaire et al. 1963), Cueva del Medio (Nami 1987), and Piedra Museo (Miotti 1992). At the Cerro La China site (Flegenheimer 1987), *Eutatus* is the fossil fauna linked to the fishtail point. In Palli Aike (Bird 1938, 1988), where *Mylodon* and fishtail points are associated, and in Arroyo Seco (Fidalgo et al. 1986), where several fossil fauna species are found without projectile points, fossil fauna were present with or without projectile points possibly as recently as the Holocene, around 8000 to 6000 years ago, if dates accurately correlate to corresponding levels. In some sites, man appears when Pleistocene fauna disappears. In Pampa de los Fósiles (Falguères et al. 1994), fossil fauna were plentiful up to 12,000 yr B.P. The vast majority of prehistoric cultural sites on the northern coast of Peru, as at Pampa de los Fósiles 13, site of the Man of Paiján—La Cumbre (Chauchaut 1988; Chauchat and Dricot 1979), occur immediately after the layer with fossil animals; in other words, without association.

Glossotherium anticipates the presence of man in the habitat, without confirmation of contemporaneity, at Cueva del Mylodon (Bird 1988; Emperaire and Laming 1954), Lapa Vermelha (Cunha and Guimarães 1978; Laming-Emperaire et al. 1975), Arroio Touro Passo, and Arroio dos Fósseis (Bombim and Bryan 1979; Milder 2000; Miller 1987).

Conclusions

The stratigraphic and topographic association of man and megafauna prior to 20,000 yr B.P., and their renewed joint presence at the Pleistocene/Holocene transition 10,000 years ago, ranks Santa Elina among important South American prehistoric sites. Unquestionably there was a lithic industry and activity in making ornaments from osteoderms. Not only was there copresence, contemporaneity, and coexistence of man and *Glossotherium*, there was interaction between them. The low density of lithic vestiges and the scarcity of fireplaces suggest the shelter was a place of temporary encampment and not a permanent dwelling. Its characteristics are similar to those of sites which do not yield projectile points, a trait that could be valid for the period 10,000 years ago because studies of central Brazil have not revealed a culture possessing projectile points or bifacial artifacts in general. The insufficiency of cultural data 14,000 years ago linked to previous occupations prevents our forming a hypothesis about the forms of adaptation of American man to the environment existing by the end of Pleistocene 30,000 to 15,000 years ago.

Acknowledgments

Acknowledgments to Ministère des Affaires Etrangères, Direction de la Coopération Scientífique, Universitaire et de la Recherche (France) and University of São Paulo, Museu de Arqueologia e Etnologia (Brazil) for the funds granted by them. We thank Laura Miotti and Monica Salemme for their revision of this paper.

References Cited

Alvarenga, C. J. S.

1990 *Phénomènes Sédimentaires, Structuraux et Circulation de Fluides* Dévellopés à la Transition Chaîne-craton. Exemple de la Chaîne *Paraguai d'Âge Protérozoique Supérieur, Mato Grosso, Brésil.* Tese de Doutorado Université de Marseille.

Benabdelhadi, M.

2002 Contribuição da Sedimentologia e da Micromorfologia para o Conhecimento dos Sítios Pré-históricos. Métodos de Estudo e Resultados. In *Pré-História do Mato Grosso*, edited by A. Vilhena Vialou, EDUSP, São Paulo. In press.

Bird, J.

1938 Antiquity and Migrations of the Early Inhabitants of Patagonia. *Geographic Review*, 28(2):250–275.

1988 *Travels and Archaeology in South Chile*, edited by John Hyslop. University of Iowa Press, Iowa City, IA.

Bombin, M., and A. Bryan

1979 *News Perspectives on Early Man in Southwestern Rio Grande do Sul, Brazil.* In Early Man in America from a Circum-Pacifc Perspective, edited by A. L. Bryan, pp. 301–302. Department of Anthropology, University of Alberta, Edmonton, AB.

Chauchat, C.

1988 Early hunters-gatherers on the Peruvian Coast. In *Peruvian Prehistory,* edited by R. W. Keatinge, pp. 41–66, Cambridge University Press, Cambridge, UK.

Chauchat, C., and J-M. Dricot
1979 Un Nouveau Type Humain Fossile en Amérique du Sud: l'Homme de Paiján (Pérou). *Comptes Rendus de l'Académie des Sciences.* Paris, 289, série II:387–389.

Cunha, F. L. de S., and M. L. Guimarães
1978 Posição Geológica do Homem de Lagoa Santa no Grande Abrigo da Lapa Vermelha (PL), Pedro Leopoldo, Estado de Minas Gerais. *Coletânea de Estudos em Homenagem a Annette Laming-Emperaire, Coleção Museu Paulista, série Ensaios,* 2:275–305, São Paulo, Brazil.

Dillehay, T. D., and M. B. Collins
1988 Early Cultural Evidence from Monte Verde in Chile. *Nature* 332:150–152.

Emperaire J., and A. Laming
1954 La Grotte du Mylodon. *Journal de la Société des Américanistes.* XLIII:173–205.

Emperaire J., A. Laming-Emperaire, and H. Reichlen
1963 La Grotte Fell et Autres Sites de la Région Volcanique de la Patagonie Chilienne. *Journal de la Société des Américanistes* LII:167–254.

Falguères, C.
2002 La Méthode U-Th In *Pré-História do Mato Grosso,* edited by A. Vilhena Vialou, EDUSP, São Paulo, Brazil. In press.

Falguères, C., M. Fontugne, C. Chauchat, and J-C. Guadelli
1994 Datations Radiométriques de l'Extinction des Grandes Faunes Pleistocènes au Pérou. *Comptes Rendus de l'Académie des Sciences, Paris,* 319, série II:261–266.

Fidalgo, F., L. M. Guzman, G. Politis, M. Salemme, E. Tonni, J. Carbonari, G. Gomez, R. Huarte, and A. Figini
1986 Investigaciones Arqueológicas en el Sitio 2 de Arroyo Seco (Pdo de Tres Arroyos – Provincia de Buenos Aires – República Argentina). In *New Evidence for the Pleistocene Peopling of the Americas,* edited by A. L. Bryan, pp.221–269. Center for the Study of Early Man, University of Maine, Orono, ME.

Figuti, L.
2002 Considerações sobre a Distribuição Espacial em Santa Elina. In *Pré-História do Mato Grosso,* edited by A. Vilhena Vialou. EDUSP, Sao Paulo, Brazil. In press.

Flegenheimer, N.
1987 Recent Research at Localities Cerro La China and Cerro El Sombrero, Argentina. *Current Research in the Pleistocene* 4:148–149.

Gruhn, R., and A. L. Bryan
1984 The Record of Pleistocene Megafauna Extinction at Taima taima, Northern Venezuela. In *Quaternary Extinctions, a Prehistoric Revolution,* edited by P. S Martin and R. G. Klein, pp. 128–137. University of Arizona Press, Tucson AZ .

Laming-Emperaire A., A. Prous, A. Vilhena de Moraes, and M. Beltrão
1975 Grottes et Abris de la Région de Lagoa Santa, Minas Gerais, Brésil. *Cahiers d'Archéologie d'Amérique du Sud* 1, EHESS, Paris.

Lavallée, D.
1995 *Promesse d 'Amérique. La Préhistoire de l'Amérique du Sud,* Hachette, Paris.

Milder, S. E. S.
2000 *Arqueologia do Sudoeste do Rio Grande do Sul: Uma Perspectiva Geoarqueológica.* Tese de Doutorado, Universidade de São Paulo, São Paulo, Brazil.

Miller, E. T.
1987 Pesquisas Arqueológicas Paleoíndias no Brasil Ocidental in Investigaciones Paleoíndias al Sur de la Línea Equatorial. *Colección Estudos Atacameños* 8:37–61.

Miotti, L.
1992 Paleoindian Occupation at Piedra Museo Locality, Santa Cruz Province, Argentina. *Current Research in the Pleistocene* 9:30–32.

Montané, J. C.
1968 Paleo-Indian Remains from Laguna de Tagua Tagua, Central Chile. *Science* 161:1137–1138.

Nami, H.G.
1987 Cueva del Medio: A Significant Paleoindian Site in Southern South America. *Current Research in the Pleistocene* 4:157–159.

Núñez L., J. Varela, and R. Casamiquela
1983 *Ocupación Paleo-india in Quereo, Reconstruccion Multidisciplinar en Territorio Semi-árido de Chile.* Universidad del Norte, Antofagasta Chile.

Ross, J. L. S.
1987 *Estudo e Cartografia Geomorfológica da Província Serrana–MT.* Tese de Doutorado Faculdade de Filosofia Letras e Ciéncias Humanas-Universidade de São Paulo, São Paulo, Brazil.

Vialou, D.
1987 Les Peintures Pariétales de Santa Elina, Mato Grosso, Brésil. *Bulletin de la Société Préhistorique Française*, 84(10-12):403–406, Paris.

Vilhena Vialou, A.
1998 Une Pendeloque Taillée dans un Os de "*Glossotherium.*" In *Universalia, Encyclopaedia Universalis*, p. 267, Paris.

Vilhena Vialou, A., and D. Vialou
1989 Abrigo Pré-histórico Santa Elina, Mato Grosso: Habitats e Arte Rupestre. *Revista Instituto de Pré-História da USP*, 7:34–53, São Paulo, Brazil.

Vilhena Vialou A., T. Aubry, M. Benabdelhadi, C. Cartelle, L. Figuti, M. Fontugne, M. E. Solari, and D. Vialou
1995 Découverte de Mylodontinae dans un Habitat Préhistorique Daté du Mato Grosso (Brésil): l'Abri Rupestre de Santa Elina. *Comptes Rendus de l'Académie des Sciences,* Paris, 320, série IIa:655–661.

Vilhena Vialou A., P. D. de Blasis, L. Figuti, P. Paillet, and D. Vialou
1999 Art Rupestre et Habitats Préhistoriques au Mato Grosso (Brésil). In *L'Amérique du Sud, des Chasseurs-cueilleurs à l'Empire Inca,* edited by A. Chevallier, L. Velarde, and I. Chenal-Velarde, pp.9–22. BAR International Series 746, Oxford, UK.

Paleoindian Components of Northern Uruguay: New Data on Early Human Occupations of the Late Pleistocene and Early Holocene

Rafael Suárez

Introduction

Uruguay is a small country, with extensive plains watered by many rivers. It is situated in the southeast of South America (lat. 30° to 35° S, long. 58° to 54° W). It is very likely the Uruguay and Negro rivers were the main entrance ways for the first humans to the plains of Uruguay during the late Pleistocene. The early archaeological sites known in Uruguay are all in the open air and situated close to important waterways (Negro River, Uruguay-Cuareim rivers, or their tributaries).

There are interesting aspects to note in the recording and archaeological context of the Pleistocene/Holocene transition in Uruguay: for sites radiocarbon-dated between 11,200 and 8600 yr B.P. (Table 1) (Hilbert 1991; MEC 1989; Suárez 2002, 2003), dozens of Fell-type points (also called fishtail projectile points or Fell's Cave stemmed) were recovered on the surface, as well as fluted and unfluted bifaces. This report presents and discusses new information about human presence during the late Pleistocene and early Holocene in Uruguay.

Research into the archaeology of Uruguay at the Pleistocene/Holocene transition is in its early stage. However, existing data and the prospect of studying colonization in this area of the continent are very encouraging. Archaeological research at Pay Paso Site 1 has identified new early sites and recovered a previously unreported Paleoindian projectile point (Pay Paso type) from the period 9500–9000 yr B.P. (Figure 1).

Investigation into early human occupations in northern Uruguay has identified two

Comisión Nacional de Arqueología (MEC), Camino Carrasco 4658, Block D, Torre 1, Apto 1302. Malvin Alto. CP 11,400. Montevideo Uruguay. e-mail: suarezra@hotmail.com

Table 1. Early archaeological localities (30° S to 31° S, 57° W to 58° W) dated by ^{14}C in Uruguay.

Site	Date (RCYBP)	Sample	Lab no.	Artifact	References
Y 58	11,200 ± 500	charcoal	Gif 4412	one core , bifacial flakes	MEC 1989:459
K87	10,420 ± 90	charcoal	Kn 2531	biface, grinding stone, flakes	Hilbert 1991:15
Pay Paso 1	9890 ± 75	charcoal	RT1445	debitage	Austral 1994:365
Pay Paso 1	9280 ± 200	charcoal	Uru 248	projectile point, flakes	Suárez 2002
Pay Paso 1	9120 ± 40	charcoal	Beta 156973	projectile points	Suárez 2002
Pay Paso 1	8570 ± 150	charcoal	Uru 246	flakes, unifacial tools, projectile points	Suárez 2002

Paleoindian components, early Paleoindian ca. 11,000–10,000 yr B.P. (Fell 1 component?) and late Paleoindian ca. 9500–8600 yr B.P. (Pay Paso component).

Fluted preforms, large bifaces exhibiting extraordinary flaking technique, excellent flake scar spacing, and "fishtail" or Fell points have been recorded in northern Uruguay (Suárez 2002). Working from the first technical and typological studies and from observations carried out in recent years, I propose an idealized model of rejuvenation for Fell-type points (Figure 2), hunting weapons used in vast areas of the Southern Cone during the late Pleistocene.

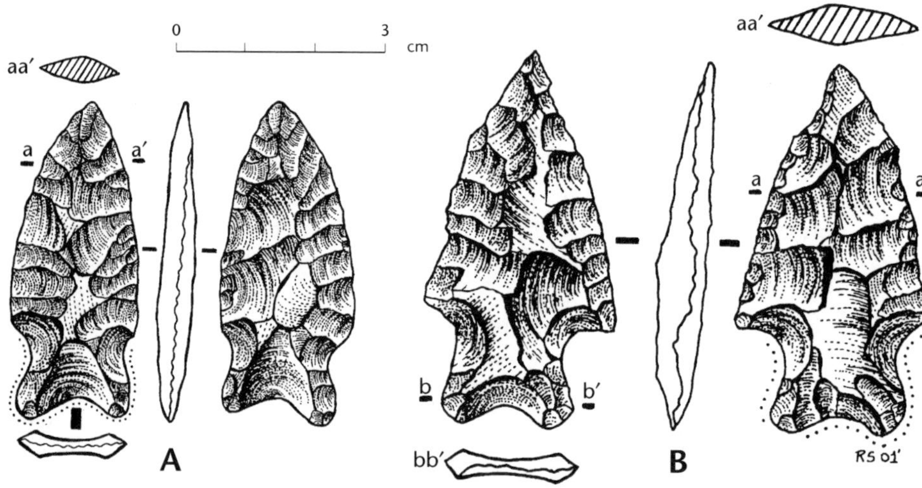

Figure 1. Most recent Paleoindian projectile points of Uruguay, Pay Paso type. **A,** from Pay Paso site 1, recovered in the lower archaeological level (Excavation 1, Level 4, C2LPVI2332), dated ca. 9500–9000 yr B.P. Note the basal thinning on both faces of the stem. **B,** from Pay Paso site 2, surface (PPII4652). Both points are made of silicified sandstone.

Raw Materials

In the center and north of the country, there is a great variety and abundance of lithic cryptocrystalline raw material, which is excellent for flaking. These archaeological regions show great concentrations of highly siliceous lithic resources, which can be obtained from primary outcrops and secondary quarries (Suárez 1998; 2000a). Outcrops of geological formations in northern Uruguay, especially the Arapey formation of volcanic rock, supplied Paleoindian knappers with geodes of chalcedony-agate, as well as vast shoals and clastic dams of silicified sandstone, jasper, and opal, which they used to manufacture toolkits (Suárez 1999). Silicified sandstone and agate-chalcedony are the raw materials that appear more frequently in radiocarbon-dated early stratified contexts in northern Uruguay.

Present Research

In recent years new data have been collected on sedimentological (Piñeiro et al. 1999), chronological, paleoenvironmental, and stratigraphic aspects (Suárez 2002) of the Pleistocene/Holocene transition in northern Uruguay. Regarding the lithic technology of early hunter-gatherers, quarries of raw material were identified and petrographic thin-section analyses were performed on primary quarries and on flakes from excavations at Pay Paso Site 1 dated during the transition (Suárez and Piñeiro 2002). Fell projectile points in the area were recorded, and technological aspects of bifacial preforms of Fell points were described (Suárez 1999, 2000b, 2001, 2002, 2003).

Archaeological research at Pay Paso (30° 16′ S, 57° 27′ W) on the Cuareim River (Uruguay-Brazil-Argentina border) may significantly improve our understanding of the most recent Paleoindian occupations in northern Uruguay at the beginning of the Holocene. The Pay Paso locality has seven sites with similar stratigraphic and sedimentological features formed by complex geomorphological processes. Research in this area is in its initial phase; preliminary data are presented here. So far 59 m^2 has been excavated in Pay Paso Site 1. Three charcoal samples taken from the lower archaeological level were recently radiocarbon-dated at 9120 ± 40 yr. B.P. (Beta 156973), 9280 ± 200 yr B.P. (Uru 248), and 8570 ± 150 yr B.P. (Uru 246) (Table 1). The sedimentary pack where the cultural remains were found was formed by fluvial (sand, slime, and clay) and eolian (loess and volcanic ash) sedimentation. In this cultural component, we found late-Pleistocene fauna in primary context and stratigraphic association with unifacial tools, red ocher, and fragments of carbonized plant (used to obtain the ^{14}C dates). Faunal remains recovered in this culture component include one *Glyptodon* sp. scute, several tooth fragments (not identified yet), and bones in an initial stage of fossilization. A long combustion structure (fire hearth) red-orange in color contained fragments of charcoal and ash from combustion. This structure is 1.05 m long, 0.6 m wide, and 0.3 m thick. The archaeological context includes flaking remains of silicified sandstone and chalcedony-agate, blade tools, end- and sidescrapers, bifaces in early and final stages of reduction, abundant charcoal, and bifacial projectile points of Pay Paso type (Figure 1A) manufactured on silicified sandstone. The point illustrated in Figure 1A is 44.1 mm long, 18.2 mm wide, and 5.8 mm thick, with prominent shoulders and triangular blade; the well-defined stem with concave edges expands towards the concave low-cut base. There is abrasion on both edges of the stem and thinning on both faces of the concave base; final sharpening of the blade was done using parallel and continuous pressure flaking. The archaeological context where this type of projectile point was recovered was dated between ca. 9500 and 9100 yr B.P. (see Table 1). In private collections of artifacts recovered from surface contexts at Pay Paso Site 1, 2, and 3 and other sites of the archaeological region of the Uruguay-Cuareim Rivers, I identified nine points whose technology and morphological features were similar to those of the point recovered in this site (Figure 1B).

The same level of the archaeological material shows strong (white) precipitations of calcium carbonate (post-depositional process) seen as subhorizontal "vein" threads measuring 2.5 to 20 mm (simple or branched); in some cases they fill small cracks formed when clay contracted with vertical development. These veins form concretionary structures (rhizoconcretions) of circular section corresponding to radicle ducts (carbonated roots) seen in the intersection of the threads. In some cases they stick to the lithic material. The presence of carbonate structures, rhizoconcretions, and carbonated threads at the same level as the archaeological material and fire hearths identified in the lower level of the site may indicate that in the early Holocene there was a paleosurface on the banks of the Cuareim River that was occupied by Paleoindians.

In the area of Pay Paso Site 4, about 7 km east of Site 1, partial remains of a young nursing *Stegomastodon* sp. were recovered in situ at the bottom of a ravine at an approximate depth of 6.7 m. The remains include a molar, a vertebra, fragments of a rib, and a complete tibia. On the surface near where the *Stegomastodon* remains were recovered, an assemblage of three bifaces 78–110 mm long with extraordinary technological features was recently reported. One, made of red chalcedony, exhibits basal fluting on one face and nipple preparation for fluting on the reverse face (see Suárez 2002: 318, Figure 3B).

Other species of megamammals identified in this region include *Hemiauchenia paradoxa, Scelidotherium leptocephalum, Glossotherium robustum, Pampatherium humboldti, Toxodon platensis, Glyptodon clavipes, Hippidion principale, Equus (Amerhippus) neogeus, Megatherium americanum, Smilodon populator, Macrauchenia patachonica, Morenelaphus brachyceros, Morenelaphus lujanensis, Paraceros fragilis,* and *Antifer ultra* (Bombin 1976:48-51; Ubilla and Perea 1999:78).

Design of Fell Points of Uruguay

Fell points recovered in surface contexts in Uruguay have been reported by different authors (Bird 1969; Bosh et al. 1974; Figueira 1892; Meneghin 1977; Nami 2001; Politis 1991; Suárez 2000a, 2001, 2002, 2003).

On a regional scale, Fell points in the Argentinean pampas are systematically dated to the late Pleistocene, 10,800–10,100 yr B.P. (Flegenheimer and Zárate 1997; Martínez 1997; Mazzanti 1997). Fell projectile points in Uruguay exhibit the following general features, especially regarding the shape of the stem and shoulders; my comments are based on observations of Fell points (n = 23) from northern and central Uruguay, most of which were probably used for hunting (some show impact and fracture damage). These weapons can be fluted or unfluted on the base; in some cases they are bifacially thinned, in others they are shaped starting from a flake; the final shaping (pressure flaking) can be marginal or laminar (Nami 1997, 2000). Two groups can be distinguished: a) in one group Fell points have clearly pronounced shoulders (angle between shoulder blade and stem 90°–110°), a defined stem with concave edges strongly expanded from a concave base, and abrasion on both edges of the stem (see Suárez and López 2003: 73–76, Figures 5 and 6A); b) in the other group Fell points have insinuated and rounded shoulders (angle between shoulder blade and stem 140°–160°), the edges of the stem are concave with abrasion, the concave base is hinted or in some cases straight (Figure 2B).

In Argentinean Patagonia as well as in the pampas, Fell points of both groups have been

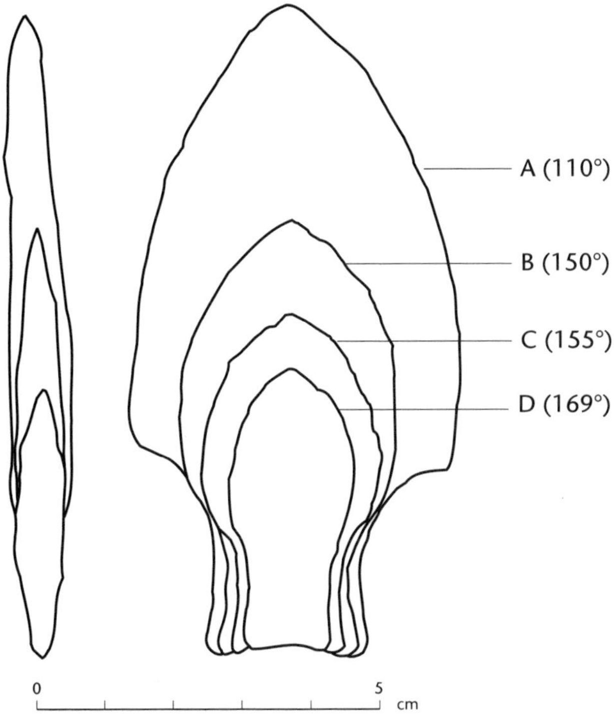

Figure 2. Idealized model of rejuvenation for Fell points of the Southern Cone. Note that the more resharpening, the more the angle of shoulder to stem increases; the size of the blade and the expansion of the stem toward the base diminish; the thickness remains unchanged (the number in parentheses indicates the angle between the shoulder blade and stem). **A**, Cerro El Sombrero site (silhouette from Flegenheimer and Zarate 1989, Figure 1B); **B**, mid-Negro River, Uruguay (silhouette from Bosh et al. 1974, Figure 2.16); **C**, Fell's Cave (silhouette from Emperaire, Laming, and Reichlen 1963, Figure 21.4); **D**, Cueva del Medio (according to Nami 1987, Figure 16a).

reported. For examples with extremely pronounced shoulders, see Flegenheimer and Zárate 1989:12 Figure 1B; Miotti 1996:36 Figure 5A; for examples with insinuated or rounded shoulders, see Bird 1969:64 Figure 2.2,3,4; Nami 1985-86:107 Figure 4. Fell points of Argentina are quite similar in these technological and morphological aspects to Fell points of Uruguay (Suárez 2000a, 2001).

Conclusion and Discussion

The projectile points recovered in the low level of Pay Paso Site 1 dated ca. 9500–9100 yr B.P. are a previously unknown type of hunting weapon for late-Paleoindian times in Uruguay (Pay Paso points, Figure 1A and 1B). Points surprisingly similar in design and flaking technique have been recovered from surface contexts in other archaeological regions (Rio Grande do Sul Brazil, see Mentz et. al 1995:207 Figure 6f and 6g).

With reference to the hunting weapons of Paleoindian groups in the north of Uruguay, Pay Paso projectile points differ culturally, chronologically, and stylistically from Fell types.

New surface findings of Fell points (Suárez 1999; 2002, 2003) clarify the chronological and stratigraphic record at sites Y58 and K87 and verify the presence of Fell components in northern Uruguay.

Some Fell points of the north of Uruguay show complete bifacial thinning and were manufactured starting with bifacial preforms, in some cases fluted (ca. 78–130 mm).

Recent technological and morphological studies of Fell points note that, in the original or primary design, these hunting weapons have very pronounced shoulders (angle between shoulder blade and stem 90º–110º) (see Suárez 2003; Suárez and López 2003: 73–74, Figures 5 and 6A). These points with markedly pronounced shoulders are generally large (100 mm long) and may be at the earliest stage of their use-life (Figure 2A). Resharpening the shoulder and blade to correct impact and fracture damage incurred in hunting activities surely led to a secondary design with rounded shoulders, which corresponds morphologically to the "classic" shape of Fell points, like those recovered in Fell's Cave (angle between shoulder blade and stem 140º–160º) (Figure 2B and 2C). Other examples, having been extremely resharpened, are at the latest stage of use-life (Bird 1969:71 Figure 5 J; Suárez 2000a:80 Figure 1B). In some cases they were discarded on hearths after suffering impact damage from use, like the point recovered from Cueva del Medio (Nami 1987:91 Figure 16B). Therefore I suggest that the differences in design noted in the shape of the shoulders of Fell points of the Southern Cone may be the result of resharpening to rejuvenate these hunting weapons during their long use-life (Figure 2). Other possible causes of the variability in the design of Fell points are: a) points made by different peoples, b) specific techno-functional requirements, c) expressions of cultural significance, d) individual knapper style, e) unique requirements for hunting specific prey.

Two Paleoindian components have been identified in Uruguay. The first component, Fell 1, is associated with the late-Pleistocene inhabitants of Uruguay who carried hunting weapons of the classic design of Fell points, in the region of the Argentine pampas and Patagonia dated ca. 10,800–10,100 yr B.P. The second component, Pay Paso, was made in more recent Paleoindian times (ca. 9500–8600 yr B.P.) in Uruguay. The future of research into Paleoindian occupations in Uruguay is quite encouraging, for there is solid stratigraphic evidence in sites dating to the Pleistocene/Holocene transition and there are still vast areas to explore in this interesting field.

Acknowledgments

Research was financed by CONICYT, Fondo Clemente Estable 1999 project Nº 5093; Comisión Nacional de Arqueología (M.E.C.). The author wishes to thank L. Miotti, N. Flegenheimer and C. Gnecco for their accurate comments and suggestions in a previous draft of this paper. Finally to the editors for their observations and corrections to this paper. The paper contents are the responsibility of the author. This paper is dedicated to the memory of Roberto Beto Moreira, who was an excellent field guide, an expert of the Uruguay-Cuareim rivers like none other, and a fine friend.

References Cited

Austral, A.

1994 La Campaña de 1989 en el Sitio Pay Paso, Río Quarai, Dpto. Artigas, Rep. Oriental del Uruguay. *Revista del Museo de Historia Natural de San Rafael (Actas y Memorias del XI Congreso Nacional de Arqueologia Argentina),* XIV (1/4):365.

Bird, J.

1969 A Comparison of South Chilean and Ecuatorial «Fishtail» Projectile Points. *The Kroeber Anthropological Society Papers* 40:52–71.

Bombin, M.

1976 Modelo Paleoecológico Evolutivo para o Neoquaternario da Região da Campaña Oeste do Río Grande do Sul (Brasil) A Formacão Touro Passo, seu Conteúdo Fossilifero e a Pedogenese Posdeposicional. *Comunicacões do Museo de Ciencias da PUCRGS,* Vol 15:1–90. Porto Alegre.

Bosh, A., J. Femenías, and A. Olivera
1974 Dispersión de las Puntas de Proyectil Líticas Pisciformes en el Uruguay. In *III* Congreso Nacional de Arqueología VI Encuentro de Arqueología del Litoral *C.E.A. S/n.*Montevideo.

Emperaire, J., A. Laming, and H. Richlen
1963 La Grotte Fell et Autres Sites de la Région Volcanique de la Patagonie Chilienne. *Journal de la Société des Américanistes. Nouvele série* (52):169–254.

Figueira, J. H.
1892 Los Primitivos Habitantes del Uruguay. *Uruguay en la Exposición Histórico Americana de Madrid.* Montevideo, Uruguay.

Flegenheimer, N., and M. Zárate
1989 Paleoindian Occupations at Cerro El Sombrero Locality, Buenos Aires province, Argentina. *Current Research in the Pleistocene* 6:12–13.
1997 Considerations on Radiocarbon and Calibrated Dates from Cerro La China and Cerro El Sombrero, Argentina. *Current Research in the Pleistocene* 14:27–28.

Hilbert, K.
1991 *Aspectos de la Arqueología en el Uruguay.* Verlang Philipp Von Zabern. Mainz Am Rhein, Germany.

Martínez, G.
1997 A Preliminary Report on Paso Otero 5, a Late Pleistocene Site in the Pampean Region of Argentina. *Current Research in the Pleistocene* 14:53–55.

Mazzanti, D.
1999 Ocupaciones Humanas Tempranas en Sierra La Vigilancia y Laguna La Brava, Tandilia Oriental, Provincia de Buenos Aires. *XII Congreso Nacional de Arqueología Argentina*, Edited by C. Diez, pp. 149–155. Facultad de Ciencias Naturales y Museo de la Universidad Nacional de La Plata.

M.E.C. (Ministerio de Educación y Cultura)
1989 *Misión de Rescate Arqueológico de Salto Grande.* Tomo 2, Primera Parte pp. 1–609. Montevideo, Uruguay.

Meneghin, H.
1977 Nuevas Investigaciones en los Yacimientos del "Cerro de los Burros". *Edited by the author.* Montevideo, Uruguay.

Mentz, P., J. Soloviy, and A. Herberts
1995 Levantamentos Arqueologicos da Região do Areal, Quarai, RS. In *VIII Congreso Nacional de Arqueología Uruguaya* :193–211. Maldonado, Uruguay.

Miotti, L.
1996 Piedra Museo (Santa Cruz), Nuevos Datos para la Ocupación Pleistocenica en Patagonia. *Arqueología Sólo Patagonia II Jornadas de Arqueología de la Patagonia*:27–38. Centro Nacional Patagonico.

Nami, H. G.
1985-86 Excavación Arqueológica y Hallazgo de una Punta de Proyectil «Fell 1» en la Cueva del Medio, Seno de Ultima Esperanza Chile. *Anales del Instituto de la Patagonia* 16:103–109.
1987 Cueva del Medio: Perspectivas Arqueológicas para la Patagonia Austral. *Anales del Instituto de la Patagonia, Serie Ciencias Sociales* (17):73–106.
1997 Investigaciones Actualisticas para Discutir Aspectos Técnicos de los Cazadores Recolectores del Ttardiglacial: El Problema Clovis-Cueva Fell. *Anales del Instituto de la Patagonia, Serie Ciencias Sociales* (25):151–186.
2000 Technological Comments on Some Paleoindian Lithic Artifacts from Ilaló, Ecuador. *Current Research in the Pleistocene* 17:104–107.

2001 Consideraciones tecnológicas preliminares sobre los artefactos líticos de Cerro de los Burros (Maldonado, Uruguay). *Comunicaciones Antropológicas Museos Nacionales de Historia Natural y Antropología*. III (21):1–24.

Piñeiro, G., R. Suárez, and A. Gascue

1999 Transición Pleistoceno-Holoceno en los Sitios Arqueológicos del Río Uruguay Medio: Sedimentos Asociados. *I Jornadas del Cenozoico en Uruguay*:19–20. Facultad de Ciencias.

Politis, G.

1991 Fishtail Projectile Points in the Southern Cone of South America: An Overview. In *Clovis: Origins and Adaptations*: edited by R. Bonnichsen and K. Turnmire, pp. 287–301. Center for the Study of Early Man, Orono, ME.

Suárez, R.

1998 *¿Tallarían Puntas de Proyectil? Los Bifaces del Catalán Chico: El Proceso Tecnológico*. Tesis de Licenciatura inédita. F.H.C.E. Universidad de la República, Montevideo, Uruguay.

1999 Cazadores Recolectores en la Transición Pleistoceno-Holoceno del Norte Uruguayo: Fuentes de Abastecimiento de Materias Primas y Tecnología Lítica. *I Jornadas del Cenozoico en Uruguay*:27–28. Facultad de Ciencias.

2000a Paleoindian Occupations in Uruguay. *Current Research in the Pleistocene* 17:78–80.

2000b Evidence of Human Occupation During the Transition Pleistocene-Holocene in the North of Uruguay: Paleoindian Sites, Fishtail Projetile Points and New Radiocarbon Dates for the Archaeological Region of Uruguay-Cuareim Rivers. *International Workshop of INQUA, The Colonization of South America during the Plesitocene/Holocene Transition,* Abstracts: 35. La Plata, Argentina.

2001 Technomorphological Observations on Fishtail Projectile Points and Bifacial Artifacts from Northen Uruguay. *Current Research in the Pleistocene* Vol. 18:56–58.

2002 Investigaciones Paleoindias en Uruguay: Estado Actual del Conocimiento y Recientes Investigaciones en la Localidad Arqueológica Pay Paso (Río Cuareim, Dpto Artigas). In *Del Mar a los Salitrales Diez Mil Años de Historia Indigena en el Umbral del Tercer Milenio.* Edited by D. L. Mazzanti, M. A. Berón, and F. W. Oliva, pp. 311–326. Mar del Plata.

2003 First Records of Pleistocene Fauna for an Archaeological Context in Uruguay: Evidences from Pay Paso Locality, Site 1. *Current Research in the Pleistocene,* Vol. 20 (in press).

Suárez, R., and G. Piñeiro

2002 La Cantera Taller del A° Catalán Chico: Nuevos Aportes a un Viejo Problema de la Arqueología Uruguaya. In *Del Mar a los Salitrales Diez Mil Años de Historia Indigena en el Umbral del Tercer Milenio.* Edited by D. L. Mazzanti, M. A. Berón, and F. W. Oliva, pp. 263–279. Mar del Plata.

Suárez, R., and J. López

2003 Archaeology of the Pleistocene-Holocene Transition in Uruguay: An Overview. *Quaternary International* 109–110:65–79.

Ubilla M., and D. Perea

1999 Quaternary Vertebrates of Uruguay: A Biostratigraphic, Biogeographic and Climatic Overview. *Quaternary of South America and Antarctic Peninsula*. 12 (1996–1997):75–90.

Geoarchaeology of Paso Otero 5 (Pampas of Argentina)

Vance Holliday[1], Gustavo Martínez[2], Eileen Johnson[3], and Briggs Buchanan[4]

The Paso Otero 5 site (38° 12′ 08″ S , 59° 06′ 58″ W) is located in the middle basin of the Quequén Grande River (Interserrana Bonaerense Area, Buenos Aires Province, Argentina). Analysis of the geology as well as the artifacts recovered from an area of 20 m² excavated and supervised by Martínez (1997, 1999, 2001) forms the basis of the reported cultural association.

The general stratigraphic sequence in the area is represented by sediments of the Luján Formation and its two members, the late-Pleistocene Guerrero Member (GM) and the early- to middle-Holocene Río Salado Member (RSM). The GM includes alluvial and aeolian facies; the RSM is a fluvial deposit representing an aggrading floodplain. Aeolian sediments of La Postrera Formation rest on top of the Luján Formation (Johnson et al. 1998; Tonni and Fidalgo 1978; Zárate et al. 1998).

Stratigraphy and Geochronology of Paso Otero 5

The geoarchaeological field work at Paso Otero 5 was carried out in 1998 by the authors. The section exposed by the excavations as well as a cutbank exposure was described using standard soil and stratigraphic nomenclature and procedures. Samples for radiocarbon analyses were collected from the upper 5–10 cm of each buried A horizon. For each sample, dates on

[1] Depts.of Anthropology and Geography, University of Arizona, P.O. Box 210030, Tucson, AZ 85721-0030. e-mail: vthollid@email.arizona.edu

[2] CONICET–INCUAPA–UNCPBA. Del Valle 5737 (7400) Olavarría, Bs. As. e-mail: gmartine@soc.unicen.edu.ar

[3] Museum of Texas Tech University, Lubbock, Texas 79409-3191. e-mail: Eileen.johnson@ttu.edu

[4] Museum of Texas Tech University, Lubbock, Texas 79409-3191. e-mail: briggs@unm.edu

the "humate" (humic acid extraction or base soluble humic acids) and on the "soil residue" (humin) fractions were run. The dates are expressed in uncorrected and corrected ^{14}C ages but not calibrated radiocarbon yr B.P. (Table 1). In each pair of corrected dates, the older is assumed to be closer to the "true" age because in general contamination by younger carbon is more likely than contamination by older carbon (Holliday 1995; Martin and Johnson 1995; Wang et al. 1996).

Table 1. Radiocarbon data from Paso Otero 5 site, organic matter and bone analysis

	Base soluble humic acids			Soil residue		
Soil	Uncorrected ^{14}C age (B.P.)	Corrected ^{14}C age (B.P.)	$\delta^{13}/_{12}C$ (‰)	Uncorrected ^{14}C age (B.P.)	Corrected ^{14}C age (B.P.)	$\delta^{13}/_{12}C$ (‰)
Ab3 (140–153 cm)	6524 ± 127 (DRI-3603)	6629 ± 129 (DRI-3603)	-18.50 ± 0.05	6331 ± 93 (DRI-3604)	6412 ± 95 (DRI-3604)	-19.98 ± 0.05
Ab4 (166–172 cm)	7253 ± 84 (DRI-3601)	7366 ± 86 (DRI-3601)	-18.02 ± 0.05	7684 ± 69 (DRI-3602)	7794 ± 71 (DRI-3602)	-18.20 ± 0.05
Ab5 (186–197 cm)	8315 ± 89 (DRI-3605)	8415 ± 91 (DRI-3605)	-18.79 ± 0.05	8683 ± 87 (DRI-3606)	8793 ± 89 (DRI-3606)	-18.20 ± 0.05
Ab6 (213–224 cm)	8767 ± 290 (DRI-3572)	8863 ± 292 (DRI-3572)	- 19.06 ± 0.05	9292 ± 114 (DRI-3573)	9399 ± 116 (DRI-3573)	-18.40 ± 0.05

Bone			^{14}C age (B.P.)	$\delta^{13}/_{12}C$ (‰)
Burned megamammal (AA-19291)	U1- SSE	2.55–2.60 m	10,190 ± 120	-20.6
Burned *Megatherium* sp. (AA-39363)	U1- SSE	2.55–2.60 m	10,440 ± 100	-19.8

The stratigraphy at Paso Otero 5 is generally representative of the upper Luján Formation with slight differences (Figure 1). The lower section exposes the green Guerrero Member (GM) (ca. 230–240 cm below the surface), a sandy loam subjected to some weathering in the form of oxidation, giving it a mottled appearance (hence Cgb6 horizon). This weathering is probably related to an overlying A horizon at the base of the RSM. This member traditionally has been interpreted as a result of lacustrine and paludal facies, although diatomaceous deposits are also recorded in different parts of the basin (e.g., La Horqueta II site, see Zárate et al. 1998:139). The RSM here is similar to that at Paso Otero 1 (Johnson et al. 1998) and traceable for hundreds of meters along the cutbanks of the river. The RSM consists of a series of carbonate layers, or "marls," each with a weakly developed soil (producing A-C or A-Bk profiles). The density of these marls is very low, likely due to a high content of volcanic ash and diatoms.

The buried soils in the RSM are indicative of six periods of landscape stability. Four of these soils are dated. The Ab6 horizon (Figure 1) separates the two members of the Luján Formation and is correlated with the regionally developed Puesto Callejón Viejo soil that separates the two members of the Luján Formation (Tonni and Fidalgo 1978). This A horizon formed at the top of the GM contains the archaeological deposit dated on bone to ca. 10,200–10,450 yr B.P. (see Figure 1 and Table 1). The top of this A horizon was dated to 9399 ± 116 yr B.P. The overlying sediments and buried soils span much of the early and middle Holocene. The Ab5 horizon dates to ca. 8800 yr B.P.; the Ab4 to ca. 7800 yr B.P.; and the Ab3 to ca. 6600 yr B.P. (Table 1). The Ab2 and Ab1 soils have not been dated. La Postrera Formation appears to be missing from the Paso Otero 5 sequence, although the

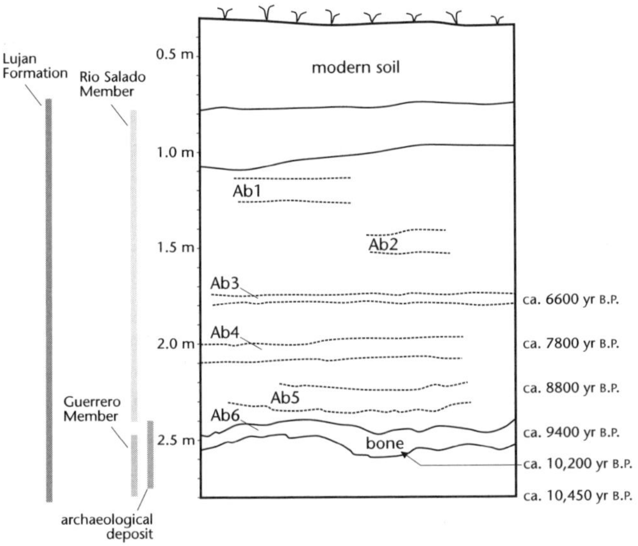

Figure 1. Stratigraphic column at Paso Otero 5 site, geological formations and its members, location of the archaeological deposit, and soil radiocarbon ages.

high sand content of the modern A horizon may be related to La Postrera deposition.

The Archaeological Record

With the exception of a few items that were recorded near the contacts between the RSM-GM and the Ab6 soil (Figure 1), the assemblage was found almost exclusively within the paleosol. The most remarkable artifact is a fishtail projectile point (Figure 2). Although the stem and the tip of this artifact are partially missing owing to fractures, the shoulders and the piece of what remains of the stem have diagnostic attributes indicating a fishtail type (e.g., stem thickness and edge grinding). No other type of projectile point on the Pampas has such attributes (N. Flegenheimer pers. comm. 1997). It is made from a red chalcedony (silica micro-cryptocrystalline) frequently found in early sites dating to 10,000–11,000 yr B.P. in the pampas. Recent studies suggest that the quarries for this raw material are located in Uruguay, where fishtail projectile points made from this rock are found in surface sites (Flegenheimer et al. 2003). Although fishtail projectile points have been reported at surface sites in the Interserrana Bonaerense Area (Flegenheimer and Bayón 1996; Politis 1991), the Paso Otero 5 specimen is the first recorded in a clear stratigraphic Pleistocene-Holocene sealed archaeological context and with megamammal bones (Martínez 2000, 2001). The projectile point and the other lithics at the site were recorded in close association with bones (see Figures in Martínez 2001).

Identified taxa are *Megatherium americanum* (giant ground sloth), *Equus neogeus* (extinct horse), *Toxodon* sp. (Toxodon), *Glossotherium* sp. (ground sloth), *Hemiauchenia* sp. (extinct camelid), *Glyptodon* sp. (giant armadillo), *Lama guanicoe* (guanaco), and Xenarthra (see Table 1 in Martínez 2001). A remarkable feature is the quantity of burned bones. They are concentrated around a calcaneum (*Megatherium americanum*) and a megamammal vertebra (Xenarthra) (see Figures in Martínez 2001). The intensity of combustion, a mixed burning con-

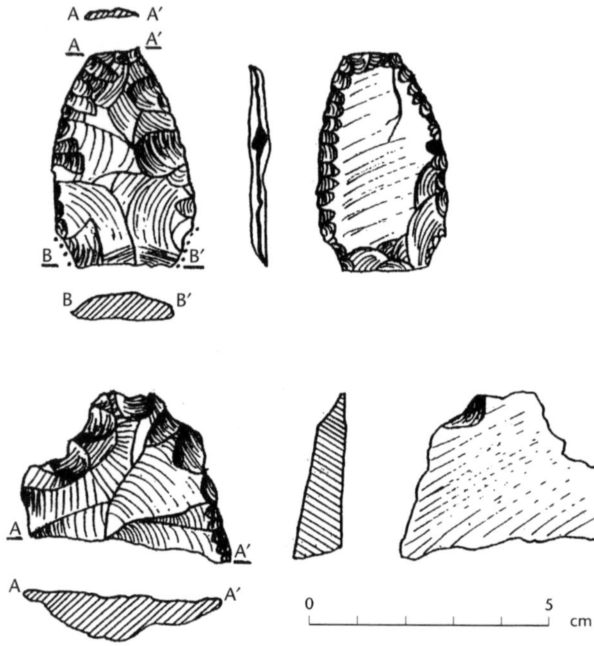

Figure 2. The fishtail projectile point and a multipurpose tool.

dition from not-burned to calcined stages, and high degree of fragmentation caused by fire support the idea that bone was used as fuel (Martínez 1999, 2001).

Discussion and Conclusions

The stratigraphy, soils, and radiocarbon dates from Paso Otero 5 provide evidence of episodic floodplain sedimentation and stability in cycles of ca. 1000 years between ca. 6600 and 9400 yr B.P. and probably throughout most of the rest of the Holocene. The soils and stratigraphy also indicate that little post-depositional alteration of the archaeological deposit and overlying sediments occurred. The age of ca. 9400 yr B.P. on the Ab6 provides a minimal age for the archaeological material contained in the soil and is probably close to the age of the burial by the overlying sediments.

Megamammal bone from the bed itself is dated to ca. 10,190 and ca. 10,440 yr B.P. The dating of the bone and associated soil shows that human activity and burial of Ab6 both took place at around the Pleistocene-Holocene boundary. Humates from the same soil at Paso Otero 1, located on the opposite bank of the river from Paso Otero 5, date to ca. 9950 yr B.P. (Johnson et al. 1998:20). Thus, the lowest soils at each site, Ab4 at PO1 (Ab3 in Johnson et al. 1998) and Ab6 at PO5, were buried at about the same time (a little less than 10,000 yr B.P.).

At La Horqueta II site, 30 km downstream, a similar stratigraphic column was studied (Zárate et al. 1998). A radiocarbon date obtained from the organic matter of the upper part of the Puesto Callejón Viejo soil yielded an age of 9000 ± 70 yr B.P. (Beta 79439; Zárate et al. 1998:142–143; Figure 3, Table 2). Gastropod shells obtained from 5 cm above the base of the RSM, near the contact with the buried soil, yielded ages of 9340 ± 110 yr B.P. (Beta

84180) and 9820 ± 100 yr B.P. (1972 AECV). The older ages of the gastropods may be due to reservoir effect, calculated in the Arroyo Tapalqué basin (200 km northwest) at ca. 1100 ± 300 yr B.P. (Figini et al. 1996). The buried soils were not subject to this age offset "because the carbon uptake of terrestrial vegetation appeared to be dominated by photosynthesis" (Figini et al. 1996; Zárate et al. 1998:142–143).

The soils provide a general perspective of environmental conditions along the Río Quequén during the past 10,000 years. The deposits probably represent episodic sedimentation in the backswamp portion of a floodplain. Thus the site was in a very low energy setting hydrologically. The iron oxidation and mottling of the Ab6 soil indicate it was subjected to a fluctuating water table following burial, and throughout much of the Holocene the soils probably formed under conditions of a high water table, indicated by the relatively high content of organic matter and the absence of leaching of the carbonates.

Radiocarbon data from bones have been difficult to obtain. From 11 processed samples, only 2 have been successful. The study of diagenetic parameters in bones (porosity, crystallinity (IRSF), diagenetic carbonate content (C/P), calcite, protein content (percent N) and histology) for Paso Otero 1, 3, and 5 indicates a pattern of differential bone preservation due to hydrolysis, microorganism action, and probably, time (Gutiérrez 1998; Gutiérrez et al. 2001). The conditions of the Ab6 paleosetting (soil subjected to a fluctuating water table) agree with the results obtained by the diagenetic study.

Bones of at least five extinct megamammal genera are present at Paso Otero 5. Their taphonomy provides some insight into the site formation processes. The bone is weathered subaerially, with some elements exhibiting exfoliation and deep desiccation cracks. Carnivore modification occurs on other bones. Given the size and amount of available edible tissues of these animals, the idea of a simultaneous procurement is difficult to support. Martínez (1999, 2001) has proposed that the site was not formed through a single event but rather by several hunting/scavenging episodes, suggesting that the same place in the landscape was reoccupied by the hunters. If bone was used for fuel, a possible procurement strategy of collecting bones from carcasses near the site may have been implemented. Such a strategy could explain the large number of taxa recovered yet each taxa being represented by only a few elements, and it would further agree with the types of natural modification recorded on the bone surfaces.

Cultural modification is present in the form of helical fractures, radial intersecting fracture fronts, and blow marks (Martínez 1999). As for the nature of the bone bed, its setting is a very low energy environment and the bones lack fluvial modification such as rounding and polishing.

Stratigraphic and chronological information obtained from Paso Otero 5 has been useful in evaluating site formation processes and aspects related to the integrity of the site. Further comparison with the other Paso Otero locality sites will allow the construction of a model for the middle stream of the Río Quequén Grande.

Acknowledgments

Support for the Paso Otero 5 stratigraphy and geochronology research was provided to Johnson by the National Science Foundation International Program (INT9603078) and Museum of Texas Tech University and represents part of the ongoing Lubbock Lake Landmark research into grasslands hunter-gatherers of the Americas. Excavations were supported by the Universidad Nacional del Centro annual budget given to INCUAPA. Radiocarbon dating was carried out at the Desert Research Institute, Las Vegas, Nevada. The soil analyses were performed in the geomorphology laboratory of the Department of Geography, University of Wisconsin-Madison, by Jemuel Ripley and James Mayer. Thanks to Dr. James Steele for including Paso Otero 5 as part of his research program "Dating the earliest human occupation of southern South America." The figures were made by Soledad Sartori and Gustavo Gómez.

References Cited

Figini, A. J., F. Fidalgo, R. Huarte, J. Carbonari, and R. Gentile
1996 Cronología Radiocarbónica de los Sedimentos de la Fm. Luján en Arroyo Tapalqué, Provincia de Buenos Aires. *IV Jornadas Geológicas Bonaerenses*, Actas 1:119–126. Junín. Argentina.

Flegenheimer, N., and C. Bayón
1996 Surface Fell's Cave Stemmed Points in the Argentine Pampas. *Current Research in the Pleistocene* 13:17–19.

Flegenheimer, N., C. Bayón, M. Valente, J. Baeza, and J. Femenías
2003 Long Distance Tool Stone Transport in the Argentine Pampas. *Quaternary International* 109–110:49–64.

Gutiérrez, M.
1998 *Taphonomic Effects and State of Preservation of the Guanaco (Lama guanicoe) Bone Bed From Paso Otero 1 (Buenos Aires Province, Argentina).* Unpublished thesis, University of Texas Tech. Lubbock, TX.

Gutiérrez, M., G. Martínez, and C. Nielsen-Marsh
2001 Alteración Diagenética y Preservación Diferencial de los Conjuntos Óseos de la Localidad Arqueológica Paso Otero (Provincia de Buenos Aires, Argentina). *Estudios Geológicos* 56:291–299. Museo Nacional de Ciencias Naturales, Madrid, Spain.

Holliday, V. T.
1995 Stratigraphy and Paleoenvironments of Late Quaternary Valley Fills on the Southern High Plains. *Geological Society of America Memoir* 186:1–136.

Johnson, E., G. Politis, G. Martínez, T. Hartwell, M. Gutiérrez, and H. Haas
1998 The Radiocarbon Chronology of Paso Otero 1 in the Pampean Region of Argentina. *Quaternary of South America and Antarctic Peninsula* 11(1995):15–25.

Martin, C., and W. Johnson
1995 Variation in Radiocarbon Ages of Soil Organic Matter Fractions from Late Quaternary Buried Soils. *Quaternary Research* 43:232–237.

Martínez, G.
1997 A Preliminary Report of the Late Pleistocene Site of Paso Otero 5 in the Pampean Region of Argentina. *Current Research in the Pleistocene* 14:53–55.

1999 *Tecnología, Subsistencia y Asentamiento en el Curso Medio del Río Quequén Grande: Un Enfoque Arqueológico.* Unpublished Ph.D. Dissertation. Facultad de Ciencias Naturales y Museo. Universidad Nacional de La Plata. La Plata, Argentina.

2000 Late Pleistocene-early Holocene Archaeological Sites in the Pampean Region: An Approach to the Organization of Early Human Occupations (Buenos Aires Province, Argentina). Book of Abstacts of the *International* Workshop of INQUA. The Colonization of South America during the *Pleistocene-Holocene Transition*, p. 23. Facultad de Ciencias Naturales y Museo. La Plata and Santa Cruz Province.

Martínez, G.
2001 "Fish-tail" Projectile Points and Megamammals: New Evidence from Paso Otero 5 (Argentina). *Antiquity* 75:523–528.

Politis, G.
1991 Fishtail Projectile Points in the Southern Cone of South America: An Overview. In *Clovis:*

Origins and Adaptations, edited by R. Bonnichsen and K. Turnmire, pp. 287–301. Center for the Study of the First Americans. Orono, ME.

Tonni, E., and F. Fidalgo
1978 Consideraciones sobre los Cambios Climáticos durante el Pleistoceno Tardío-Reciente en la Provincia de Buenos Aires. Aspectos Ecológicos y Zoogeográficos Relacionados. *Ameghiniana* 15 (1-2): 235–253.

Wang, Y., R. Amundson, and S. Trumbore
1996 Radiocarbon Dating of Soil Organic Matter. *Quaternary Research* 45:282–288.

Zárate, M., M. Espinosa, and L. Ferrero
1998 Paleoenvironmental Implications of the Holocene Diatomite, Pampa Interserrana, Argentina. *Quaternary of South America and Antarctic Peninsula* 11(1995):135–152.

Survival of Pleistocene Fauna: New Radiocarbon Dates on Organic Sediments from La Moderna (Pampean Region, Argentina)

Gustavo G. Politis[1], Eileen Johnson[2], María A. Gutierrez[3], and William T. Hartwell[4]

La Moderna was the first recorded archaeological site from the Pampean region where the stratigraphic association between lithic artifacts and extinct faunal remains was confirmed in the early 1970s (Palanca and Politis 1979; Palanca et al. 1972, 1973). Archaeological material recovered at this site from the lithostratigraphic unit (a′) was identified as the lower component (Politis 1984). This material constituted an important source of information for understanding the early peopling of the region and discussing the role of humans in Pleistocene faunal extinction. The majority of the archaeological material recovered during the initial field seasons, however, was lost as the result of relocating the collections to the local museum in Olavarría (Buenos Aires Province); two floods inundated the city and museum in 1979 and 1981. Thereafter, new excavations and results from faunal, taphonomic, and technological analyses improved the characterization of the human occupation of the site (Politis and Gutierrez 1998).

Based on these results, the lower component of La Moderna has been interpreted as a procurement site, where in a single event *Doedicurus clavicaudatus* (Glyptodontidae) was butchered at the edge of an ancient swamp. In order to carry out this activity, expedient tools

[1] CONICET–INCUAPA. Facultad de Ciencias Sociales (UNCPBA) and Facultad de Ciencias Naturales y Museo (UNLP). Avda. del Valle 5737. B7400JWI. Olavarría, Bs. As., Argentina. e-mail: gpolitis@museo.fcnym.unlp.edu.ar

[2] Museum of Texas Tech University, Lubbock, Texas, 79409-3191. e-mail: eileen.johnson@ttu.edu

[3] CONICET–INCUAPA. Facultad de Ciencias Sociales (UNCPBA). Avda. del Valle 5737. B7400JWI. Olavarría, Bs. As., Argentina. e-mail: mgutierr@soc.unicen.edu.ar

[4] Desert Research Institute, Quaternary Sciences Center, Las Vegas, Nevada 89132. e-mail: tedh@dri.edu

of crystalline quartz (a raw material whose source is located a few kilometers from the site) and some curated tools of quartzite and chert (an outcrop of which is located over 17 km from the site) were used (Politis and Gutierrez 1998). The archaeological materials, both lithic and faunal, were recorded within the Luján Formation in a transitional unit (a′) between the Río Salado and Guerrero Members (Zetti et al. 1972).

The chronology of this occupational event has always been problematic and controversial. Consequently, multiple dates have been run on *Glyptodon* bone collagen. The first dating result, a standard date processed by Beta Analytic, yielded an age considered too young: 6550 ± 160 yr B.P. A second date of 12,350 ± 370 yr B.P. was obtained by AMS from the ISOTRACE radiocarbon laboratory in Toronto. However, two additional dates on the same bone sample from the same laboratory, but with a more appropriate pretreatment, yielded dates of 7010 ± 100 yr B.P. and 7510 ± 370 yr B.P. (Beukens 1992). Finally, a radiocarbon date on another bone fragment gave a result close to these dates, 7460 ± 80 yr B.P. As a consequence, this series of dates has established the proposed chronology of the lower component from La Moderna at 7000–7500 yr B.P. (Politis and Gutierrez 1998).

As part of a regional approach to taphonomy and geochronology of early pampean sites (Gutierrez et al. 1997; Johnson and Politis 1993; Johnson et al. 1997, 1998, 2000), organic sediment samples from La Moderna were dated. The samples were taken from the north wall of the stratigraphic column of unit 8, following procedures outlined by Haas et al. (1986). Sample C-MQ8-1 came from sediments with a high content of organic matter (a buried A-horizon) that occur immediately above the archaeological level (Figure 1). This sample was located 1.57–1.62 m below the surface. Sample C-MQ8-2 came from sediments directly associated with the archaeological material, 1.62–1.65 m below the surface (Figure 1). Both samples were taken from lithostratigraphic unit (a′). Two quartz microflakes were recovered from this unit during the radiocarbon sampling. Analyses were carried out only on the soil humates fraction, the results of which are shown in Table 1.

Table 1. Radiocarbon dates from the soil humates fraction of La Moderna sediments.

Field no.	DRI date no.	$\delta^{13}/_{12}C$ (‰)	Uncorrected ^{14}C age (B.P.)	Corrected ^{14}C age (B.P.)
C-MQ8-1	3012	-20.51	8284 ± 63	8356 ± 65
C-MQ8-2	3013	-23.07	7417 ± 107	7448 ± 109

Discussion and Conclusions

These new radiocarbon results should be regarded with caution for two main reasons. First, dates from organic matter from sediments represent the mean residence time of these organic constituents plus the time since burial of the dated sediments (Martin and Johnson 1995). Because young carbon is continuously incorporated into the sediments (Martin and Johnson 1994; Wang et al. 1996), the results obtained from this type of dating are considered the *minimum* age of the soil formation. A limitation of this type of dating when dealing with archaeological sites is that the probability of obtaining a "true age" for the archaeological event is low. What is dated is the development of the concentration of organic matter by

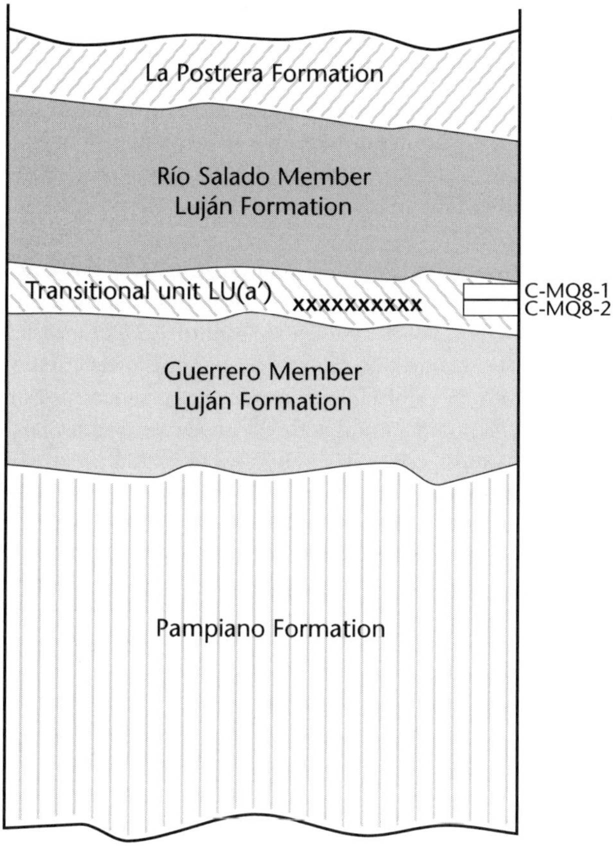

Figure 1. Idealized stratigraphic profile showing the location of sediment samples LU(a′) taken for radiocarbon dating. Samples for bone collagen dating were taken from archaeological deposits recovered within LU(a′).

whichever process that formed it (e.g., pedogenesis, accumulation at the bottom of a lagoon) that does not necessarily reflect the time of the archaeological occupation. The date provides an upper bracketing age (i.e., older than the date) for an occupation.

Second, the inverse position of the dates (the older date is stratigraphically above the younger one) suggests specific problems of contamination due either to methodology or to differential addition of organic matter to the samples. However, the latter seems unlikely since both samples came from the same transitional unit (a′) and only about 5 cm apart. The more likely cause of the problem is that only one fraction was dated. Paired dating (humates and residue) provides the opportunity to evaluate the results and use the older of the two dates as the more reliable age. In the pair, the older date is considered closer to the "true age" because in general contamination by younger carbon is more likely than contamination by older carbon (Holliday 1995; Martin and Johnson 1994; Wang et al. 1995).

Dates for bone and organic sediments are now available for La Moderna. Many things can affect the results of radiocarbon assays of bone and soils (Taylor 1987). Ultimately the issue is site specific and even sample specific. In order to compare effectively the dates for bone and organic sediments from La Moderna, the sediments would have to be resampled and both fractions tested. Nevertheless, the result from sample C-MQ8-2 is synchronic with the estimated age from the deposit based on dates of LM 2.4 and LM 1.4, that is, ca. 7000–7500 yr B.P. (see Politis and Gutierrez 1998). This result generally supports the early-Holocene chronology of the lower component.

Pleistocene faunal survival in South America is currently a matter of debate. Empirical support is provided by evidence of megamammal remains from pampean archaeological sites dated to the Holocene (Miotti and Salemme 1999; Politis et al. 1995; Tonni 1992). One of the strongest candidates in this discussion, and the one most commonly cited, is the lower component of Arroyo Seco 2, where three radiocarbon dates of Holocene age have been obtained on bones of extinct horse (*Equus [Amerhippus] neogeus*) and ground sloth (*Megatherium americanum*): 8890 ± 90 (TO-1504), 8470 ± 240 (LP-53), and 7320 ± 50 (TO-1506) yr B.P. However, 10 new AMS dates on megamammal bone from Arroyo Seco 2 from different radiocarbon laboratories range from 10,500 ± 90 yr B.P. to 12,240 ± 110 yr B.P. (Gutierrez et al. 2000; Steele et al. 2001). Among these, the date of 12,200 ± 170 yr B.P. (CAMS-58182) is particularly significant as it was obtained on *Megatherium americanum* bone previously dated to 7320 ± 50 (TO-1506) yr B.P. Consequently, this group of mammals does not appear to support a Holocene faunal survival as was proposed previously (i.e., Martínez 1999; Miotti and Salemme 1999; Politis and Beukens 1991; Politis and Gutierrez 1998; Politis et al. 1995).

Several aspects of radiocarbon dates on organic sediments should be considered when evaluating the results, especially when comparing them with results obtained on other organic samples (Taylor 1987). For the pampas, these other samples are primarily bone collagen. Although the issue is far from resolved, a series of radiocarbon dates from different types of samples appears to be one of the most promising approaches. As such, the new dates generally support the current accepted chronology of the lower component of La Moderna of ca. 7000–7500 yr B.P. and as a consequence confirm the survival of one Pleistocene megamammal into the early Holocene.

Acknowledgments

Support for the La Moderna geochronology research was provided to Johnson by the National Science Foundation International Program (INT9603078) and Museum of Texas Tech University and represents part of the ongoing Lubbock Lake Landmark research into grasslands hunter-gatherers of the Americas. Radiocarbon dating was carried out at the Desert Research Institute, Las Vegas, Nevada. This paper is part of the INCUAPA (Investigaciones Arqueológicas y Paleontólogicas del Cuaternario Pampeano) Research Program which receives funds from CONICET (PIP- nro. 4721/96), Agencia Nacional de Promoción Científica y Tecnológica (Proyecto nro. 04-00000-01566) and Universidad Nacional del Centro de la Pcia. de Buenos Aires (Argentina).

References Cited

Beukens, R. P.

1992 Report on the Results of the Radiocarbon Dates to Gustavo Politis. Ms. in the Department of Archaeology, Facultad de Ciencias Naturales, Universidad Nacional de La Plata, La Plata, Argentina.

Gutierrez, M. A., G. G. Politis, and E. Johnson
2000 La Ocupación Más Temprana en Arroyo Seco 2. Paper presented at the II Congreso de Arqueología de la Región Pampeana Argentina. Mar del Plata. November 27–30, 2000.

Gutierrez, M. A., G. Martínez, E. Johnson, G. G. Politis, and W. Hartwell
1997 Nuevos Análisis Óseos en el Sitio Paso Otero 1. In *La Arqueología de la Región Pampeana en la Década de los '90*, edited by M. Berón and G. Politis, pp.213–228. Museo de Historia Natural de San Rafael, (Mendoza)- INCUAPA, FACSO, UNICEN.

Haas, H., V. T. Holliday and R. Stuckenrath
1986 Dating of Holocene Stratigraphy with Soluble and Insoluble Organic Fractions at the Lubbock Lake Archaeological Site, Texas: An Ideal Case Study. *Radiocarbon* 28(2A):473–485.

Holliday, V. T.
1995 Stratigraphy and Paleoenvironments of Late Quaternary Valley Fills on the Southern High Plains. *Geological Society of America Memoir* 186:1–136.

Johnson, E., M. A. Gutierrez, G. G. Politis, G. A. Martínez, and W. T. Hartwell
1997 Holocene Taphonomy at Paso Otero 1 on the Eastern Pampas of Argentina. In *Proceedings of the 1993 Bone Modification Conference, Hot Springs, South Dakota*, edited by A. Hannus, L. Rossum, and P. Winham, pp. 105–121. Augustana College, Archaeology Laboratory, Occasional Paper.

Johnson, E., and G. Politis
1993 New World Grasslands Hunter-Gatherers in the Late Pleistocene and Early Holocene. *Current Research in the Pleistocene* 10:24–27.

Johnson, E., G. G. Politis, and M. A. Gutierrez
2000 Early Holocene Bone Technology at the La Olla 1 Site, Atlantic Coast of the Argentine Pampas. *Journal of Archaeological Science* 27:463–477.

Johnson, E., G. G. Politis, G. A. Martínez, W. T. Hartwell, M. A. Gutierrez, and H. Haas
1998 The Radiocarbon Chronology of Paso Otero 1 in the Pampean Region of Argentina. *Quaternary of South America & Antarctic Peninsula* 11(1995):15–25.

Martin, C., and W. Johnson
1995 Variation in Radiocarbon Ages of Soil Organic Matter Fractions From Late Quaternary Buried Soils. *Quaternary Research* 43:232–237.

Martínez, G. A.
1999 *Tecnología, Subsistencia y Asentamiento en el Curso Medio del Río Quequén Grande: Un Enfoque Arqueológico*. Unpublished Doctoral Dissertation. Facultad de Ciencias Naturales, Universidad Nacional de La Plata, La Plata, Argentina.

Miotti, L., and M. Salemme
1999 Biodiversity, Taxonomic Richness and Specialists-Generalists During Late Pleistocene/Early Holocene Times in Pampa and Patagonia (Argentina, Southern South America). *Quaternary International* 53/54:53–68.

Palanca, F., L. Daino, and E. Benbassat
1972 Yacimiento "Estancia La Moderna" (Pdo. de Azul, Provincia de Buenos Aires). Nuevas Perspectivas para la Arqueología de la Pampa Bonaerense. *Etnia* 15:19–27. Olavarría, Argentina.

Palanca, F., L. Gau, and A. Pankonin
1973 Yacimiento "Estancia La Moderna" (Pdo. de Azul, Provincia de Buenos Aires). Nuevas Perspectivas para la Arqueología de la Pampa Bonaerense. *Etnia* 17:1–11. Olavarría, Argentina.

Palanca, F., and G. G. Politis
1979 Los Cazadores de Fauna Extinguida en la Provincia de Buenos Aires. *Prehistoria Bonaerense*, pp. 70–91. Municipalidad de Olavarría, Olavarría, Buenos Aires, Argentina.

Politis, G. G.
1984 *Arqueología del Area Interserrana Bonaerense*. Unpublished Doctoral Dissertation. Facultad de Ciencias Naturales, Universidad Nacional de La Plata, La Plata, Argentina.

Politis, G. G., and R. P. Beukens
1991 Cronología Radiocarbónica de la Ocupacióu Humana del Área Interserrana Bonaerense. *Actas del X Congreso Nacional de Arqueología Argentina*. *Shincal* 3:151–157. San Fernando del Valle de Catamarca, Argentina.

Politis, G. G., and M. A. Gutierrez
1998 Gliptodontes y Cazadores-Recolectores en la Región Pampeana de Argentina. *Latin American Antiquity* 9(2):111–134.

Politis G. G., J. L. Prado, and R. P. Beukens
1995 The Human Impact in Pleistocene-Holocene Extinctions In South America. In *Ancient Peoples and Landscapes*, edited by E. Johnson, pp. 187–206. Museum of Texas Tech University, Lubbock, TX.

Steele, J., G. G. Politis, and P. Pettitt
2001 AMS Radiocarbon Dating of the Earliest Paleoindian Occupation of the Southern Cone of South America. Paper presented at the 66th SAA Annual Meeting. New Orleans, April 18–22, 2001.

Taylor, R. E.
1987 *Radiocarbon Dating*. Academic Press, New York.

Tonni, E. P.
1992 Mamíferos y Clima del Holoceno en la Provincia de Buenos Aires. In *El Holoceno en la Argentina*, edited by M. Iriondo, pp. 64–78. CADINQUA 1.

Wang, Y., R. Amundson, and S. Trumbore
1996 Radiocarbon Dating of Soil Organic Matter. *Quaternary Research* 45:282–288.

Zetti, J., E. P. Tonni, and F. Fidalgo
1972 Algunos Rasgos de la Geología Superficial en las Cabeceras del Arroyo del Azul (Provincia de Buenos Aires). *Etnia* 15:28–34. Olavarría, Argentina.

Cerro El Sombrero: A Locality with a View

Nora Flegenheimer

In the last two decades evidence has accumulated of an important occupation in the Tandilia Ranges of the Argentine pampas during the Pleistocene-Holocene transition. Several sites separated by about 50 km, with some similarities in their lithic assemblages and chronology, show considerable variation in human activity and artifact density (Flegenheimer 1994). The sites have been grouped according to the intensity of their occupations (Mazzanti, this volume). Currently known sites include larger domestic sites (Tixi Cave, Los Pinos Shelter, El Abra Cave, and Cerro La China 1 and 3), more ephemeral sites (La Brava Cave and Burucuyá Cave), and sites with a very low density of specific activities (Amalia 2 and La China 2, which probably is a hunting site). Los Helechos possibly also belongs to this latter group (Flegenheimer and Bayón 2000; Flegenheimer and Zárate 1997; Mazzanti 1999, this volume). In this report we describe Cima and Abrigo 1, the two sites currently excavated at Cerro El Sombrero, and discuss the characteristics of their occupation.

All these sites are rockshelters except Sombrero Cima and La China 2 and 3. The living space ranges from about 20 to 200 m^2, only Cima being larger. The living space is limited by the size of the rockshelter or the slope of the surrounding hill; sites in the plains have no natural size restrictions. Two sites of similar chronology are reported from the plains: Paso Otero 5, a site related to hunting, processing, and consuming megamammals (Martínez 1999); and Arroyo Seco 2, an extensive campsite (Politis and Madrid 2001). These sites lie 50 km and 150 km, respectively, from sites in the Ranges. Paso Otero 5 is clearly related to the sites in the Ranges; whether Arroyo Seco 2 is also still being discussed (Politis and Madrid 2001). Isolated finds of fishtail points suggest that other areas of the plains were probably also occupied at this time (Flegenheimer and Bayón 1996; Politis 1991).

Cerro El Sombrero, one of the highest hills in the Tandilia Ranges (429 m a.s.l.), stands out 200 m above the surrounding plains. Its flat top is formed by an orthoquartzite outcrop

CONICET-Area Arqueol. y Antrop., Museo Municipal de Ciencias Naturales de Necochea, C.C. 275, 7630 Necochea, Argentina. e-mail: noraf@necocheanet.com.ar

(Flegenheimer and Zárate 1989). Madrazo (1972) first published the locality as a surface open-air site with an early occupation characterized by fishtail or Fell 1 projectile points. We now know it includes both surface and stratigraphic contexts. Also, some of the small rock-shelters surrounding the hilltop contain sedimentary filling. Six shelters containing archaeological remains were identified during surveys; the largest, 10 minutes' walk from the hilltop, was chosen for excavation.

Abrigo 1

The shelter is 4 m wide and 3 m long. This area of 12 m^2 has been excavated. A small back portion with lower roof, which remains unexcavated, is frequently covered by water that percolates from the orthoquartzites. Two units have been identified in the sedimentary filling (Flegenheimer et al. ms). The lower, Unit 1, overlies the quartzitic bedrock and has high clay content. It contains quartz grains resulting from rock disaggregation and a high proportion of clasts (Figure 1A). Evidence of occupation is concentrated within this Unit 1 in a layer about 10 cm thick, which lies 2–3 cm above the bedrock, suggesting that human occupation probably occurred soon after sediments started accumulating at the end of the late Pleistocene. Overlying Unit 2 is a clayey silt that contains a smaller proportion of clasts and supports a dense fern cover. It contains very few lithic artifacts, indicative of a recent occupation.

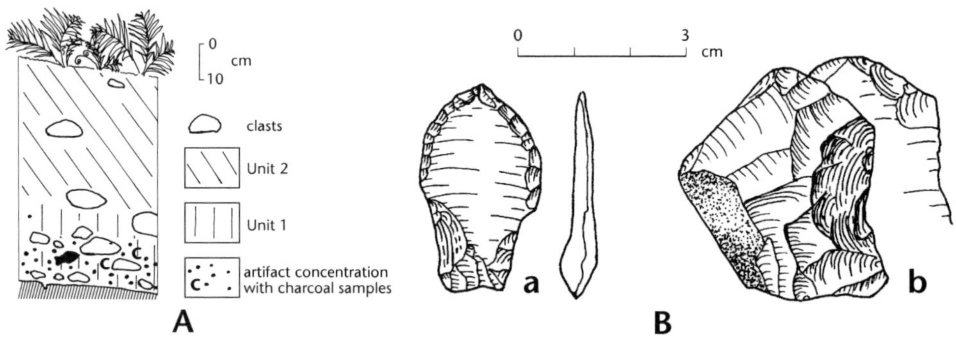

Figure 1. **A,** schematic profile of Abrigo 1; **B(a),** Fishtail projectile point (No. C7-134); **(b),** concave scraper (No. C10-95)

No organic remains have been preserved at the site. The excavation yielded 27 tools, 6 cores, 392 flakes, and 39 ocher fragments in Unit 1 (Figure 1B). Tools include two fishtail points, one complete and one broken, three bifacial fragments, a bifacial knife, seven scrapers, four raclettes, a limace, a backed knife, six unidentified retouched flakes, and two conjoining bipolar fragments. The principal toolstone is good-quality local orthoquartzite from about 40 km towards the west; a substantial proportion (35 percent) of the assemblage is made of immediately available orthoquartzite and quartz of poor quality. Rocks found within 10 km of the sites are considered immediately available; rocks found 10–40 km distant are considered local (Flegenheimer et al. 2003). Cortex is present in 12 percent of the artifacts and is more frequent on immediately available rocks.

Charcoal was found within the occupation level as small flecks, which were dated using

AMS. Five samples yielded dates of 10,725 ± 90 yr B.P. (AA-4765), 10,270 ± 85 yr B.P. (AA-4766), 10,675 ± 110 yr B.P. (AA-4767), 10,480 ± 70 yr B.P. (AA-5220), and 8060 ± 140 yr B.P. (AA-5221) (Flegenheimer and Zárate 1997; Flegenheimer et al. ms). Four of the dates are quite consistent; the fifth, more recent, may either be contaminated or evidence of a long-term occupation at the site. Water, organic matter from modern vegetation, or even charcoal from fires that frequently occur nowadays in the hills could have been the agent causing contamination. Since charcoal for this sample was obtained within the occupation level, even beneath other dated charcoal fragments, and since most dates associated with assemblages in the area are consistently earlier, I assume the sample is contaminated and recommend it not be used until its significance is better understood.

The presence of different tool types, cores, and flakes corresponding to different steps in the reduction sequence suggests that several activities, possibly domestic, were carried out at the site. The largest ocher fragments were found cached on a shelf in the rock wall, indicating the inhabitants must have intended to reoccupy the site. However, from current information it is difficult to assess whether the site was reoccupied or not.

Cima

Cerro El Sombrero, Cima, is a large open-air site where surface finds are scattered throughout the hilltop. The quartzitic bedrock outcrops along the edges of the summit. Artifacts with rounded edges and covered with lichens or oxide stains are frequently found on rocks and in crevices. The first excavations were planned in an area with high density of surface artifacts (Figure 2, AI and BI) (Flegenheimer and Zárate 1989); a sampling was also designed to assess site size and density (Flegenheimer 1995). A total area of 35 m^2 is currently excavated. All the pits yielded archaeological remains, confirming that the entire hilltop was used.

The excavated deposits are of variable thickness, from a few centimeters to more than a meter thick (Figure 2B). In some sectors the lowermost section of profiles corresponds to an undated well-developed soil, equivalent to Unit 1 at La China, probably of late-Pleistocene age (Zárate and Flegenheimer 1991). Sometimes it contains a level of colluvium in its upper portion; in other sectors a $CaCO_3$ layer was observed. Overlying either the well-developed soil or the $CaCO_3$ layer, or directly on the bedrock, is an eolian deposit up to 50 cm thick on which an A soil horizon has developed. Archaeological remains are found in this uppermost level; that is, they lie within the present soil. All buried remains are free of lichens and stains and have fresh edges with visible use-wear damage (M. Leipus pers. comm. 2000); that is, they have not suffered long exposure or redeposition.

Since no carbon has been recovered for dating, the site has been assigned a late-Pleistocene/early-Holocene chronology based on the following characteristics shared by the surface and excavated assemblages: diagnostic artifacts including points, thin double-side scrapers, and large sidescrapers; raw materials with a significant proportion of colored regional orthoquartzites (Flegenheimer and Bayón 1999) and a low proportion of quartz, chalcedony, and other rocks; a very low proportion of silcretes transported from a long distance; a high proportion of bifacial tools and bifacial thinning flakes with strong platform abrasion; isolated platforms, lips, and diffuse bulbs indicative of frequent platform preparation and soft hammerstones. The site has yielded a collection of 109 fishtail points and stems from surface and

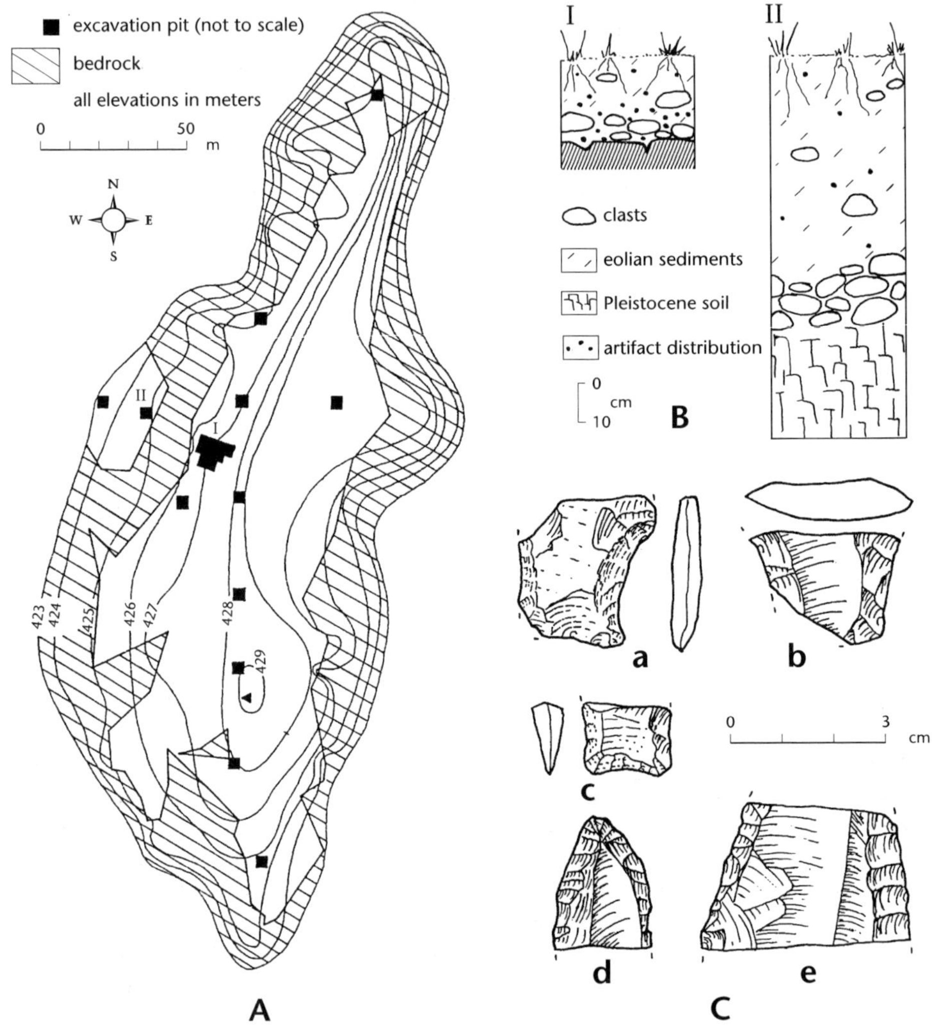

Figure 2. **A,** location of excavations and profiles I and II at Cima; **B,** schematic profiles I and II; **C(a),** surface Fishtail projectile point with rounded edges and lichens (Col. Noseda No.95A-34); **(b),** surface stem of Fishtail point, one face with lichens (Col. Noseda No. 95A-20); **(c),** surface stem of Fishtail point, with lichens (Col. Noseda No. 95A-15); **(d),** broken limace (No.S12-106-5); **(e),** broken double sidescraper (No.S12-105-4).

stratigraphic finds (Figure 2C). These artifacts have proved useful in correlating other early occupations in the region; the recurrence of silcretes at these sites is currently being analyzed to infer long-distance social relationships among early groups (Flegenheimer et al 2003). Surface and excavated assemblages also share traits that are diagnostic of the final stages of tool manufacture and replacement (Flegenheimer 1995).

Of 678 tools recovered in the excavated area, 25 are fishtail points or fragments. Artifacts are unevenly distributed; pits have yielded from 46 to 2 tools per m^2 and from 145 to 4 flakes with platforms per m^2, and the excavated portion of the site (less than 1 percent of its surface) is not at all representative. Therefore it would be inaccurate to estimate the total quantity of artifacts still buried at the site from our current data. Furthermore, many artifacts were removed by amateur collectors in years prior to the first report. Yet, taking into account the large size of surface and excavation collections, it is clear that a great number of tools were discarded at Cima.

Discussion

As we have elsewhere discussed, people at the Pleistocene-Holocene transition in the Tandilia Ranges were well acquainted with specific resources in their environment and did not use them randomly (Flegenheimer and Bayón 1999). Certain features of the landscape, such as the hilltop of Cerro El Sombrero, were thus selected and used for specific purposes. A pattern of great intersite variability—larger domestic sites and smaller more transitory sites—has been proposed for the area. Abrigo 1 belongs to the second group, but Cerro El Sombrero Cima stands out as a large special-purpose site; the entire hilltop is covered with remains associated with toolkit re-equipping. Furthermore, the site probably served as a lookout, for its privileged topographic location commands the view over a 30-km radius of landscape, animals, and people. This distinctive feature and the large space available would have justified working on a flat summit without shelter or water, both of which were available in neighboring rockshelters. The high density of artifacts and the large size of the site have led me to propose that it could have either been reoccupied in several occasions or served as an aggregation site where several groups met (Flegenheimer 1994).

Abrigo 1 was probably used by the same groups that discarded their tools at Cima, but for different functions. Living space in the shelter is naturally limited, yet several shelters could have been in use at the same time if necessary. Also, no open-air early sites have been identified in the plains immediately surrounding the ranges. If these sites exist, they could be located in the middle and lower sections of present-day soils and would therefore have very low visibility (Zárate 1997). Related sites in the plains are farther away, but isolated surface finds of fishtail points suggest the area closer to the Ranges was probably also used.

According to current information available from the low stratigraphic resolution at studied sites, contexts at Cerro El Sombrero locality can be interpreted as evidence of several transitory occupations by small groups, or of an occupation by a larger group if several shelters were used simultaneously. A periodic or seasonal occupation by small groups recently proposed for the Ranges (Politis and Madrid 2001) may be the case, but inconclusive data from Cerro El Sombrero could be interpreted otherwise. Current evidence suggests these sites in the Ranges were not isolated; rather, it appears their occupants in the Pleistocene–Holocene transition must have also used the plains and established relationships with distant groups.

Acknowledgments

Cristina Bayón, Mónica Salemme, and Laura Miotti read and generously commented on previous drafts of the paper. Different stages of this research were supported by CONICET, Wenner Gren Foundation, and Fundación Antorchas, and datings were financed by the Accelerator Facility at the University of Arizona.

References Cited

Flegenheimer, N.

1994 Consideraciones sobre el Uso del Espacio en las Sierras de Lobería (Provincia de Buenos Aires) Argentina. *Actas y Memorias del XI Congreso Nacional de Arqueología Argentina* XIII(1/4):14–18.

1995 The Hilltop of Cerro El Sombrero, Argentina, Revisited. *Current Research in the Pleistocene* 12:11–13.

Flegenheimer, N., and C. Bayón

1996 Surface Fell's Cave Stemmed Points in the Argentine Pampas. *Current Research in the Pleistocene* 13:17–19.

1999 Abastecimiento de Rocas en Sitios Pampeanos Tempranos: Recolectando Colores. In *Los Tres Reinos: Prácticas de Recolección en el Cono Sur de América*, edited by C. Aschero, M. Kostanje, and P. Vuoto, pp. 95–107. Instituto de Arqueología y Museo FCN e IML-UNT Ediciones Magna Publicaciones, Tucumán.

2000 New Evidence for Early Occupations in the Argentine Pampas, Los Helechos Site. *Current Research in the Pleistocene* 17:24–26.

Flegenheimer N., and M. Zárate

1989 Paleoindian Occupation at Cerro El Sombrero Locality, Buenos Aires Province, Argentina. *Current Research in the Pleistocene* 6:12–13.

1997 Considerations on Radiocarbon and Calibrated Dates from Cerro La China and Cerro El Sombrero, Argentina. *Current Research in the Pleistocene* 14:27–28.

Flegenheimer, N., M. Zárate, and A. Jull

nd. Abrigo 1, Cerro El Sombrero: An Early Site in Eastern Argentina. Unpublished report, 1992.

Flegenheimer, N., C. Bayón, M. Valente, J. Baeza, and J. Femenías

2003 Long Distance Tool Stone Transport in the Argentine Pampas. *Quaternary International* 109–110:49–64.

Madrazo, G.

1972 Arqueología de Lobería y Salliqueló (Provincia de Buenos Aires). *Etnía* 15:1–18.

Martínez, G.

1999 *Tecnología, Subsistencia y Asentamientos en el Curso Medio del Río Quequén Grande: Un Enfoque Arqueológico*. PhD Thesis, Universidad Nacional de La Plata.

Mazzanti, D. L.

1999 Ocupaciones Humanas Tempranas en Sierra La Vigilancia y Laguna La Brava, Tandilia Oriental, Provincia de Buenos Aires. *Actas XII Congreso Nacional de Arqueología Argentina*, edited by C. D. Marín, III:149–155.

Politis, G.

1991 Fishtail Projectile Points in the Southern Cone of South America: an Overview. In *Clovis Origins and Adaptations*, edited by R. Bonnichsen and K. Turnmire, pp. 287–307, Center for the Study of the First Americans, Oregon State University, Corvallis, OR.

Politis, G., and P. Madrid

2001 Arqueología Pampeana: Estado Actual y Perspectivas. In *Historia Argentina Prehispánica*, Volume II, edited by E. Berberián and A. Nielsen, pp. 737–814. Editorial Brujas, Córdoba, Argentina.

Zárate, M.

1997 Late Pleistocene Geoarchaeology of the Southern Pampas, Buenos Aires Province, Argentina. *Anthropologie* XXXV/2:197–205.

Zárate, M., and N. Flegenheimer

1991 Geoarchaeology of Cerro La China Locality (Buenos Aires, Argentina): Site 2 and Site 3. Geoarchaeology: An International Journal 6(3):273–294.

Human Settlements in Caves and Rockshelters during the Pleistocene-Holocene Transition in the Eastern Tandilia Range, Pampean Region, Argentina

Diana L. Mazzanti

This study is a synthesis of the archaeological characteristics of six sites found in the Tandilia Range (Buenos Aires Province) dated at the Pleistocene-Holocene transition. The geoarchaeological descriptions are presented in Martínez and Osterrieth (in this volume). This report presents data that can contribute to our understanding of the settlements and mobility patterns of the early hunter-gatherers of the Pampean region. Our research is based on discerned socioeconomic aspects of archaeological and faunal assemblages found in rockshelters, viewed from a regional perspective.

The Tandilia Range cuts across the Pampean plains from southeast to northwest for 300 km; its easternmost limit is the Atlantic Ocean. Its low tabular hills do not form a barrier and therefore are easily traversed by human travelers. In the eastern portion of Tandilia, a systematic survey located several caves and shelters with stratigraphy and early archaeological evidence. The Atlantic coast lies approximately 40 km from the sites under study.

The sites studied are Tixi Cave, El Abra Cave, Los Pinos Shelter, Burucuyá Cave, La Brava Cave, and Amalia site 2. All were dated by ^{14}C by LATYR of the Universidad Nacional de La Plata and by the AMS Facility at the University of Arizona. Most of the plant charcoal samples were processed by the AMS method. The first evidence of human occupation in this eastern sector is dated between 9570 and 10,465 yr B.P. (Mazzanti 1999). The archaeological contexts are hearths, dispersed charcoal, or lithic artifacts. Evidence of abundant mineral pigments was found in three sites; faunal remains were found in only two sites. The contexts

Laboratorio de Arqueología de la Universidad Nacional de Mar del Plata, Bélgica 2293, 7600 Mar del Plata, Provincia de Buenos Aires, Argentina. e-mail: quintana@copetel.com.ar

are sedimentary deposits within the rockshelters. The Pleistocene-Holocene transition can be detected in the light, yellowish brown color of sediments attributable to the late Pleistocene; in many cases the transition is quite distinct (Martínez and Osterrieth this volume).

It appears that Paleoindians exploited the numerous and varied natural resources (animals, water, wood, rocks, shelters, etc.) of the interior valleys of the Range. One hill in particular, La Vigilancia, was an "oasis" that was intensely exploited by domestic groups. Four sites in the interior valleys, Tixi Cave, Los Pinos Shelter, Burucuyá Cave, and El Abra Cave, show abundant evidence of lithic technology during the Pleistocene-Holocene transition.

The six sites mentioned earlier were systematically excavated. Based on information about the functions performed during human occupation, I divide the sites into two groups. In the first group are sites that show evidence of extensive occupation; the second group includes sites that were minimally occupied, perhaps in a single event.

Extensively Occupied Sites

The first group of sites comprises three campsites, Tixi Cave, El Abra Cave, and Los Pinos Shelter, strategically integrated into the mountain landscape of the principal valleys of the "La Vigilancia" massif. These sites share gentle slopes accessible to all members of a domestic group. They are all located in the vicinity of critical resources including water, and all command a view of the internal valleys, which must have served as natural pathways for people and animals. These two valleys, both quite fertile at present, extend for 10 and 8 km and cut through the massif-like wedges. The lower component of El Abra Cave, located at the entrance to La Vigilancia Creek Valley, was dated at 9834 ± 65 yr B.P. (AA-38098); Los Pinos Shelter, at the source of La Vigilancia Creek Valley, yielded dates of 9570 ± 150 yr B.P. (LP-630); 10,465 ± 65 yr B.P. (AA-24045), and 10,415 ± 70 yr B.P. (AA-24046). The third site, Tixi Cave, in the intermediate sector of the San Pedro Creek Valley, was dated at 10,045 ± 95 yr B.P. (AA-12131) and 10,375 ± 90 yr B.P. (AA-12130). These three base camps yielded a profusion of lithic artifacts in various stages of production (Mazzanti 1999)—2,670 in Tixi Cave, 2,746 in Los Pinos Shelter, and 8,433 in El Abra Cave. The widely varying instruments (Figure 1), one-sided for the most part, include cores, flakes, and microflakes. This last category is the most abundant, constituting 67.41 percent of all artifacts found in Tixi Cave, 52.07 percent in Los Pinos Shelter, and 76.52 percent in El Abra Cave. Bipolar flaking is present in assemblages from all three sites. Fine- and medium-grained quartzites are the most utilized rocks. The first material may have come from the Sierras Bayas group in the north-central sector of Tandilia Range (Bayón et al. 1999); medium-grained quartzite, defined as local, comes from the Balcarce Formation. Basalt and silica, the least abundant materials found in the assemblages, may have come from the Atlantic coast. The most remarkable of the vast variety of stone instruments found in this group of sites are a preform and a fishtail projectile point manufactured of fine quartzite from Los Pinos Shelter (Figure 1A). Scrapers of fine quartzite with alternating retouch are the most abundant artifacts found in Tixi Cave. Scrapers and unclassified instruments, also of fine quartzite, were discovered in El Abra Cave.

Research was done in these three sites on the extensive use of red and yellow mineral pigments in ornamental uses (paintings) and utilitarian uses (the tanning of hides, among

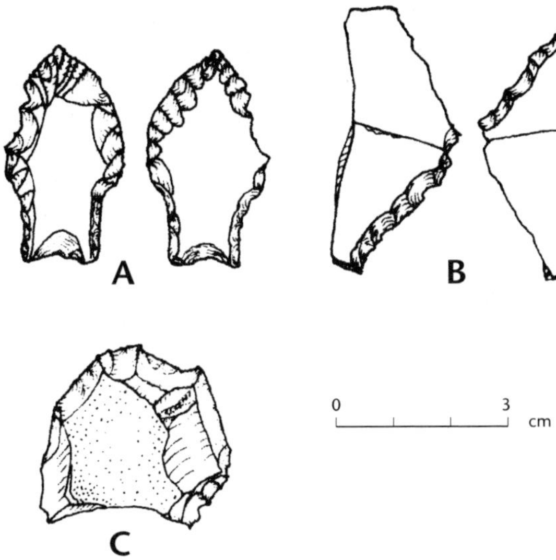

Figure 1. **A,** fishtail projectile point from Los Pinos Shelter; **B,** alternating scraper from Tixi Cave; **C,** scraper from El Abra Cave.

others). Olive (1987) theorizes that burnt ocher powder was used as a drying agent for tanning hides or as an ingredient of the additive used to create handles for instruments. Pigments appear as angular instruments with edges or faces showing wear caused by abrasion; they appear in the form of coarse chunks (raw material) and numerous small fragments (waste). Six pieces showing abrasive wear and 319 small fragments were found in Tixi Cave; 13 pieces showing wear and 32 small fragments were found in Los Pinos Shelter; and 20 pieces showing wear and 255 small fragments were found in El Abra Cave.

The record of faunal remains in El Abra Cave is poor and characterized by large splinters, some burnt. Species that show evidence of consumption are deer (*Ozotoceros bezoarticus*) and armadillos (*Chaetophractus villosus* and *Zaedyus pichiy*). Rodents (*Lagostomus maximus* and *Ctenomys talarum*) are also recorded. At Tixi Cave the record is more numerous and of better quality; it documents a generalized strategy of subsistence that depended for food on two ungulates (*Ozotoceros bezoarticus* and *Lama guanicoe*), species of less than 10 kg (*Lagostomus maximus, Myocastor coypus, Chaetophractus villosus, Zaedyus pichiy* and *Dasypus hybridus*), the American ostrich of around 30 kg (*Rhea americana*), and a very large extinct armadillo (*Eutatus seguini*) (Mazzanti and Quintana 1997; Quintana and Mazzanti 2001). The following fauna associated with this occupation do not show evidence of human use: Rodentia (*Akodon azarae, Necromys obscurus, Oxymycterus rufus, Reithrodon auritus, Calomys* sp., *Holochilus brasiliensis, Cavia aperea, Galea* sp. nov., *Ctenomys talarum* and *Dolichotis patagonum*); Mustelidae (*Galictis cuja*); Canidae (*Lycalopex gimnocercus, Canis avus, Canis* sp. A and *Canis* sp. B); Felidae (*Puma concolor*); Didelphidae (*Monodelphis* sp. A, *Thylamys* sp., *Lestodelphys halli*); Reptilia (*Bothrops alternatus* and *Tupinambis* cf. *merianae*); and indeterminate amphibians and birds.

Minimally Occupied Sites

Sites in the second group show evidence of specific, ephemeral activities. One site, Burucuyá

Cave, is located in a valley of the La Vigilancia Range; the other two sites, which lie outside this hilly massif, are La Brava Cave and a very narrow chasm-like shelter located in Site 2 of the Amalia archaeological locality.

La Brava Cave, located in the high portion of the Valdés hill across from La Brava Lake, enjoys a vast overview of the region and its lacustrine resources. It lies approximately 14 and 20 km from the aforementioned campsites. The Burucuyá Cave is located in the intermediate span of the La Vigilancia Creek Valley and the middle portion of the slope. Both caves have ample chambers (190 and 90 m^2, respectively) in their roofed areas, although access to them is somewhat more difficult than to that of the base camp. Archaeological contexts, which are only found in the lower layers of the stratigraphic sequences, comprise a single human occupation. Lithic remains are fewer than at the base camps, 128 artifacts at La Brava Cave and 105 artifacts at Burucuyá Cave. At both sites only some stages of stone flaking are present. At La Brava Cave, secondary flaking on fine-grained quartzite predominates; at Burucuyá Cave, rabots, notches, denticulate sidescrapers, and other instruments of fine-grained quartzite were found (Figure 2). Both sites have basin-shaped fireplaces with abundant charcoal. Radiocarbon dating yielded ages of 9670 ± 120 B.P. (LP-550) and 10,000 ± 120 B.P. (LP-863), respectively.

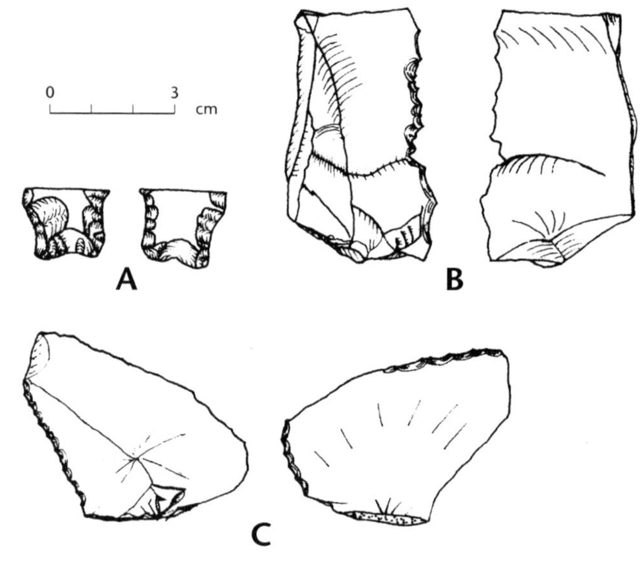

Figure 2. **A,** stem of Fishtail projectile point of Amalia site 2; **B,** scraper from Burucuyá Cave; **C,** scraper alternate from La Brava Cave.

The third site in this second group, Amalia Site 2, is located 15 and 20 km south of the base camps of La Vigilancia Range. It is a very narrow chasm at the top of a small peak surrounded by open landscape and pronounced hills. The sedimentary profile of this site is very deep (2.1 m) compared with others of the region. In the base of the sequence were found the stem of a fishtail projectile point made of fine quartzite (Figure 2A), seven stone pieces (two instruments, four flakes, and a core fragment), and dispersed charcoal. This assemblage dates to 10,425 ± 75 yr B.P. (AA-35499).

Conclusions

The sites in the first group show evidence of intense use characteristic of camps used for multiple activities and were reutilized during extensive periods of time. Sites in both groups were favorably located, with manageable landscapes and access to natural resources. This system of settlements may have depended on the use of other shelters, occupied only when activities required travel over long distances.

Studies of these sites indicate an age consistent with other sites in the vicinity, Cerro La China and Cerro El Sombrero (Flegenheimer 1994) and Paso Otero 5 (Martínez 1999). Furthermore, these sites have yielded other data that serve to explain intersite differences in such activities as lithic production and processing of extinct megafauna.

The information gathered by these research groups is contributing to our knowledge of the settlement systems of the Paleoindians who inhabited the Pampas during the Pleistocene-Holocene transition.

References Cited

Bayón C., N. Flegenheimer, M. Valente, and A. Pupio

1999 Dime Cómo Eres y Te Diré de Dónde Vienes: Procedencia de Rocas Cuarcíticas en la Región Pampeana. *Relaciones* 24:187–217. Sociedad Argentina de Antropología. Buenos Aires, Argentina.

Flegenheimer, N.

1994 Consideraciones sobre el Uso del Espacio en las Sierras de Lobería (Provincia de Buenos Aires). *Revista del Museo de Historia Natural de San Rafael* 13(1-4):14–18, Mendoza, Argentina.

Martínez, G.

1999 Tecnología, Subsistencia y Asentamiento en el Curso Medio del Río Quequén Grande: Un Enfoque Arqueológico. Unpublished Ph.D. Dissertation , Facultad de Ciencias Naturales, Universidad Nacional de La Plata.

Mazzanti, D.

1999 Ocupaciones Humanas Tempranas en Sierra La Vigilancia y Laguna La Brava, Tandilia Oriental, Provincia de Buenos Aires. *Actas del XII Congreso Nacional de Arqueología Argentina* 3:145–148.

Mazzanti, D., and C. Quintana

1997 Asociación Cultural de Fauna Extinguida en el Sitio Arqueológico Cueva Tixi, Provincia de Buenos Aires, Argentina. *Revista Española de Antropología Americana,* 27:11–21.

Olive, M.

1987 Le Traitement de l'Ocre. In *"Le Feu Aprrivoisé. Le Feu dans las Vie Quotidienne des Hommes Préhistoriques,"* Musée de Préhistoire D'Ile-De-France, pp. 44–46. Nemours, France.

Quintana, C., and D. Mazzanti

2001 Selección y Aprovechamiento de Recursos Faunísticos. In *"Cueva Tixi:* Cazadores y Recolectores de las Sierras de Tandilia Oriental. 1. Geología, *Paleontología y Zooarqueología,"* edited by D. Mazzanti and C. Quintana. Publicación Especial 1, Laboratorio de Arqueología, Universidad Nacional de Mar del Plata, Cap. 12:181–209.

The Pleistocene-Holocene Stratigraphic Record from Early Archaeological Sites in Caves and Rockshelters of Eastern Tandilia, Pampean Region, Argentina

Gustavo A. Martínez[1] and Margarita L. Osterrieth[2]

Introduction

Caves and rockshelters play a very important role in furnishing archaeological data of prehistoric human behavior and paleoecology because of their special geologic characteristics, such as relatively rapid sedimentation, protection of deposits from erosion and weathering, and their attraction for fauna in the absence of human occupation (Farrand 1985). In order to understand the prehistoric interaction between humans and their environment in our study area, it is important first to understand the evolution of rockshelters that were occupied (Donahue and Adovasio 1990). Using different analytical techniques, we can construct a synthetic interpretation of the origin and paleoenvironmental significance of cave and rockshelter sediments (Farrand 1985).

The caves and rockshelters of eastern Tandilia Range constitute an environment of archaeological importance all out of proportion with the limited space they occupy. These protected areas have been frequently occupied since the initial settlement of the region (see Mazzanti, this volume). Although rockshelters and caves have been defined as highly efficient sediment traps (Colcutt 1979), only a few rockshelters from eastern Tandilia Range possess a sedimentary record.

[1] Grupo de Arqueología Regional Bonaerense, Fac. de Humanidades, Universidad Nacional de Mar del Plata, Bélgica 2293, 7600 Mar del Plata. e-mail: gamarti@mdp.edu.ar

[2] Centro de Geología de Costas y del Cuaternario, Universidad Nacional de Mar del Plata, C.C. 722, 7600 Mar del Plata, Argentina. e-mail: mosterri@mdp.edu.ar

This report discusses the stratigraphic and sedimentological aspects of six sites with records of Paleoindian occupation. The archaeological context has been studied by Mazzanti (this volume). Stratigraphic analysis explores sedimentary and post-depositional processes caused by natural forces (e.g., weathering and erosion) and cultural activity (e.g., hearths and human introduction of material). By integrating all such information, we hope to reconstruct the past environment at the site and increase our store of paleoenvironmental information on the Pleistocene-Holocene transition in the area.

Geological Background

The Tandilia Range is one of two main ranges on the pampas plain in Buenos Aires Province. The Range is a group of table-like hills of flat summit. These elevations (no more than 300 m a.s.l.) are composed of subhorizontal quartzite strata of lower-Paleozoic age (Balcarce Formation, Dalla Salda and Iñiguez 1979).

The caves and rockshelters of eastern Tandilia Range are found on quartzite cliffs near the summit. Several authors relate their origin to ancient fluvial erosion (Dumovich and Moneda 1965; Tapia 1937). Their origin is also linked to dissolution of quartzite that occurred during wet periods throughout the Cenozoic (Martínez et al. 1999; Teruggi 1968). Colluvial deposits are usually present at the base of the shelters. The interrange wide valleys and flat summits of some ranges are covered by loess deposited during different cycles throughout the late Pleistocene and Holocene. These eolian silts of volcaniclastic origin, which derive from the Andean region about 1,100 km to the west, have been called Médano Invasor (Tapia 1937), Las Animas Formation (Rabassa 1973), La Postrera Formation (Fidalgo and Tonni 1981), and Médano Invasor and E1 Aloformations (Martínez 2001). Part of these sediments created the sedimentary sequences of the caves and rockshelters.

Tapia (1937) was the first author who proposed a stratigraphic framework for archaeological sites in the Ojo de Agua and Las Hachas caves of the Tandilia Range. Other studies of these sites were carried out by Menghin and Bórmida (1950), Dumovich and Moneda (1965), Madrazo (1968), Teruggi (1968), Carbonari (1972), Carbonari and Sierra (1974), Orquera et al. (1980), Figini et al. (1985), Zárate and Flegenheimer (1991), Martínez and Osterrieth (1996–98), Martinez et al. (1999).

The Archaeological Sites

In this report we analyze Los Pinos Rockshelter, Burucuyá Cave, La Brava Cave, Tixi Cave, El Abra Cave, and Amalia Site 2 (Figure 1). Stratigraphic units were defined for each site based on grain size, color, shape and type of limit, pedogenetic features, etc. The main lithostratigraphic characteristics are summarized in Figure 1. A detailed description can be found in Martínez and Osterrieth (1996–1998) and Martínez et al. (1999, in press).

Los Pinos Rockshelter, area 30 m^2, is located near the summit of La Vigilancia Range (37° 56′ 36″ S, 58° 05′ 02″ W) at 200 m a.s.l. Four stratigraphic units were defined (Martínez et al. 1999). Burucuyá Cave, area 90 m^2, is also located in La Vigilancia Range 4 km from Los Pinos Rockshelter. La Brava Cave, area 120 m^2, is located in De Valdes Range. Tixi Cave, area 45 m^2, located in La Vigilancia Range, is an especially relevant archaeological site because of its long-term sequence with minor post-depositional modifications. An important fauna collection of autochthonous and extinct taxa has been recovered (Mazzanti 1997).

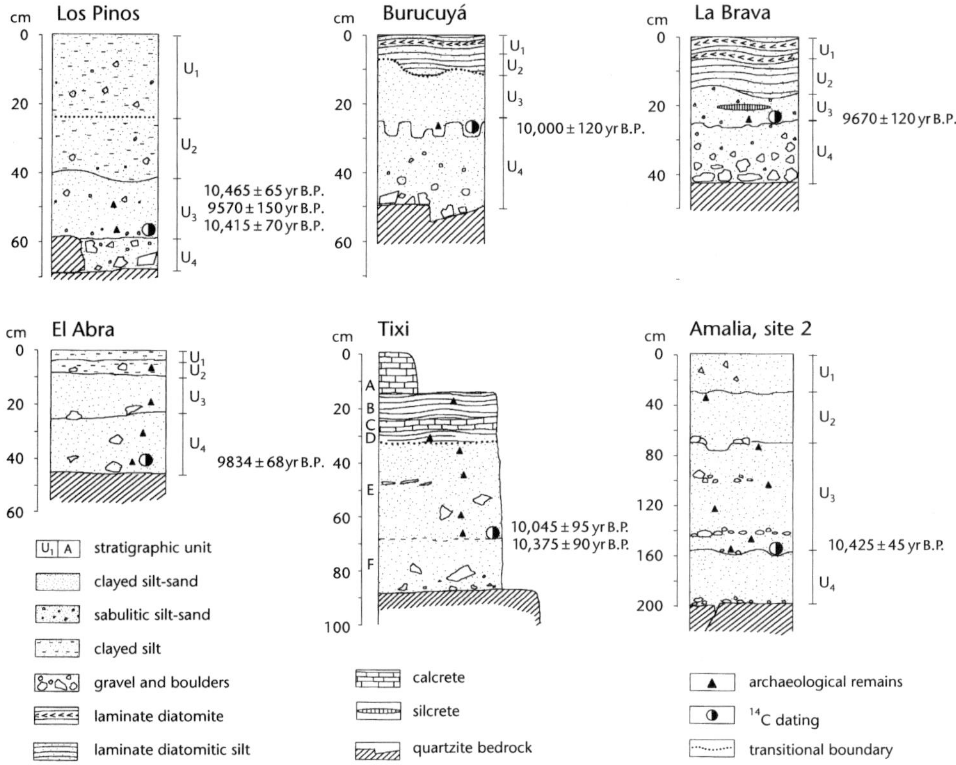

Figure 1. Stratigraphical diagram for the archaeological sites.

El Abra Cave (35 m^2) lies in the La Vigilancia Range (37° 58′ 08″ S, 58° 09′ 05″ W); Amalia Site 2, area 8 m^2, is located on Amalia Hill (38° 02′ 55″ S, 58° 11′ 38″ W) at 93 m a.s.l. This site is a vertical crevice, 0.8 m wide and 1.6 m high, developed on quartzite (Balcarce Formation). The major feature of this site is the cavity, which served as a sediment trap during the deposition process.

Radiocarbon dates from charcoal derived mainly from hearths are available for the Pleistocene-Holocene transition (Mazzanti, 1995–96, 2002, this volume). Dates from the base of Unit 3 span the interval 9500–10,000 yr B.P. for La Brava, El Abra, Burucuyá, and Tixi sites, and 9500–10,500 yr B.P. for Los Pinos and Amalia sites.

Using stratigraphic, sedimentological, and geochronological data, we can infer the endogenous and exogenous sedimentary history and post-depositional modifications of each rockshelter.

The stratigraphic record for the late-Pleistocene/Holocene period in some caves and rockshelters appears to be continuous and is a major source of information on human settlements and paleoclimatic conditions.

Caves and rockshelters capture a record of local environmental conditions. Moreover, they are a source of evidence about the processes that form cavities and other lithostratigraphic features that are unambiguous indicators of the Pleistocene-Holocene boundary.

Cave and rockshelter stratigraphic sequences do not reveal evidence of sediments older than the late Pleistocene, the period of interest in the region. However, the origin of cavities appears to be much older; dissolution processes probably took place throughout the Cenozoic or even before (Martínez 2001). Endogenous sediments are derived from the ceiling and walls by dissolution and collapse; exogenous sediments are carried in by drainage from the cave exterior or blown in by the wind. The preservation of sediments is determined by the size, configuration, exposure, and internal topography of the rockshelter. Post-depositional modification of sediments within the rockshelter may have been caused by bioturbation, which includes human construction of hearths and animal-induced transformations (e.g., mammal burrows or footprints at Burucuyá Cave; Quintana et al. 2001). Processes linked to pedogenesis have also been recorded (e.g., Los Pinos and Burucuyá Rockshelters).

Discussion

The Pleistocene-Holocene transition is usually characterized by an abrupt boundary that separates Units 4 and 3 (F and E in Tixi Cave). This marker usually coincides with a stratigraphic limit indicated by a transition from stone-rich to relatively stone-free sediments (Figure 1). In the case of Unit 4, the trend is associated with an increase in rock fragment size with depth; Units 1, 2 and 3, on the other hand, have a finer sediment fraction. A phenomenon similar to that of Unit 4 has been observed in many European caves and rockshelters, where coarse angular rock fragments have been traced to the effect of freezing and thawing on the walls and ceiling (Farrand 1985). However, there is no evidence of geocryogenic action in the studied area in the late Pleistocene. In Unit 4, it seems likely this coarser fraction is the result of more intense mechanical weathering during the late Pleistocene. For this period (Isotopic Stage 2, Clapperton 1993), colder and drier conditions in the area were noted by many authors (Alberdi et al. 1989; Bonadonna et al. 1999; Martínez 2001; Prado et al. 1987; Tonni and Fidalgo 1978). A pattern of mechanical weathering is therefore consistent with suggested palaeoclimatic conditions.

Sediment color is another distinctive feature that differentiates Units 1, 2, and 3 from 4. Overlying Holocene deposits vary from dark brown (10 YR 4/3) to grayish brown (10 YR 5/2); the sediments from Unit 4 are light yellowish brown (10 YR 7/4).

The Holocene deposits in the area show indications of wetter conditions such as pedogenetic horizons with organic matter (e.g., Los Pinos and Burucuyá) ranging between 1.56 percent and 4.96 percent (Unit 1) and the presence of diatomite levels (e.g., La Brava and Burucuyá).

To sum up, lithostratigraphic evidence mentioned above seems to be a useful method for recognizing the Pleistocene-Holocene transition in local settings such as caves and rockshelters in Tandilia Range. Archaeological, stratigraphic, and paleoclimatic information converge to reconstruct paleoclimatic conditions of the late Pleistocene and early Holocene in the area. In other words, synthesizing different lines of evidence from related disciplines seems to be the most reliable method for detecting the Pleistocene-Holocene transition.

References Cited

Alberdi, T., A. Menegaz, J. L. Prado, and E. P. Tonni
1989 La Fauna Local Quequén Salado-Indio Rico (Pleistoceno Tardío) de la Provincia de Buenos Aires, Argentina. Aspectos Paleoambientales y Bioestratigráficos. *Ameghiniana* 25 (3):225–236.

Bonadonna, F. P., G. Leone, and G. Zanchetta
1999 Stable Isotope Analyses on the Last 30 ka Molluscan Fauna from Pampa Grassland, Bonaerense Region, Argentina. *Palaeogeography, Palaeoclimatology, Palaeoecology* 153:289–308.

Carbonari, J.
1972 Estratigrafía y Arqueología en la Sierra de Valdés, Pdo. de General Pueyrredón, Provincia de Buenos Aires. Unpublished Report, *C.I.C*, La Plata, Argentina.

Carbonari, J., and I. Sierra
1974 Estratigrafía y Arqueología de la Caverna del 10 (Pdo. de General Pueyrredón, Provincia de Buenos Aires). Unpublished Report *C.I.C.* La Plata, Argentina.

Clapperton, C. M.
1993 *Quaternary Geology and Geomorphology of South America.* Elsevier, New York.

Colcutt, S.
1979 The Analysis of Quaternary Cave Sediments. *World Archaeology* 10:290–301.

Dalla Salda, L., and M. Iñiguez.
1979 La Tinta, Precámbrico y Paleozoico de Buenos Aires. *VII Congreso Geológico Argentino*, Actas I: 539–550. Buenos Aires, Argentina.

Donahue, J., and J. M. Adovasio.
1990 Evolution of Sandstone Rockshelters in Eastern North America; A Geoarchaelogical Perspective. In *Archaeological Geology of North America,* edited by N. P. Lasca and J. Donahue, pp. 231–251. Geological Society of America, Centennial Special Volume 4, Boulder, CO.

Dumovich, O. A., and C. P. Moneda.
1965 Cavernas de la Provincia de Buenos Aires. *Anales de la Comisión de Investigaciones Científicas*, vol. VI. La Plata, Argentina.

Farrand, W. R.
1985 *Rockshelter and Cave Sediments. Archaeological sediments in context.* Center for the Study of Early Man, Orono, ME.

Fidalgo, F., and E. Tonni,
1981 Sedimentos Eólicos del Pleistoceno Tardío y Reciente en el Area Interserrana Bonaerense. *VIII Congreso Geológico Argentino*, Actas 3:33–39.

Figgini, A. J., R. A. Huarte, J. E. Carbonari, G. J. Gomez, A. C. Zubiaga, E. Tonni, and F. Fidalgo.
1985 Edad Isotópica de Carbonatos de la Cueva Tixi, Partido de General Alvarado, Provincia de Buenos Aires. *Primeras Jornadas Geológicas Bonaerenses*, Actas: 128–130.

Madrazo, G. B.
1968 Hacia una Revisión de la Prehistoria de la Pampa Bonaerense. *Etnía* No. 7.

Martínez, G.
2001 Geomorfología y Geología del Cenozoico Superior de las Cuencas de Drenaje de los Arroyos Los Cueros y Seco, Sierras Septentrionales de la Provincia de Buenos Aires. Doctoral Thesis. Universidad Nacional del Sur, Bahia Blanca, Argentina.

Martínez, G., and M. Osterrieth.
1996–98 Marco Geológico-Estratigráfico del Sitio Arqueológico Los Pinos, Sierra de la Vigilancia, Sierras Septentrionales de la Provincia de Buenos Aires. *Palimpsesto. Revista de Arqueología*, N° 5:160–166.

Martínez, G., M. Osterrieth, and D. Mazzanti.
1999 Estratigrafía de Sitios Arqueológicos en Reparos Rocosos en las Sierras de La Vigilancia y Valdés, Sistema de Tandilia, Provincia de Buenos Aires. *XII Congreso Nacional Arqueología Argentina* Actas III: 139–144. September 1997, La Plata, Argentina.

2002 Ambientes de Sedimentación y Uso del Espacio en la Localidad Arqueológica Amalia, Provincia de Buenos Aires. *I Congreso de Arqueología de la Región Pampeana Argentina*. October 1998, Venado Tuerto, Santa Fe, Argentina, In press.

Mazzanti, D.

1995-96 Arqueología del Borde Oriental de Tandilia. Cambios y Continuidades en el Uso del Espacio. *Shincal. Revista de la Escuela de Arqueologia,* 5:7–24, Universidad de Catamarca, Argentina.

1997 Excavaciones Arqueológicas en el Sitio Cueva Tixi, Buenos Aires, Argentina. *Latin American Antiquity* 8 (10):55–62.

2002 Secuencia Arqueológica del Sitio 2 de la Localidad Arqueológica Amalia (Provincia. de Buenos Aires). In *Del Mar a los Salitrales Diez Mil Años de Historia Pampeana en el Umbral del Tercer Milenio.* Edited by D. Mazzanti, M. Berón, and F. Oliva, pp. 327–339. Mar del Plata, Argentina.

Menghin, O. F., and M. Bórmida.

1950 Investigaciones Prehistóricas en las Cuevas de Tandilia (Provincia de Buenos Aires). *RUNA*, vol. III, pt. 1-2:5–36.

Orquera, L. A., E. L. Piana, and A. E. Sala.

1980 La Antigüedad de la Ocupación Humana de la Gruta del Oro (Partido de Juarez, Provincia de Buenos Aires): un Problema Resuelto. *Relaciones de la Sociedad Argentina de Antropología,* T. XIV, No. 1, N.S. Bs. As.

Prado, J. L., A. Menegaz, E. P. Tonni, and M. Salemme.

1987 Los Mamíferos de la Fauna Local Paso Otero (Pleistoceno Tardío), Provincia de Buenos Aires. Aspectos Paleoambientales y Bioestratigráficos. *Ameghiniana* 24:217–233.

Quintana, C., G. Martínez, M. Osterrieth, and D. Mazzanti.

2001 Mammal Footprints in a Cave on the Eastern Edge of Tandilia Range, Late Pleistocene of Buenos Aires Province, Argentina. *Current Research in the Pleistocene*, Vol. 18:110–111.

Rabassa, J.,

1973 Geología Superficial en la Hoja "Sierras de Tandil", Provincia de Buenos Aires. *LEMIT*, Anales, Serie II, 240: 115–150. La Plata, Argentina.

Tapia, A.

1937 Las Cavernas de Ojo de Agua y Las Hachas. *Dirección Nacional de Geología y Minería,* Boletín No. 43. Buenos Aires, Argentina.

Teruggi, M. E.

1968 Geología y Sedimentología de las Cuevas de La Cuchilla de las Aguilas (Sierras de Tandil, Provincia de Buenos Aires). *Etnia* 7:13–25, Olavarría Argentina.

Tonni, E. P., and F. Fidalgo

1978 Consideraciones sobre Cambios Climáticos durante el Pleistoceno Tardío-Reciente en la Provincia de Buenos Aires. Aspectos Ecológicos y Zoogeográficos Relacionados. *Ameghiniana* 15 (1-2):235–253. Buenos Aires, Argentina.

Zárate, M., and N. Flegenheimer

1991 Geoarchaeology of the Cerro La China Locality (Buenos Aires, Argentina): Site 2 and Site 3. *Geoarchaeology,* 6(3):273–294.

The Craniofacial Morphology of Early- to Middle-Holocene Human Populations from the Pampean Region, Argentina: Getting a New Insight into the Morphological Variability of Early Americans

Gustavo Barrientos[1], Héctor M. Pucciarelli[2], Gustavo G. Politis[3], Sergio I. Perez[4], and Marina Sardi[5]

During the last 25 years human bone remains of at least 44 individuals of both sexes and various ages at death were recovered from the Arroyo Seco 2 site (Buenos Aires, República Argentina). On the basis of several radiocarbon dates from human bone collagen, an early- to middle-Holocene age was attributed to most of these burials (ca. 8000–6300 yr B.P.) (Barrientos 1997; Politis and Barrientos 2000). With the sole exception of an exploratory analysis carried out in the early 1980s (Marcellino n.d.), the cranial remains from this site have not been used in morphometric studies owing to extensive postdepositional modification suffered by a significant number of skulls. However, by employing a craniofacial reconstruction technique

[1] Facultad de Ciencias Naturales y Museo, UNLP, INCUAPA, Facultad de Ciencias Sociales, UNCPBA. Paseo del Bosque 1900, s/n, La Plata, Argentina. e-mail: barrient@museo.Fcnym.unlp.edu.ar

[2] CONICET, Facultad de Ciencias Naturales y Museo, UNLP. Paseo del Bosque 1900, s/n, La Plata, Argentina. e-mail: hmpucci@Fcv.unlp.edu.ar

[3] CONICET, Facultad de Ciencias Naturales y Museo, UNLP, INCUAPA, Facultad de Ciencias Sociales, UNCPBA. Paseo del Bosque 1900, s/n, La Plata, Argentina. e-mail: gpolitis@museo.Fcnym.unlp.edu.ar

[4] Facultad de Ciencias Naturales y Museo, UNLP. Paseo del Bosque 1900, s/n, La Plata, Argentina. e-mail: lperez@museo.Fcnym.unlp.edu.ar

[5] Facultad de Ciencias Naturales y Museo, UNLP. Paseo del Bosque 1900, s/n, La Plata, Argentina. e-mail: msardi@museo.Fcnym.unlp.edu.ar

based on the analysis of digitized images (Barrientos and Perez 1999) we were recently able to reliably measure 8 Howellian facial variables on a subsample of 10 adult individuals. These specimens were AS5 (male, ca. 6500–6300 yr B.P.), AS6 (female, ca. 6500–6300 yr B.P.), AS7 (female, ca. 6500–6300 yr B.P.), AS8 (female, 6500–6300 yr B.P), AS19 (male, ca. 7000 yr B.P.), AS22 (male, chronology unknown), AS24 (male, ca. 7800 yr B.P.), AS31 (male, ca. 7600 yr B.P.), AS39 (male, ca. 7600 yr B.P.), and AS40 (female, ca. 7000 yr B.P.) (Barrientos 1997; Perez 2002). The measured variables were OBH (orbital height), OBB (orbital breadth), DKB (interorbital breadth); FMB (bifrontal breadth), ZMB (bimaxillary breadth), NLB (nasal breadth), NLH (nasal height), NPH (nasion-prosthion height) (Howells 1973, 1989). In one case (AS19), an almost complete set of Howellian lineal variables could be measured (n = 42) owing to good preservation of the cranial vault.

In order to assess the biological affinities of the Arroyo Seco sample with respect to prehistoric and modern North and South American populations, comparisons were performed by means of principal component analysis based on shape information alone. Correction for size was done using a double Z standardization technique (by columns and by rows). All the multivariate analyses were accomplished using the SYSTAT 7.0 program.

We started by comparing 42 craniofacial variables of AS19 with those of 22 modern Asian, African, European, American, and Pacific samples published by Howells (1973, 1989) and of 5 prehistoric (Holocene) South American samples to assess the distinctiveness of the Arroyo Seco morphology relative to global human variation. A plot of the factor scores for the first two principal components (Figure 1) shows a clear morphological relationship between AS19 and

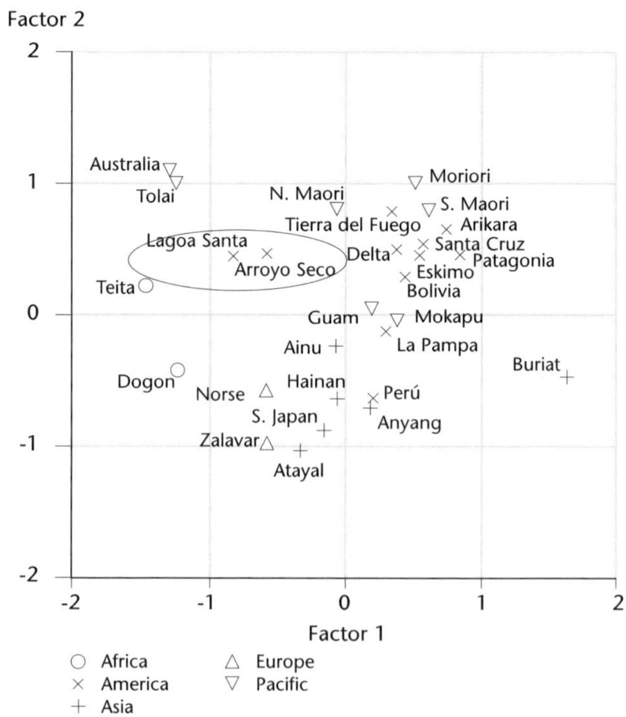

Figure 1. Scatterplot of the factor scores (standardized) of the first two principal components (analysis based on shape alone) for 22 Asian, African, European, American, and Pacific modern samples, and 6 prehistoric (Holocene) South American samples, including Arroyo Seco 2. Plot based on 42 linear Howellian craniometric variables, male individuals.

the average value of a composite sample from Lagoa Santa (Minas Gerais, Brazil) with an estimated age of ca. 10,000–8500 yr B.P. (W. Neves 2001 pers. comm. to G.B.). The graph also demonstrates that along the first component both these earlier specimens tend to differ from both modern populations and other prehistoric New World populations; they occupy an intermediate position between them and some South Pacific and African populations. Along the second component the earlier specimens tend to deviate from most modern Asiatic populations, which is consistent with results previously obtained by Neves and Pucciarelli (1989, 1991), Neves et al. (1998, 1999), and Neves and Blum (2000).

The second step was to compare the male and female subsamples from Arroyo Seco 2 with a set of North and South American crania of late-Pleistocene and early- to middle-Holocene age in order to assess morphological affinities at the facial level. The latter samples were derived from specimens from the following archaeological sites and localities (the entire list of radiocarbon dates for each skeleton is not detailed here; for a complete account, see the references below): Buhl (Idaho, U.S.A.), a female skeleton, ca. 10,800 yr B.P. (Green et al. 1998); Wizards Beach (Nevada, U.S.A.), a male skeleton, ca. 9500–9200 yr B.P. (Owsley and Jantz 1999); Spirit Cave (Nevada, U.S.A.), a male skeleton, ca. 9400 yr B.P. (Owsley and Jantz 1999); Brown's Valley (Minnesota, U.S.A.), a male skeleton, ca. 8900 yr B.P. (Owsley and Jantz 1999); Kennewick (Washington, U.S.A.), a male individual, ca. 8000 yr B.P. (Chatters 2000); Pelican Rapids (Minnesota, U.S.A.), a female skeleton, ca. 7800 yr B.P. (Owsley and Jantz 1999); Baño Nuevo (Aisén, Chile), a male individual, ca. 8700 yr B.P. (Mena and Reyes 1998; this study); Lagoa Santa (Minas Gerais, Brazil), six male and eight female individuals, ca. 8000–10,000 yr B.P. (Harold Walter Collection, G. Ozolins pers. comm. to H.M.P.); Tequendama (Cundinamarca, Colombia), four male and three female individuals, ca. 7000–5000 yr B.P. (Correal Urrego and van der Hammen 1977); and Sueva (Cundinamarca, Colombia), a female individual, ca. 10,000–9000 yr B.P. (Correal Urrego 1979).

The plot of the factor scores for the first two principal components for males (Figure 2) shows that the samples from Arroyo Seco and Tequendama exhibit a very high degree of morphological affinity along the two principal components; these account for 56.2 percent of the total variance. The other two samples from South America, Lagoa Santa and Baño Nuevo, and the North American sample differ from Arroyo Seco and Tequendama mainly in the second principal component. Notwithstanding the evidence of some deviation in the first principal component among all the North American and some of the South American crania, the first sample tends to differentiate them from the bulk of the South American crania. The variables that influence this component the most are NLH (-.798), ZMB (.708), and DKB (.698). For the second principal component, the most influencing variables are OBB (.930), and NLB (-.597). The faces from Arroyo Seco and Tequendama are characterized by a narrower orbital breadth, a wider interorbitary region, and a wider nasal breadth compared with most of the North American specimens, with which they share a similar high nasion-prosthion height. On the other hand, the Lagoa Santa crania, compared with those from Arroyo Seco and Tequendama, have a wider bifrontal breadth and wide bimaxillary and interorbital breadths (Figure 2).

Among females the main differentiation occurs in the first principal component, which accounts for 37.7 percent of the total variance. The entire sample from Lagoa Santa lies on the positive side of this axis; almost all the remaining cases fall on the negative side with the

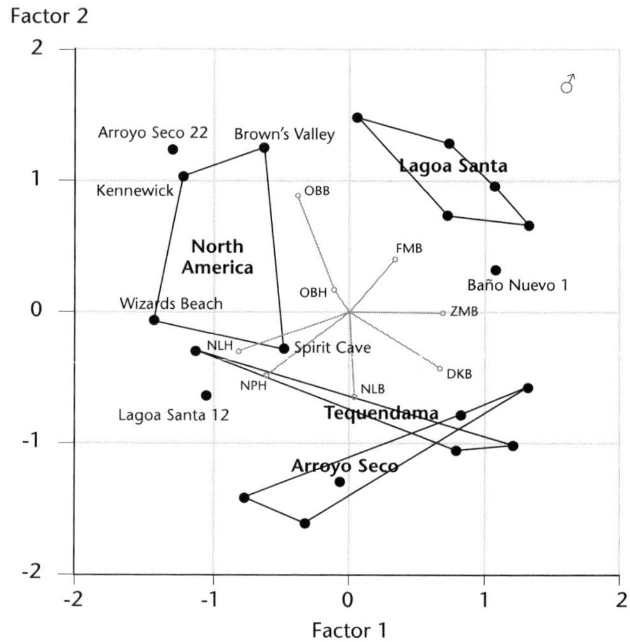

Figure 2. Scatterplot of the factor scores (standardized) of the first two principal components (analysis based on shape alone) for 21 male individuals from North and South America based on 8 linear Howellian facial variables. Superimposed in gray, the plot of factor loadings for each component.

sole exception of one specimen from Tequendama. Along the second principal component, which accounts for 22.3 percent of the total variance, there is no discernible differentiation among the samples. The variables that most influence differences in the first principal component are FMB (.835), NPH (-.819), and OBH (-.766). In the second principal component, the most influencing variables are NLB (.871) and DKB (-.709). The female faces from Arroyo Seco, Sueva, Buhl, Pelican Rapids, and some from Tequendama have higher nasion-prosthion, nasal, and orbital heights compared with those from Lagoa Santa, which have wider nasal, bimaxillary, and bifrontal breadths.

The results indicate that, despite the remarkable overall morphological similarity among most of the early- to middle-Holocene South American samples compared with worldwide populations (Neves and Pucciarelli 1989, 1991), there is a consistent pattern of differentiation within these samples on a continental scale. For both the male and the female subsamples, a close morphological affinity at the facial level was found between Arroyo Seco and both Colombian samples, Tequendama and Sueva. The Brazilian and Chilean samples clearly differ from the other two South American samples, and particularly from all the North American specimens included in this analysis. It is important to note that the North American samples used in this study exhibit a great deal of variability; whereas some specimens share a number of features with early South Americans populations, others have morphological features similar to those of modern American Indians (e.g., Owsley and Jantz 1999:93; see also Jantz and Owsley 2001 for a recent analysis of the variation among early North American crania). Among males the component that better discriminates between a modern (late-Holocene) Amerindian morphology and that described as non-Mongoloid by several authors (e.g., Neves and Pucciarelli 1991; Soto-Heim 1994), is

Component 1. For instance, all the individuals with scores for the first principal component lower than -1 in Figure 2 (Arroyo Seco 22, Lagoa Santa 12, Tequendama 12 and 13, Kennewick, and Wizards Beach) fall well within the range of variation of late-Holocene populations from the southeastern Pampean region in Argentina (Barrientos and Perez 2001). Although most of the early South American samples have a relatively low range of internal variation, some specimens are clearly outliers relative to the distribution of each geographic sample on the multivariate morphospace (e.g., Arroyo Seco 22, Lagoa Santa 12; see Figure 2). Moreover, as we already pointed out, they fall well within the range of variation of later populations; so it is evident that at least three to four different morphologies, including one similar to that of modern Amerindians, are present among the early- to middle-Holocene North and South American populations. To get a better understanding of this geographic and temporal (synchronous and asynchronous) pattern of variation, it is important to note that none of the available samples was drawn from the earliest populations that inhabited the sampled regions at the end of the Pleistocene. Indeed, there is an average temporal gap of ca. 2,000 to 4,000 years between the earliest probable date for the initial population of each region and the date of the human skeletal remains included in this and other morphological studies. Since there is an increasing body of evidence, albeit circumstantial, supporting the hypothesis of a rather rapid expansion of populations after the initial entry into the continent (probably not before 14,000–13,000 yr B.P.) (Anderson and Gillan 2000; Surovell 2000), we think the pattern of morphological variation observed among early North and South American samples is consistent with variation that would result from microevolutionary and adaptive change. This change might have occurred if each geographic location were settled by a single variable, heterogeneous ancestral population. If a population of such characteristics first entered the continent some 14,000 to 13,000 years ago and quickly expanded into empty landscapes within a matter of centuries or even a few millennia, it is reasonable to expect that most of the morphological differentiation across North and South America during the late Pleistocene and early Holocene would be the result of the interaction of subpopulations from different environments and the outcome of selection and genetic drift operating on small and more or less isolated local groups (see Steele and Powell 1999). The existence of different morphologies, an acknowledged fact in both subcontinents, could be the result of sampling biases (i.e., founder effect) operating over the original range of variability of the hypothetical ancestral population during geographic expansion. We think the combined effects of sampling biases acting over the original variability and of microevolutionary and functional-adaptive processes operating for several millennia on each regional population can account for the pattern of craniofacial differentiation observed among early- to middle-Holocene samples. The extent to which subtle biases introduced by our archaeological research designs (e.g., sampling and dating), analytical techniques (e.g., multivariate statistical analysis), and our conceptual tools are influencing the emerging picture is an issue that needs to be addressed more deeply in the future.

Acknowledgments

We wish to express our gratitude to Francisco Mena and Erik Ozolins for kindly sharing their data about Baño Nuevo 1 and Lagoa Santa, respectively, and to María Amelia Barreiro for her assistance in improving the English manuscript.

References Cited

Anderson, D. G., and J. C. Gillam

2000 Paleoindian Colonization of the Americas: Implications from an Examination of Physiography, Demography, and Artifact Distribution. *American Antiquity* 65(1):43–66.

Barrientos, G.

1997 *Nutrición y Dieta de las Poblaciones Aborígenes Prehispánicas del Sudeste de la Región Pampeana.* Unpublished Doctoral dissertation. Facultad de Ciencias Naturales y Museo, Universidad Nacional de La Plata, La Plata, Argentina.

Barrientos, G., and I. Perez

1999 Reconstrucción del Esqueleto Craneofacial de Restos Óseos Humanos del Sitio Arroyo Seco 2 (Holoceno Temprano del Sudeste de la Región Pampeana): Una Aproximación Mediante el Manejo de Imágenes. *Programa y Resúmenes de las IV Jornadas Nacionales de Antropología Biológica,* p. 65. San Salvador de Jujuy.

2001 Dinámica del Poblamiento Humano de la Región Pampeana: Implicaciones para la Discusión de un Modelo de Reemplazo Poblacional de Escala Continental durante el Holoceno Medio. Paper presented at the *XIV Congreso Nacional de Arqueología Argentina,* Rosario, Argentina.

Chatters, J. C.

2000 The Recovery and First Analysis of an Early Holocene Human Skeleton from Kennewick, Washington. *American Antiquity* 65(2):291–316.

Correal Urrego, G.

1979 *Investigaciones Arqueológicas en Abrigos Rocosos de Nemocón y Sueva.* Fundación de Investigaciones Arqueológicas Nacionales. Banco de la República, Bogotá, Colombia.

Correal Urrego, G., and T. van der Hammen

1977 *Investigaciones Arqueológicas en los Abrigos Rocosos del Tequendama.* Biblioteca Banco Popular, Bogotá, Colombia.

Green, T., J. Green, B. Cochran, T. Fenton, J. Woods, G. Titmus, L. Tieszen, M. Davis, and S. Miller

1998 The Buhl Burial: A Paleoindian Woman from Southern Idaho. *American Antiquity* 63(3):437-456.

Howells, W. W.

1973 Cranial Variation in Man. A Study by Multivariate Analysis of Patterns of Difference among Recent Human Populations. *Papers of the Peabody Museum of Archaeology and Ethnology,* Vol. 67. Harvard University, Cambridge, MA.

1989 Skull Shapes and the Map. Craniometric Analyses in the Dispersion of Modern *Homo. Papers of the Peabody Museum of Archaeology and Ethnology,* Vol. 79. Harvard University, Cambridge, MA.

Jantz, E,. and D. Owsley

2001 Variation among Early North American Crania. *American Journal of Physical Anthropology* 114(2):146–155.

Marcellino, A.

n.d. Los Esqueletos Humanos Aborígenes de Arroyo Seco (Partido de Tres Arroyos, Provincia. de Buenos Aires). Unpublished report. Córdoba, Argentina.

Mena, F., and O. Reyes

1998 Esqueletos Humanos del Arcaico Temprano en el Margen Occidental de la Estepa Centropatagónica (Cueva Baño Nuevo, XI Región). *Boletín de la Sociedad Chilena de Arqueología* 25(1):19–24.

Neves, W., and M. Blum

2000 The Buhl Burial: A Comment on Green et al. *American Antiquity* 65(1):191–194.

Neves, W. A., and H. M. Pucciarelli

1989 Extra-continental Biological Relationships of Early South American Human Remains: A Multivariate Analysis. *Ciencia e Cultura* 41(6):566–575.

1991 Morphological Affinities of the First Americans: An Exploratory Analysis Based on Early South American Human Remains. *Journal of Human Evolution* 21(2):261–273.

Neves, W. A., J. F. Powell, and E. G. Ozolins

1999 Modern Human Origins as Seen from the Peripheries. *Journal of Human Evolution* 37(1):129–133.

Neves, W. A., A. Prous, J. F. Powell, and E. G. Ozolins

1998 Lapa Vermelha IV: Morphological Affinities of the Earliest Known American. *American Journal of Physical Anthropology,* Supplement 26:169.

Owsley, D. W., and R. Jantz

1999 Databases for Paleoamerican Skeletal Biology Research. In *Who Were the First Americans? Proceedings of the 58th Annual Biology Colloquium*, edited by R. Bonnichsen, pp. 79–96. Oregon State University, Center for the Study of the First Americans, Corvallis, OR.

Perez, I.

2002 Variabilidad Temporal en la Morfología Craneofacial en Muestras de Restos Humanos del Sudeste de la Región Pampeana: Implicaciones para la Discusión del Poblamiento Regional durante el Holoceno. *Actas del II Congreso de Arqueología de la Región Pampeana Argentina*, Mar del Plata. In press.

Politis, G., and G. Barrientos

2000 La Cronología Radiocarbónica de los Entierros Humanos de Arroyo Seco 2. Unpublished report. La Plata, Argentina.

Soto-Heim, P.

1994 Les Hommes de Lagoa Santa (Brésil). Caractères Anthropologiques et Position parmi d'Autres Populations Paléoindiennes d'Amérique. *L'Anthropologie* 98:81–109.

Steele, D. G., and J. Powell

1999 Peopling of the Americas: A Historical and Comparative Perspective. In *Who Were the First Americans? Proceedings of the 58th Annual Biology Colloquium*, edited by R. Bonnichsen, pp. 97–126. Oregon State University, Center for the Study of the First Americans, Corvallis, OR.

Surovell, T.

2000 Early Paleoindian Women, Children, Mobility, and Fertility. *American Antiquity* 65(3):493–508.

Evaluating Evidence of Cultural Associations of *Mylodon* in the Semiarid Region of Chile

Donald Jackson S.

The only well-recognized Paleoindian archaeological site in the northern semiarid region of Chile is Quebrada de Quereo (31° 55′ S), a settlement located in a ravine at the edge of a paleolacustrine environment, where evidence is found of two independent hunting and butchering events of extinct fauna dating towards the end of the Pleistocene. The first event, dated prior to 11,000 yr B.P., would account for presumed anthropic activity mainly on a horse (*Equus* sp.) and a camelid (*Palaeolama* sp.), even though indications of cultural activity (lithic and bone record) are ambiguous (Núñez et al., 1994). In the second event, dated ca. 11,000 yr B.P., cutmarks and fractures, supposed lithic instruments, and bone concentrations point more clearly to human intervention on at least two horses (*Equus* sp.) in association with stone blocks (Montané and Bahamondes, 1973; Núñez et al., 1994).

In both events, besides the fauna mentioned, mastodon (*Cuvieronius* sp.), mylodon (*Mylodon* sp. or *Glossotherium* sp.), deer (*Antifer niemeyeri*), guanaco (*Lama* sp.), a carnivore (*Felidae*), a canid (*Dusicyon* sp.), as well as amphibians, rodents, birds, and molluscs were recorded, but their presence does not necessarily verify cultural activity.

A new project focusing on early occupation of the same locality at Los Vilos, Provincia de Choapa, has detected six new sites yielding extinct fauna on the surface and in stratigraphy. All include remains of *Mylodon* as well as equid, camelid, and other taxas still in study. In some of these sites the surface presence of lithic instruments, together with extinct faunal remains, implies cultural associations, particularly in the case of Quebrada El Membrillo site.

This site, located 2 km east of Quebrada de Quereo, is situated on an ancient marine terrace, 120–140 m a.s.l., which generates a depression oriented northeast-southwest. Quebrada El Membrillo is dissected by an old slide in a specific sector. Slime-clay sediments

Departamento Antropología, Facultad Ciencias Sociales, Universidad de Chile, CC 10115, Santiago, Chile. e-mail: djackson@uchile.cl were deposited on top of the terrace and the depression, and upon these, the ancient sandy deposits of dunes. Eolian processes have subsequently partially uncovered the sedimentary sequence containing the extinct faunal evidence and cultural remains.

Surface collection and stratigraphic excavation of 26 m^2 evidenced the presence of *Mylodon* sp., *Palaeolama* sp., equid, molluscs (*Concholepas concholepas* and *Fissurella* sp.), remains of minor fauna now under study, and various lithic instruments and ceramic pieces.

The mylodon remains of two different-sized individuals were found in two well-limited loci in the interface between the slime-clay and sandy deposits at a depth no more than 10 cm. One of these loci, Unit I, yielded vertebrae, ribs, and fragments of large and unidentified bones, together with cobbles and rocks that outcropped from the top of the terrace. There is no clear evidence of their use as lithic tools, even though some bones show fresh fractures and a fragment of an epiphysis clearly bears a cut mark, interpreted as the result of processing (Figure 2). One of the vertebrae gave an AMS date of 13,500 ± 65 yr B.P. (NSRL-11081, University of Colorado). In the second locus, Unit IV, 21 m northeast of Unit I, were found a mandibular branch, five vertebrae and splinters, and six mollusc fragments. About 70 flakes refitted and knapping debitage were found close by the bone concentration, and several osteoderms were found dispersed towards the middle and most deflated part of the settlement (Figure 1).

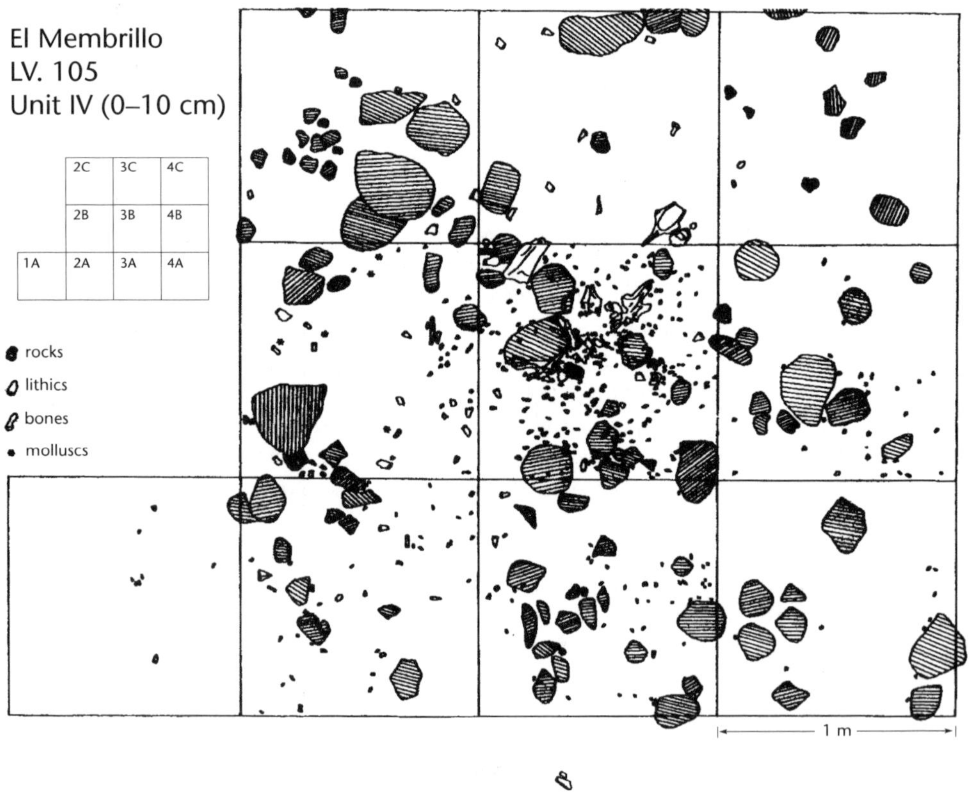

Figure 1. Artifacts associated with *Mylodon* sp. vertebrae.

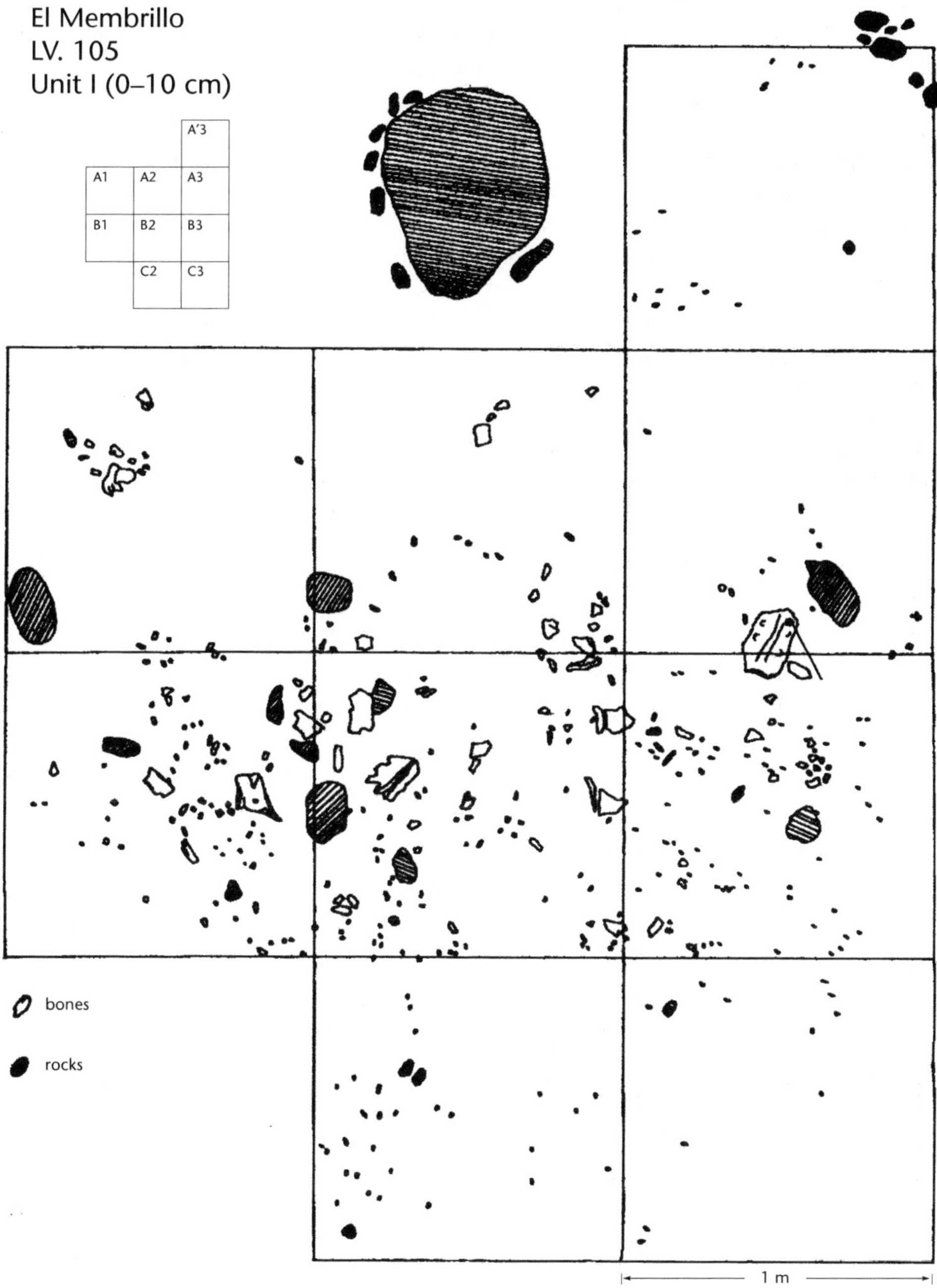

Figure 2. *Mylodon* bone record dated ca. 13,500 yr B.P.

Near Unit III towards the east of the site, on the sandy deposits of the dune undergoing eolian erosion, were found a disperse and undefined assortment of vertebrae, scapulae, ribs, and teeth of *Palaeolama* sp., some bearing probable evidence of antropic fresh fractures. At the southeastern limit of the site near Unit V, some equid teeth and fragments of large bones were detected.

Dispersed on the surface were observed extinct fauna bones, probably equids, with clear-cut fractures and splintering upon the large bones, and lithic instruments including ovoidal cobbles without modifications, cores, core flakes, some with intentional modifications, planes, scrapers, a sidescraper with extreme marginal chipping; some lithic instruments show evidence of intense tempering. Ceramic items, even though disperse, were concentrated in two loci, one towards the northwest, the other towards the southeast.

The site was apparently created by a series of complex formation processes (Schiffer, 1996:239) involving at least three depositing events; deflation action partially obliterated evidence of the previous event before the next occurred. Nevertheless, it is possible to distinguish a first event associated with the remains of *Mylodon* sp. (13,500 ± 65 yr B.P.) located in the slime-clay and sandy interface next to the top of the marine terrace. In a second event (posterior to 13,500 yr B.P.), the remains of *Palaeolama* sp. and an equid were deposited exclusively on the sandy substrate and distant to the top of the marine terrace. A third event (late-Ceramic period, or posterior to A.D. 1,000), which occurred upon the eroded sandy substrate, is associated with the ceramic items.

It is possible to infer cultural associations with regards to the first and second extinct fauna depositional events based on the following factors:

1. The strategic location with access to the Quebrada el Membrillo, which had forage resources and water, was favorably situated for stalking and killing prey, a situation similar to other Paleoindian sites like Quereo (Núñez et al., 1994) and Tagua Tagua (Núñez et al., 1994).
2. Two distinct loci, temporally unrelated, of extinct fauna, in one case of at least two individuals of *Mylodon* sp., in the other case of individuals of diverse species (*Palaeolama* sp. and an equid.), are associated with stone blocks, a situation similar to other Paleoindian sites (Quereo and Tagua Tagua).
3. The probable association of extinct fauna (*Mylodon* sp.) with lithic instruments (more than 70 flakes and debitage) in at least one locus (Unit IV) within a slime-clay and sandy ephemeral deposit is difficult to attribute to natural processes.
4. The bones of *Mylodon* sp. bear evidence of fresh fractures and sharp cutmarks, morphologically compatible with the action of a sidescraper with extreme marginal chipping. Fresh fractures with impact marks and chipping (continuous and conchoidal) are found on vertebrae and large bone fragments of *Palaeolama* sp. and equid.
5. Skeletal pieces with much economic yield are absent; the skeletal elements in situ are of low economic yield (Mengoni, 1999).
6. Evidence of typologically early lithic instruments (an extreme marginal chipping sidescraper, choppers, planes, and thick scrapers, some of them strongly tempered) is distinct from other later lithic evidence.
7. A first taphonomic approach to the bone record (Lyman, 1994:523) shows only evi-

dence of rodent gnawing posterior to the outcrop of one of the bone assemblages (*Mylodon* sp.). There is no evidence of carnivore marks that would explain the presence of spiral fractures, nor is it likely these were produced by trampling, since the soft substrate of sand would offer little resistance to any force of impact.

Judging by the complexity of the extinct faunal record, its associations and marks, eventually anthropic, it is reasonable to infer they are evidence of at least two hunting and butchering events by human groups at the end of the Pleistocene. If this hypothesis is correct, then both events might be associated with the two levels at the Quereo site (Núñez et al., 1994), with two levels of extinct fauna found at the Las Monedas site (in study), located just 500 m southeast of Quebrada El Membrillo, and with four surface sites in the locality. The implied spatial patterns are thus especially relevant.

An alternative hypothesis to account for the faunal record might be constructed based on the territory of big carnivores; however, evidence of their presence is quite meager. The presence of osteoderms of *Mylodon* sp. in some sites might be related to the depositing of their faeces, which has been shown in the paleontological record. In the particular case of the *Mylodon* sp. individuals, as well as those recorded at other Paleoindian contexts for which human hunting or "human-scavenging" has been hypothesized, it would be necessary to form an alternative explanation to account for the archaeological and paleontological evidence.

The early dating of the events associated with the *Mylodon* sp. (13,500 yr B.P.) and other compelling evidence of Paleoindian hunting and butchering of extinct fauna like camelids and equids justify modeling the "pre-Clovis" archaeological record.

References Cited

Lyman, L.
1994 *Vertebrate Taphonomy*. Cambridge University Press, Cambridge, U.K.

Mengoni, G.
1999 *Cazadores de Guanaco de la Estepa Patagónica*. Sociedad Argentina de Antropología, Buenos Aires, Argentina.

Montané, J., and R. Bahamondes.
1973 Un Nuevo Sitio Paleoindio en la Provincia de Coquimbo, Chile. *Publicaciones del Museo Arqueológico de La Serena,* Boletín N°15:215–222.

Núñez L., J. Varela, R. Casamiquela, and C. Villagrán.
1994 Reconstrucción Multidisciplinaria de la Ocupación Prehistórica de Quereo, Centro de Chile. *Latin American Antiquity* 5(2):99–118.

Schiffer, Michael B.
1996 *Formation Processes of the Archaeological Record*. University of Utah Press, Salt Lake City, UT.

Exploitation Territory at Agua de la Cueva (Southern Area) Site (11,000–9000 RCYBP)

Alejandro García

Agua de la Cueva is an extensive rockshelter located in the precordillera of Mendoza (32° 37′ S, 69° 09′ W, 2,900 m a.s.l.). At one of the corners of the site, named "Southern Area," numerous lithic and faunal remains dating to the late Pleistocene and early Holocene were discovered (García et al. 1999). Most of the evidence of early occupations was found in layer 2b (Figure 1), which extends in time from 10,950 ± 190 yr B.P. (Beta 61,409) to a little after 9210 ± 70 yr B.P. (Beta 64,539) (García 1998). In this layer 16,071 pieces of lithic debris and 732 lithic tools were recovered. A sample of 2,546 debris pieces, taken from the first and last archaeological levels of the layer, was analyzed as well as all the tools. Moreover, 1,887 bone specimens were recovered, of which only 908 were identifiable at genus or species levels. Some of the data here presented are useful in assessing the size of the exploitation territory and in drawing inferences about other components of the settlement system into which the site was integrated during the period ca. 11,000–9000 yr B.P.

Lithic Resources Acquisition

The lithic debitage is of quartz (n = 1,632), rhyolite (625) or chalcedony (232); other rocks are basalt (14), quartzite (7), schist (1) and obsidian (1). In 34 cases the rocks are unidentified.

Most of the lithic tools (Figure 2) are made of rhyolite (425), quartzite (137) and chalcedony (107). A few are of quartzite (19), basalt (13), schist (4), obsidian (1) and other local rocks including tufa (7). In 19 cases the raw material was not identified.

Several potential sources of this material were discovered in the mountain area surrounding the site. Sources of rhyolite, quartz, chalcedony, and schist lie within 5 km of the site. Quartzite and basalt are found 10–20 km south of Agua de la Cueva; the nearest source of obsidian is at least 100 km south.

CONICET (Universidad Nacional de San Juan) – UNCuyo. E. Echeverría 1030, B° Universitario, Rivadavia (5400), San Juan, Argentina. e-mail: agarcia@logos.uncu.edu.ar

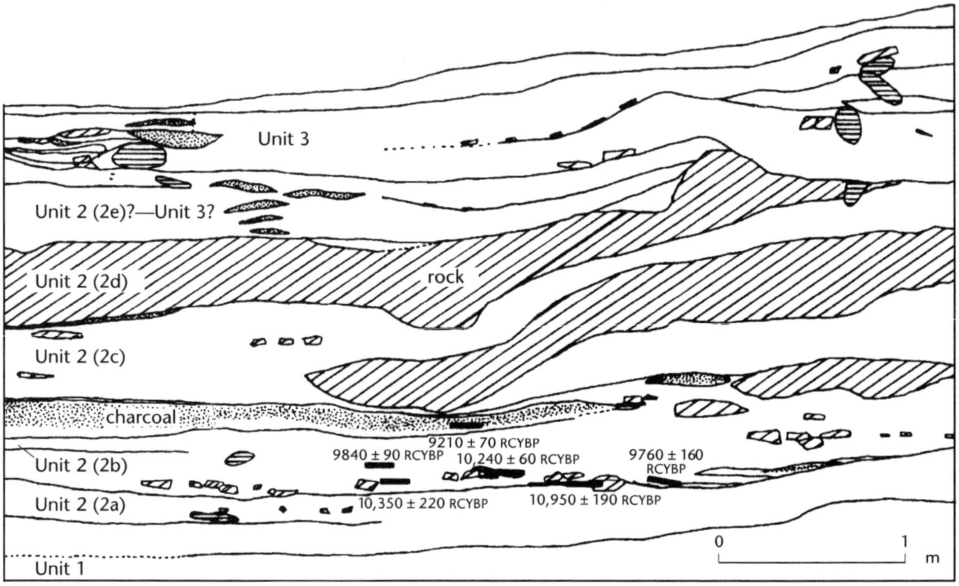

Figure 1. Stratigraphic profile and radiocarbon dates.

According to Meltzer's classification (1989), 98.29 percent (n = 3,170) of the analyzed artifacts (excluding unidentified items) are made of local rocks, 1.64 percent (n = 53) of regional rocks (source 10–40 km distant), and 0.06 percent (n = 2) of exotic rocks (source more than 40 km distant). This distribution suggests restricted mobility in acquiring rocks during the occupation of the shelter and restricted range of movement of the residents, and a special interest in keeping a few tools made of high-quality distant rocks.

Acquiring Faunal and Vegetable Resources

Preliminary archaeofaunal analysis of the remains (Gil et al. 1997) notes the predominance of Artiodactyla (n = 942) and large mammals (n = 608) and a low frequency of *Chaetophractus vellerosus*, *Lagidium* sp., Rodentia, and Rheidae. Most Artiodactyla remains are of *Lama* sp. and *Lama guanicoe*. Also present are a few specimens of *Lama* (*Vicugna*) (n = 16) belonging to the extant *L. Vicugna* (vicuña) or possibly to the extinct *L. gracilis*.

Except for *Lama* (*Vicugna*), the faunal record comprises the same animals observed today in the area. According to the analyzed record, the main faunal resource was the guanaco (*Lama guanicoe*). Paleoenvironmental studies (Zárate et al. 1998) indicate that by the late Pleistocene and early Holocene the precordillera was a shrubby steppe capable of supporting a population of camelids equal to or greater than that of modern times. So guanaco could have been an abundant and highly predictable resource for the shelter inhabitants. Other likely resources were smaller species, like *Lagidium viscacia*, that lives near the site. A complementary activity was the gathering of ñandú (Rheidae) eggs; in fact, shells have been recovered along the entire early archaeological sequence.

Since the colder and probably wetter conditions prior to ca. 9000 RCYBP (García et al.

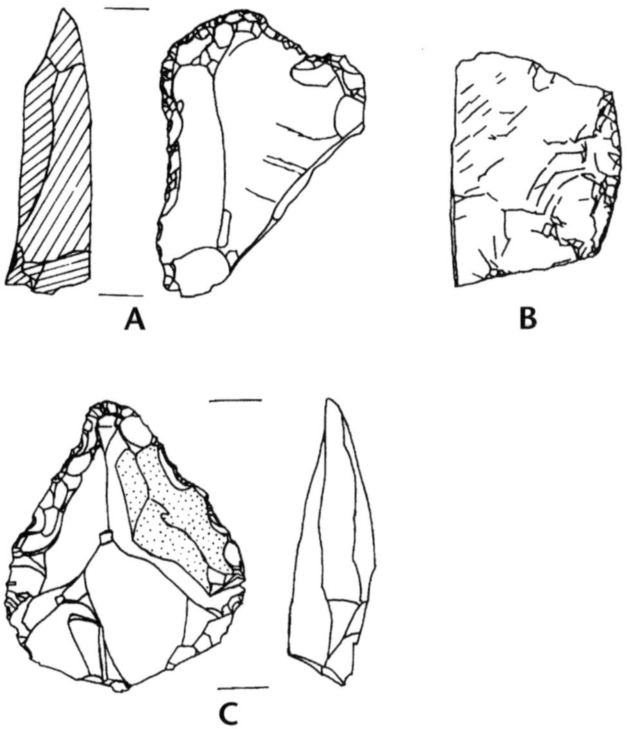

Figure 2. A, end- and sidescraper, rhyolite, 60 x 43 x 15 mm; B, double knife, rhyolite, 48 x 42 x 8 mm; C, multiple scaper, basalt, 60 x 50 x 10 mm.

1999) fostered grassy (*Stipa* sp.) and shrubby vegetation, only firewood and some cactaceous plants would have been available in the area; fruits of *Prosopis* sp. and *Schinus* sp., species from the phytogeographical Monte province, were occasionally gathered; they must have been more numerous in the extramontane zone farther east.

Conclusions

The present-day structure of resources in the precordilleran region, where Agua de la Cueva is located, suggests inhabitants were restricted in movement in their principal activities, acquiring lithic raw material and big-game hunting, during the period ca. 11,000–9000 RCYBP.

This pattern of resource exploitation mainly at the local level is similar to that observed in other early South American sites (Borrero 1996:348). Rocks for making tools were generally available from sources within 5 km of the site. Utilization of regional rocks means that sources in the precordilleran region were exploited at distances up to ca. 20 km. The few obsidian artifacts could signify the bounds of the settlement system or the existence of social or interchange networks spreading through a vast area of western Argentina as early as the late Pleistocene.

Acknowledgments

Recent studies at Agua de la Cueva site were supported by CONICET and PICT 01391 (ANPCyT) directed by M. Zárate. I especially thank the editors for their work on the manuscript.

References Cited

Borrero, L.

1996 The Pleistocene-Holocene Transition in Southern South America. In *Humans* at the End of the Ice Age: The Archaeology of the Pleistocene-Holocene *Transition,* edited by L. G. Straus, B. V. Eriksen, J. M. Erlandson, and D. R. Yesner, pp. 339–354. Plenum Press, New York.

García, A.

1998 Geocronología del Alero «Agua de la Cueva - Sector Sur». *Revista de Estudios Regionales* 17:49–64. Mendoza, Argentina.

García, A., M. Zárate, and M. Páez

1999 The Pleistocene-Holocene Transition and Human Occupation in the Central Andes of Argentina: Agua de la Cueva locality. *Quaternary International* 53/54:43–52.

Gil, A., G. Neme, and A. García

1997 Preliminary Zooarchaeological Results at Agua de la Cueva-Sector Sur Shelter. *Current Research in the Pleistocene* 14:139–140.

Meltzer, D.

1989 Was Stone Exchanged among Eastern North American Paleoindians? In *Eastern Paleoindian Lithic Resource Use,* edited by C. Ellis and J. Lothrop, pp. 11–39. Westview Press, Boulder, CO.

Zárate, M., M. Páez, and A. García

1998 Condiciones Ambientales entre los 14000 y los 5000 Años C14 en la Precordillera de Mendoza, Argentina: Localidad Agua de la Cueva. In *Ressumos Expandidos:*517–521, VI Congresso da Associacão Brasileira de Estudos do Quaternário (ABEQUA) e Reuniao sobre o Quaternário da América do Sul. Curitiba, Brazil.

Geochronology of the Arroyo Malo 3 Site and the First Human Occupations in North Patagonia in the Early Holocene

Sergio Diéguez[1] and Gustavo Neme[2]

Paleoindian occupations in Mendoza province, central-west Argentina, have been recorded since the 1960s in Gruta del Indio. At this site have been found bone specimens of taxa *Mylodon* sp., *Hippidion* sp., and Megatheriidae, associated with four lithic tools, some flakes, and furnaces (Lagiglia 1968, 1977; Lagiglia and García 1999). Recent excavations in Agua de la Cueva Rockshelter, in the north of this province, recovered a component radiocarbon-dated at earlier than 10,000 yr B.P. Numerous lithic materials and charcoal associated with bone specimens of present fauna were recovered from this site (García 1992; Gil et al 1997).

Excavations at the Arroyo Malo 3 site, in the southern Andean range of Mendoza, reveal a continuous human occupation sequence throughout the Holocene. The sequence starts with a cultural component from the early Holocene in association with Pleistocene faunal remains. Radiocarbon data and the stratigraphic profile show it was necessary to solve a range of problems of geoarchaeological nature. In this report we reconstruct the site formation history and discuss its stratigraphy. We also introduce the most recently obtained radiocarbon dates and identify extinct fauna.

The Arroyo Malo 3 site is a rockshelter developed at the base of andesitic outcrops with an opening 13 m long and 7.5 m deep oriented in an east-west direction. It is located on the border of the Arroyo Malo stream, a tributary of the Atuel River (34° 51′ 00″ S, 69° 53′ 05″ W, about 2,000 m a.s.l.) (Figure 1). The study area lies within the "Cordillera Principal"

[1] Museo de Historia Natural de San Rafael, Parque Mariano Moreno s/n (5600) San Rafael, Mendoza. Argentina. e-mail: sdieguez@infovia.com.ar

[2] Facultad de Ciencias Naturales y Museo, Universidad Nacional de La Plata y Museo de Historia Natural de San Rafael. Parque Mariano Moreno, (5600) San Rafael, Mendoza. Argentina. e-mail: ananeme@infovia.com.ar

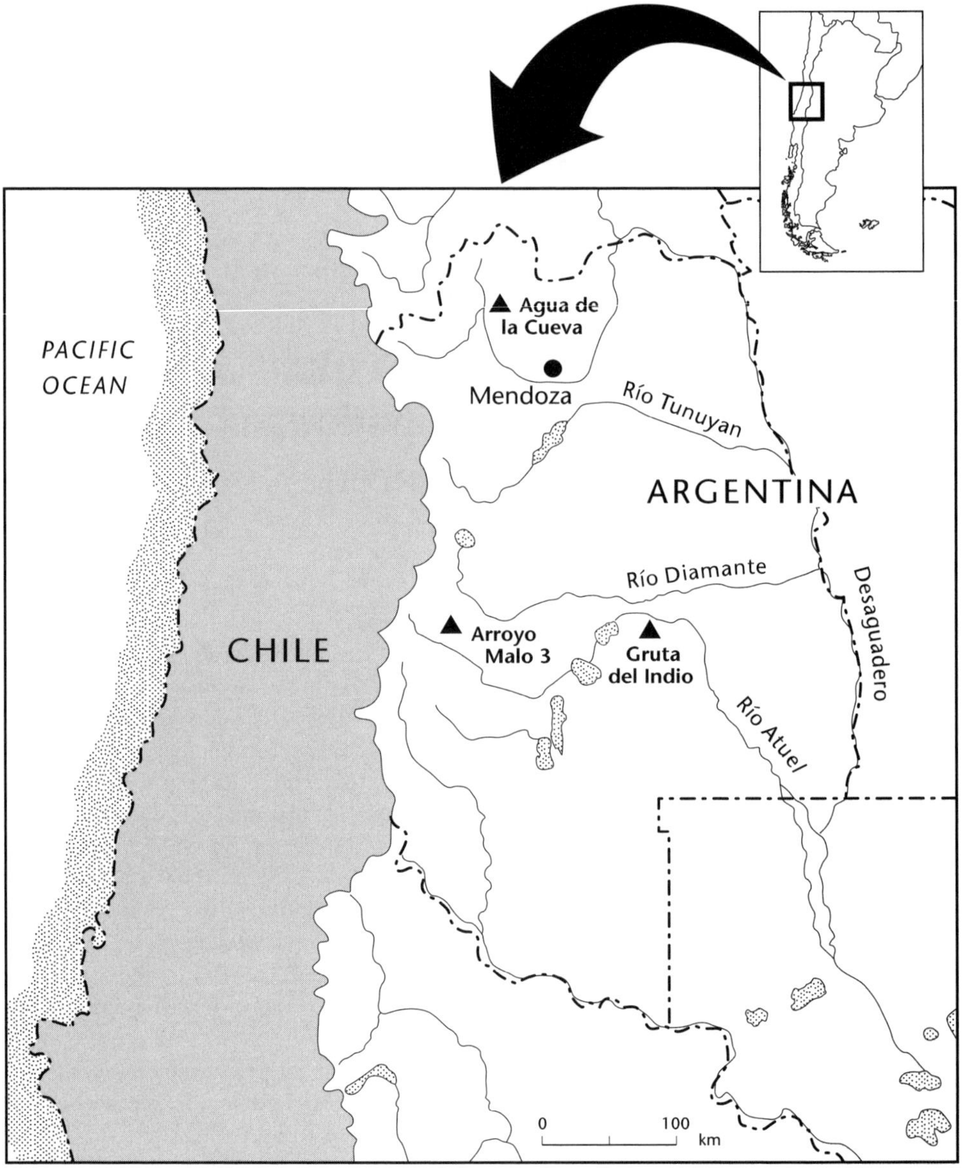

Figure 1. Late-Pleistocene/early-Holocene archaeological sites.

geological province (Yrigoyen 1978). Jurassic-Cretaceous lands predominate the eastern half; the western half is covered by volcanic material from the lower Tertiary-Cretaceous and the upper Tertiary-Quaternary. Three geomorphological units can be recognized within the region of our study (Volkheimer 1978): anticlinal relief of Atuel; volcanic relief related to the structuring of the Sosneado Mountain; and glacial relief with U-shaped valleys and a series of terminal moraines that end near the Arroyo Malo 3 site.

This site is one of a series of rockshelters and caves belonging to the "Cerro Guanaquero" Formation (Volkheimer 1978) or "Chapualitense inferior y general" Formation (*sensu* Groeber 1980). The rockshelters develop mainly in basaltic breaches at the base of outcrop of variable thickness. Because of their formational characteristics, these breaches are subject to weathering; over time blocks collapse, creating rockshelters.

The excavation, covering an area of 6 m^2, was dug in four archaeological field works between 1992 and 2000. Material was removed in increments of 5 cm until reaching bedrock at a maximum depth of 2 m. Important cultural materials, sediment characteristics, and postdepositional structures were mapped in three dimensions. Sediment samples were taken, and the profiles of the walls were mapped with determination of fits and sedimentary structures.

Although the sediment that composes the site is quite homogeneous, it is possible to differentiate three units (A, B, C) on the basis of variations in grain size, color changes, and the presence of sedimentary structures (Figure 2). Blocks of different sizes have fallen from the ceiling on the surface of the shelter; variations in the magnitude of such falls could be observed in the sequence.

The first important stratigraphic characteristic that can be distinguished is a change in the color of sediments within 45 cm of the present surface, from dark gray to light gray. Sandy sediments with clasts of different sizes, from sabule to blocks of 250 mm, predominate the deposit. Most subangular clasts are formed of ceiling rock (basaltic breach and andesite). Recovered artifacts, such as millingstones, manos, and flakes, are made of sandstone and basalts.

On the west wall of the excavation, at an approximate depth of 75–145 cm, are poorly

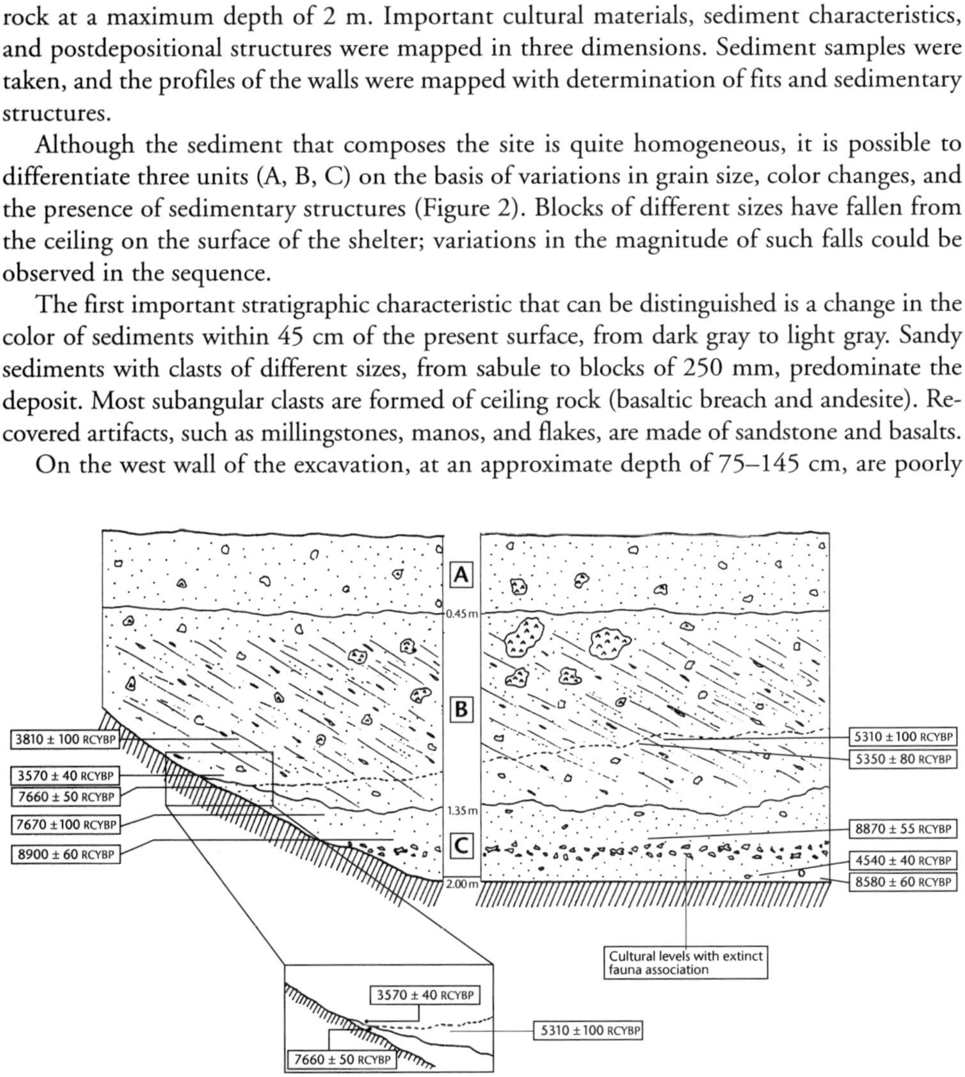

Figure 2. Arroyo Malo 3 stratigraphy.

defined areas where sedimentary unit B inclines 22° towards the north. This characteristic is observed mainly in the disposition of the grain-sized fraction between 1 mm and 3 cm. Numerous millingstones also display similar values of dip. Above this depth big and medium-sized blocks are concentrated in the south sector of the rockshelter, coinciding with the line of dripping, and diminish gradually towards the interior.

Below this depth the sediment becomes finer and more homogeneous, dark gray in color when moist. There is a discernible decrease in the psephite fraction of the unit. This is not true of the psammite fraction proportion, which in general remains stable throughout the profile. Concerning postdepositional processes, it is noteworthy that the record has been significantly altered by the fall of great blocks and the presence of rodent caves. This last unit between levels 35 and 38 (175–190 cm deep), deposited during the early Holocene, contains the oldest occupation, with evidence of furnaces associated with flakes and basalt instruments, some silica and obsidian flakes, and a bone specimen of extinct fauna (Xenartra cf. Tardígrada); other faunal remains include bone specimens of *Lama guanicoe,* armadillos, birds, and carnivores (Neme 2002).

Beneath level 38 the sediment is sterile in cultural materials with the exception of two carbonaceous areas containing cultural materials and bone specimens, which continue until bedrock. In one of these areas, lying on base rock, charcoal speckles were dated at 4540 ± 40 yr B.P. (NSRL-11719). The distribution of materials in the layers and the sediment composition indicate the speckles and cultural materials correspond to migrations resulting from fossorial animal activity. This date had been discussed deeper in another paper (Dieguez and Neme MS).

Results and Discussion

Two series of samples were radiocarbon dated. The first from grid A-1, and four years later (after new excavations) the second from grid B-1, yielded a total of 11 dates, all Holocene (Table 1).

Table 1. Radiocarbon datings.

Grid	Level	^{14}C age (RCYBP)	Material	Lab code
A-1	12	2200 ± 50	charcoal	LP 958
A-1	24	3810 ± 100	charcoal	LP 946
A-1	27	3570 ± 40	charcoal	NSRL-11721
A-1	28	7660 ± 50	charcoal	NSRL-11722
A-1	31, 32, 33	7670 ± 100	charcoal	LP 783
A-1	35	8900 ± 60	charcoal	AA 26193
B-1	23 N	5350 ± 80	charcoal	LP-1279
B-1	23 S	5310 ± 100	charcoal	LP-1267
B-1	35	8870 ± 55	charcoal	NSRL-11723
B-1	39	8580 ± 60	charcoal	NSRL-11720
B-1	40	4540 ± 40	charcoal	NSRL-11719

The stratigraphic observations and radiocarbon datings reveal two problematic issues: the absence of dates in the middle Holocene in grid A-1; and the sediment inclination observed in stratigraphy in the midsection of the sedimentary profile.

Absence of mid-Holocene dates in grid A-1 The dates obtained for the first set of samples (grid A-1, levels 27 and 28, separated in depth by 5 cm), disclose a hiatus of about 3,000 years in the sedimentary and cultural record. This discontinuity does not appear in the samples for grid B-1 (within 2 m of grid A-1), which yielded two radiocarbon dates of ca. 5300 yr B.P. The rockshelter bedrock topography, the present topography of the land, the locations from which the samples were obtained, and the events of fallen blocks around the present drip line suggest the likely existence of differential deposits in mid-Holocene sediments, which could account for anomalies like the one observed. The homogeneity of the sedimentary package prevents our visually corroborating these alternatives in the profiles.

Inclination of sediments The inclination of layers observed in the midsection of the profile (levels 23 to 28) is not reflected in the radiocarbon-dating samples taken from the north and south sectors of level 23, grid B-1. Several possibilities arise from this observation: 1) the inclination of the sediment may be a postdepositional change, not a primary characteristic; 2) such a dip may be a localized problem (e.g., fallen blocks) that did not affect the entire rockshelter record; 3) the horizontal range from where the samples were taken was not wide enough to reflect the change between the different deposition events.

Formation History of the Deposits

Erosion of the basaltic front deposited by the end of the Pleistocene created the rockshelter. Immediately after, eolian deposition of sandy sediments began. The main source of sedimentary material was the alluvial plain of the Atuel River, without any contribution from the ceiling rock. This sedimentation continued after the first human occupations of the rockshelter about 9000 yr B.P. These inhabitants coexisted with the last representatives of Pleistocene fauna in the region. Local basalts were the main source of raw material for making instruments; *Lama guanicoe* was the main species exploited.

After 7600 yr B.P. sediments of the middle Holocene were differentially deposited on the rockshelter (probably the result of a change either in the transport agent or in the source at the alluvial plain of the Atuel River) without completely covering the surface (see Figure 2). This created lenticular structures according to the distribution of fallen ceiling blocks or to paleotopographic conditions. Finally, the rockshelter was completely filled by 2200 yr B.P.; ceiling rock contributed substantially to fill material. Human occupations and sedimentary filling of the rockshelter occurred simultaneously and without interruption during the entire Holocene.

The record for the beginning of the Holocene shows an early hunter-gatherer occupation in the high environment of north Patagonia. This occupation began just after glacier regression (Markgraf 1989). The archaeological record since 9000 years ago shows complete use of regional resources, including faunal (perhaps Pleistocene fauna) and lithic resources, which indicates a keen awareness of the area. The occupation was probably contemporary with the Mendocina Foothill Paleoindian site.

This record of Pleistocene fauna associated with early Holocene human occupations deviates from our previous knowledge of Paleoindian settlements in the region. The survival of extinct species, observed only in high-altitude environments, has not been recorded either in the piedmont or in the plains (García 1992; Lagiglia 1968; Lagiglia and García 1999).

Acknowledgments

The excavations were carried out with the support of Fondo Provincial de la Cultura de Mendoza and Agencia Nacional de Promoción Científica y Tecnológica. We want to thank especially INSTAAR laboratories (University of Colorado and Arizona AMS facility), who processed the samples for radiocarbon dates within their special programs. Thanks to Sergio Vizcaíno and Claudia Tambussi for the determination of Xenartra specimen and to Adolfo Gil for the critical reading of the manuscript.

References Cited

Dieguez, S., and G. Neme
2000 Geoarqueología del Sitio Arqueológico Arroyo Malo 3. Unpublished paper presented at *XV Congreso Nacional de Arqueología Chilena*, Arica, Chile.

Garcia, A.
1992 Early Occupations at Agua de la Cueva-Sector Sur, Province of Mendoza, Argentina. *Current Research in the Pleistocene* 9:13–14.

Gil A., G. Neme, and A. Garcia
1997 Preliminary Zooarchaeological Results at Agua de la Cueva-Sector Sur Shelter. *Current Research in the Pleistocene* 14:139–140.

Groeber, P.
1980 Observaciones Geológicas a lo Largo del Meridiano 70°. *Asociación Geológica Argentina. Serie C*, Reimpresiones número 1. Buenos Aires, Argentina.

Lagiglia, H.
1968 Secuencias Culturales del Centro Oeste Argentino: Valles del Atuel y del Diamante. *Revista Científica de Investigaciones* 1(4):159–174.

1977 *Arqueología y Ambiente Natural de los Valles del Atuel y del Diamante*. Ph.D. Dissertation. 2 volumes. Facultad de Ciencias Naturales y Museo. Universidad Nacional de La Plata. La Plata, Argentina.

Lagiglia, H., and A. Garcia
1999 Las Ocupaciones Tempranas del Atuel (Nuevos Estudios en la Gruta del Indio*). Actas del XII Congreso Nacional de Arqueología Argentina* III:251–255.

Markgraf, V.
1989 Paleoclimates in Central and South America since 18,000 BP Based on Pollen and Lake Level Records. *Quaternary Science Reviews* 8:1–24.

Neme, G.
2002 Arqueología del Alto Valle del Río Atuel: Modelos, Problemas y Perspectivas en el Estudio de las Regiones de Altura del Sur de Mendoza. In *Arqueología del Sur de Mendoza*, edited by A. Gil and G. Neme, pp. 65–83.

Volkheimer, W.
1978 *"Cerro El Sosneado." Hoja 27 b. Carta Geológico-económica de la República Argentina*. Ministerio de Economía. Secretaría de Estado de Recursos Naturales y Ambiente Humano. Subsecretaria de Minería, Servicio Geológico Nacional. Buenos Aires, Argentina.

Yrigoyen, M.
1978 Cordillera Principal. *Segundo Simposio de Geología Regional Argentina. Academia Nacional de Ciencias* I:651–694. Córdoba, Argentina.

Stratigraphy and Environmental Geology of Monte Verde: Classic Uniformitarianism and Multiple Scales of Research

Mario Pino

When studying the geoarchaeology of early-man sites, the researcher must first develop a precise understanding of present archaeological and environmental conditions in order to assess the circumstances encountered by the first Americans in their environment.

This report examines the regional context of the stratigraphy of the Monte Verde site and the local conditions that were responsible for preserving the archaeological remains; the temporal-spatial relationships between the different strata and the human occupation of 12,500 yr B.P.; the Pleistocene environment represented; and the moment when, regardless of their real depositional age, there were surfaces available for use by the inhabitants.

Fundamental interpretations are presented, based on comparison with current geological phenomena.

Some photos and outlines are available on Web page www.ciencias.uach.cl/user/monteverde

The Regional Scale (e.g., 1:25,000)

The Monte Verde site is located on a plain interrupted by the Chinchihuapi Creek in the middle of a little valley (about 6 m deep and 200 m wide). The surface of the plain, corresponding to the youngest beds of an outwash deposit, is dated about 33,000 RCYBP, which means they are synchronic with the Llanquihue Glaciation (Heusser et al. 1999). These outwash deposits are referred to as the Salto Chico Formation (Pino 1984, 1989; Pino and Dillehay 1988). At the outcrop of the Salto Chico village, near the base of the cutbanks of the Chinchihuapi Creek, and in our trenches and pits we noted gravels and sands with a matrix (less than 15 percent) composed of volcanic ash and thin lenses and laminas of pure

Instituto de Geociencias. Universidad Austral de Chile. Casilla 567. Valdivia. Chile. e-mail: mariopino@uach.cl

volcanic ash. Well-rounded intraclasts of peat are frequent. Small channels about 1 m deep with cross-stratification are a very common structure. These shallow, gravel-bed braided river deposits are very similar to the "Scott type" fluvial style (Miall 1977).

The Local Scale (e.g., 1:2,500)

Another type of sediment outcrops at both borders of the Chinchihuapi Creek. The Monte Verde Formation (Pino 1989), only a couple of kilometers long, a few hundred meters wide, and with deposits about 1 m thick, is characterized by a mixture of clastic, orthochemical, and biogenic sediments. We recognized six strata from bottom to top (Figure 1) (for details see Dillehay and Pino 1986, 1989; Dillehay et al. 1982).

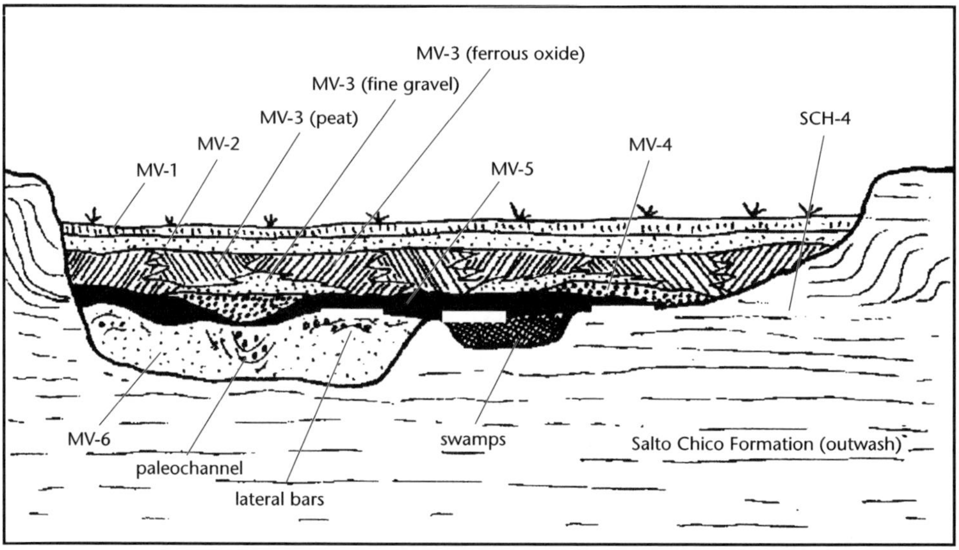

Figure 1. Stratigraphic and facies outline (without scale) of the Monte Verde site. The white rectangles indicate the occupational surface of 12,500 yr B.P.

Salto Chico Formation, Erosion Unconformity

MV-6: Clean gravel interfingered with sand (fine matrix less than 15 percent). Stratification is mostly horizontal, and the old channels are flat and no more than 1 m wide. Very tiny fragments of leaves and wood are deposited behind gravel clasts. Most of these gravel particles have a patina of red iron oxides in the upper face. There is no clast imbrication.

MV-5: Dark brown peat, very plastic, composed mostly of vegetable fragments with a subordinate mineral fraction.

MV-4: Clean gravel, also interfingered with sand (fine matrix less than 15 percent). This layer is very discontinuous and most of the times appears as lenses. There is no patina on these clasts.

MV-3: This stratum is composed of three different facies. The most frequent corresponds to sedimentary iron oxides. These oxides interfinger with black peat and fine gravel, the latter completely weathered.

MV-2: Mostly medium sand, without matrix or structures. This layer is also discontinuous and frequently outcrops as lenses.

MV-1: *Sensu stricto* this is a soil, but we usually think of it as a stratum because it includes evidence of the big forest fire made about 1950 by the first Chilean settlers.

The Site Scale (e.g., 1:10)

At the Monte Verde site there is an erosional unconformity between the outwash deposits of the Salto Chico Formation (locally SCH-4) and bed MV-6 of the Monte Verde Formation. The uppermost 6 m of the outwash deposits was eroded by the very first Chinchihuapi Creek (Chinchihuapi I) about 20,000 years ago (Pino 1993); consequently the sediments beneath the unconformity are not weathered and have a very typical blue-gray color, which contrasts with the fine white ash layers. In this bed (SCH-4, formerly also MV-7 and MV-8) there are no archaeological remains. All the gravel and sand of the MV-6 bed derived from the Salto Chico outwash, and at the time of human occupation by 12,500 yr B.P. (Dillehay and Pino 1997a) the Chinchihuapi Creek lateral and point bar sediments represent a lag deposit (Chinchihuapi II). The settlement was mainly restricted to the surface of this point and lateral bars of the Chinchihuapi Creek (the top of MV-6). The iron oxide patina and very tiny deposits of leaves and wood at the border of the paleochannel indicate a flat creek with a very low energy flux. Today it is possible to observe the same situation in spring and summer when the rainfall is low or nearly absent. We observed that in other creeks with swifter current or greater water flow it is impossible to produce iron hydroxides in a colloidal stage. Although it is not possible to prove it, the production of the iron colloids may have been the first step in forming the swamp where MV-5 was deposited.

The deposits of MV-4 also correspond to a creek environment (Chinchihuapi III), short in time span and low in energy compared with the creek in MV-6. After this erosion-deposition event a very large swamp formed, with deposits of peat and the ferrous orthochemical sediments. The latter became completely impermeable rock that protected the archaeological remains, preventing lixiviation by the annual 1.5 m of rainfall. Creek erosion caused by Chilean settlers after 1950 exposed the layers of the Monte Verde Formation and the archaeological remains (Chinchihuapi IV)

The Human Scale

To the north and south of the Chinchihuapi axis there were other microenvironments also available at 12,500 yr B.P. (Dillehay and Pino 1997b) (Figure 1). Between the borders of the lateral and point bars and the old surface of the outwash there were some minor erosional depressions where little wetlands and swamps formed. Also available was a flat surface over the outwash deposits near the lateral bars. An important fact, which was earlier misunderstood, is that most of the surfaces over the outwash deposits were available about 20,000 years ago. Now it is possible to find above this surface (weathered and supporting soil development, quite different from the fresh blue-gray SCH-4) objects belonging to settlements found during the 1977–1987 excavations, as well as Huilliche or Archaic artifacts. Of course, it was possible for the Monte Verde people to walk on this old surface.

It is also necessary to understand another geological process that occurred at Monte Verde, the rapid development of a wetland and later a swamp, where organic-rich peat was deposited. This stratum (MV-5), today 1–25 cm thick, was created after 12,500 yr B.P. (Dillehay and Pino 1997a) in a strong anoxic environment that preserved organic natural and cultural materials including bone, wood, seeds, meat, hide, etc. Moreover, not only was the MV-5 layer responsible for remarkable preservation, it also established a time scale for the Monte Verde settlement. The MV-5 layer overlies the lateral and point bars of MV-6, and also the older swamps and the 20,000 yr B.P. surfaces of the Salto Chico outwash (Figure 1). Thus we excavate and interpret between two surfaces well defined in space and time: a lower surface formed mainly by the lateral and point bars (MV-6) and also by the 20,000 yr B.P. erosional surface on the outwash; and an upper surface delimited by the base of the MV-5 peat.

The rapid change between the creek and the wetland-swamp environment was recreated temporarily during the very dry 1979 summer. We built a barrier of gravel and sand in a shallow zone of the Chinchihuapi Creek; as a result the water current was nearly zero, and the water level rose about 20 cm over the lateral bars of the Chinchihuapi Creek. A few days later a large number of aquatic plants were growing, rapidly covering most of the surface of our little wetland. In the past a rise in the local base level (the Maullin River) was the cause of the change in environment from creek to wetland-swamp.

In actuopaleontology it is possible to make different interpretations depending on whether you find a biocoenosis, thanatocoenosis, or taphocoenosis. It is possible to say the rapid preservation of the 12,500 yr B.P. Monte Verde camp produced a kind of biocoenosis assemblage, with a perfect representation of the most important activities of daily life of the Monte Verde Culture.

References Cited

Dillehay, T., and M. Pino

1986 Monte Verde: An Early Man Site in South-central Chile. *Andean Archaeology, Monograph* XXVII: 1–17. Institute of Archaeology, University of California Los Angeles, Los Angeles, CA.

1989 Stratigraphy and Chronology. In *Monte Verde. Palaeoenvironment and Site Context*, edited by T. Dillehay, Vol. I, pp. 133–146 Smithsonian Institution Press, Washington, D.C.

1997a Radiocarbon Chronology. In *Monte Verde. Archaeological Context and Interpretation*, edited by T. Dillehay, Vol. 2, pp. 41–52. Smithsonian Institution Press, Washington, D.C.

1997b Site Settings and Stratigraphy. In *Monte Verde. Archaeological Context and Interpretation*, edited by T. Dillehay, Vol. 2, pp. 25–40. Smithsonian Institution Press, Washington, D.C.

Dillehay, T., M. Pino, M. Davis, S. Valastro, A.Varela, and R. Casamiquela

1982 Monte Verde: Radiocarbon Dates from an Early-man Site in South-Central Chile. *Journal of Field Archaeology* 9:547–550.

Heusser, C., L. Heusser, and T. Lowell

1999 Paleoecology of the Southern Chilean Lake District - Isla Grande de Chiloe during Middle-late Llanquihue Glaciation and Deglatiation. *Geografiska Annaler* 81A(2):231–284.

Miall, A. D.

1977 A Review of the Braided River Depositional Environment. *Earth Science Review* 13:1–62.

Pino, M.

1984 Geological and Chronostratigraphical Relationships of the Monte Verde Site. *Geological Society of America. Abstracts and Programs* 16(6):524.

1989 Regional and Site Geology. In *Monte Verde. Palaeoenvironment and Site Context*, edited by T. Dillehay, Vol. I, pp. 189–132. Smithsonian Institution Press, Washington, D.C.

1993 Estratigrafía, Cronología e Interpretación Ambiental del Sitio Monte Verde, Centro Sur de Chile. *Taller Internacional "El Cuaternario de Chile"* Universidad de Chile, SUDAMQUA, Santiago, Chile.

Pino, M., and T. Dillehay
1988 Monte Verde, South-Central Chile: Stratigraphy, Climate Change and Human Settlement. *Geoarchaeology* 3(3):177–191.

Radiocarbon Chronology at Piedra Museo Locality

Laura Miotti[1], Mónica Salemme[2] and Jorge Rabassa[3]

Piedra Museo locality is located at 47° 53′ 42″ S, 67° 52′ 04″ W, in the Central Plateau of Santa Cruz province, Argentine Patagonia. Several open-air sites and rockshelters were surveyed in this area across the Zanjón Elornia, which flows to Laguna Grande. The area of excavated site AEP-1 is an enclosed basin; it constitutes a real topographic trap for fauna today and probably was so during the studied period.

Archaeological Evidence

Rockshelter AEP-1 yielded two main archaeological contexts, the older one dated between 12,800 and 9200 RCYBP, the younger occupation about 7400 RCYBP on average (Table 1). An area of 50 m^2 was excavated (approximately 70 percent of the surface under the rockshelter).

Two strata are evident in the excavation. The upper one (Unit 1) is an eolian unit; the lower stratum (Unit 2 to Unit 6, from top to bottom) is a paleosol containing five units, distinguished by their sedimentological characteristics (texture, color, structures, granulometry, and lateral and vertical boundaries) (Miotti 1992, 1996). The degree of preservation of bones, their spatial distribution, and bone modifications in each layer also served to distinguish this deposit (Blasi et al. 1997; Miotti et al. 1999). The profile is described as an edaphic profile. There is a remarkable unconformity only between Units 1 and 2; the other boundaries are gradual and transitional, since they are different horizons of a paleosol (Figure 1).

Two archaeological components were identified in this paleosol, the upper component

[1] Departmento de Arqueología, Facultad de Ciencias Naturales y Museo, Universidad Nacional de La Plata–CONICET. e-mail: miotti@netverk.com.ar

[2] Laboratorio de Geología del Cuaternario, CADIC–CONICET, and Universidad Nacional de la Patagonia, Ushuaia, Argentina. e-mail: labcuat@satlink.com

[3] Laboratorio de Geología del Cuaternario, CADIC–CONICET, and Universidad Nacional de la Patagonia, Ushuaia, Argentina. e-mail: jrabassa@infovia.com.ar

Table 1. Radiocarbon Datings from AEP-1.

Stratigraphic unit	Sample no.	^{14}C age (B.P.)	$\delta^{13}/_{12}C$ (‰)	Material	Taxa
2 middle	NSRL11167 ■	7470 ± 140	n/d	charcoal	indet.
2 bottom	LP 450 ▲	7670 ± 110	n/d	bone	*Lama guanicoe*
4 top	LP 949 ▲	9230 ± 105	-20	bone	*Lama guanicoe*
4 bottom	LP 859 ▲	9710 ± 105	n/d	bone	*Lama guanicoe*
5 middle	AA-8428 ■	10,400 ± 80	-25.8	bone	Camelidae
5 bottom	OxA9249 ■	10,470 ± 65	-26.6	charcoal	indet.
5/6 top of block	OxA9508 ■	Both samples under redating process at Arizona Lab.			
5/6 bottom of block	OxA9509 ■	(Dr. J. Steele, pers. comm. November 2000)			
6 bottom	GRA9837 ■	10,470 ± 60	n/d	charcoal	indet.
6 middle	OxA8527 ■	10,390 ± 70	-18.1	bone	*Lama guanicoe*
6 bottom	OxA8528 ■	10,925 ± 65	-19.3	bone	*Hippidion saldiasi*
6 bottom	AA-27950 ■	11,000 ± 65	-23.4	charcoal	indet.
6 bottom	AA-20125 ■	12,890 ± 90	-25	charcoal	indet.

Processing methods: ■AMS ▲standard

(Holocene) and the lower component (Pleistocene/Holocene transition). In the lower component, at least two occupation events were confirmed by radiocarbon dating. Unit 6, dated between 12,890 ± 90 RCYBP (AA-20125) and 10,470 ± 65 RCYBP (OxA-9249), is confirmed as the initial late-Pleistocene occupation in southernmost Patagonia. Unit 4/5, dated between 10,400 ± 80 RCYBP (AA-8428) and 9230 ± 105 RCYBP (LP-949), represents the stage of effective colonization of the region. However, there are no technological differences be-

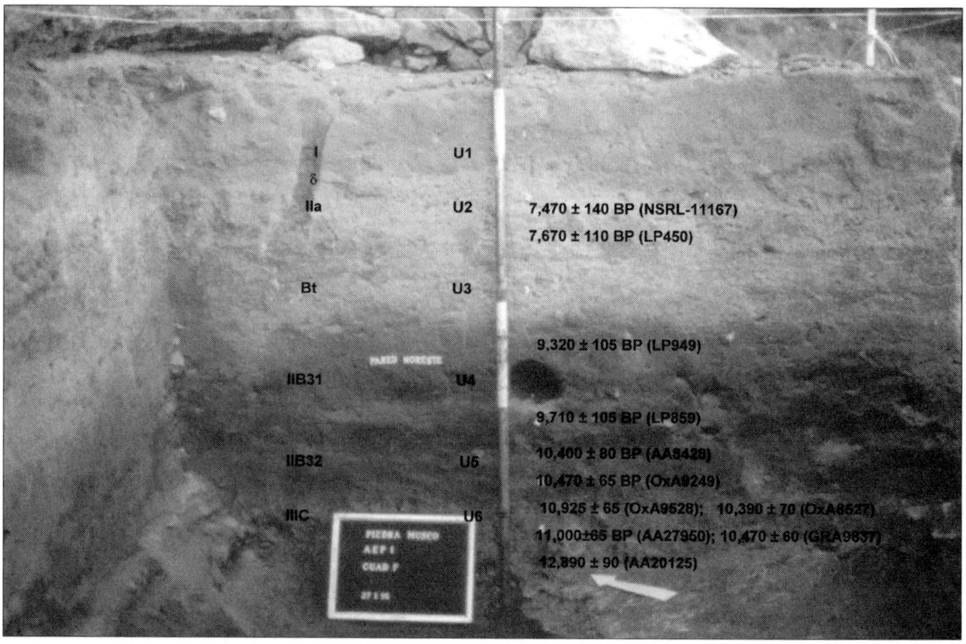

Figure 1. Profile from excavation unit F. Vertical distribution of radiocarbon datings is shown.

tween these levels; the differences between U4/5 and U6 would be merely the result of two distinct butchering events (Miotti and Cattáneo 1997; Miotti et al. 1999), separated by an interval of few decades.

Unit 3 is archaeologically sterile; the few materials found in it could just be the result of vertical displacement from the unit above it.

Two samples from the upper component of Unit 2 (Holocene) were dated at 7670 ± 110 RCYBP (LP-450) and 7470 ± 140 RCYBP (NSRL-11167). This assemblage is related to the territorial consolidation phase of the local hunter-gatherer societies (Miotti 1998; Miotti and Salemme 1999). According to data gathered from the faunal assemblage, stratigraphic position, and radiocarbon dating, U2 represents the latest occupation in the site during the mid-Holocene, following a massive collapse of the roof. Different occupational events are defined in part by radiocarbon data and also by taphonomic, taxonomic, spatial, and statistical archaeozoological analyses and study of the technology of lithic and bone artifacts. Taxonomic analysis finds greater biodiversity (a higher proportion of extinct taxa) in U6 than in U4/5. Although U4/5 are considered a block in a cultural sense, from a geological point of view there are pedogenetic differences between U5 and U4 (Figure 1). Moreover, there are more extinct species represented in U5 than in U4. Finally, there is no evidence of extinct species in Unit 2, in which *Lama guanicoe* (guanaco) dominates the spectrum.

Two alternative interpretations are considered for the decrease in biodiversity from U6 to U4, sample bias, and differential extinction of Pleistocene fauna. Based on comparative studies of other archaeological contexts of similar antiquity in the Patagonian region, we consider the second hypothesis the more reliable. Likewise, analyses of bone refitting and spatial distribution of archaeological materials indicate that U4/5 has the best archaeological resolution and highest integrity of the entire sequence. Conversely, U6 has lower integrity and archaeological resolution (Miotti et al. 1999). Therefore it is assumed that the occupations are separated by a brief interval of time, one or a few centuries, during the Pleistocene/Holocene transition.

In summary, radiocarbon dating, different depths below the surface of the site (Table 1 and Figure 1), and differences in sedimentation suggest the remains of U6 and U4/5 are associated with different depositional events separated in time. Both depositional zones contain evidence of two episodes of hunting and carcass processing during human colonization of the region.

Radiocarbon-dating Evidence

AEP-1 is the first site in the extra-Andean Patagonian region of Argentina where two fragments of fluted projectile points—fishtail projectile points, or FPPs (Miotti 1992)—were found in the later occupation of the oldest component, clearly associated with a high resolution faunal assemblage and bone instruments (Miotti 1995, 1996; Miotti and Cattáneo 1997). Radiocarbon analyses by the AMS method place the earliest human occupation between 13,000 and 10,500 RCYBP (Table 1), whereas the second occupational event dates between 10,400 and 9200 RCYBP; all these datings are discussed below.

So far 11 radiocarbon datings have been obtained from the excavations in AEP-1 site. Two additional samples from the transitional zone between the bottom of U4/5 and the top of U6, OxA-9508 and OxA-9509 (Table 1), are being redated at the Radiocarbon Laboratory of the University of Arizona because of possible contamination by organic matter related to pedogenetic processes, which could have rejuvenated them (J. Steele, University of Southampton, UK, m.s. report to L. M. November 2000).

Below we discuss the provenance and analysis of the radiocarbon samples following their association with weakened and slim burning zones, mixing with organic matter in the soil, structures, and archaeological materials; we follow the stratigraphy proposed in Zárate et al. (2000).

The first radiocarbon date (AA-8428, Table 1) was published with the announcement of the primary association between the fragment of a fishtail projectile point and a late-Pleistocene context (Miotti 1992:33); we now know this dating identifies the second occupational event in U4/5. After this first dating, eight other radiocarbon datings have confirmed this early context and allow us to identify at least two early occupation events in this area of the Central Plateau of Patagonia.

The two events identified for the early component have been dated through bone and charcoal samples; however, only small charcoal speckles were found in excavations in 1995, 1996, and 1997. In a latter excavation (field season 1997) sectors B and C yielded a probable area of burning at the contact of Unit 5 (bottom) and Unit 6 (top). A sample (OxA-9249) from the earliest occupations was obtained close to this structure, and another two were obtained from the top and bottom of this lens of charcoal-like organic matter (Table 1). However, sedimentological and taphonomic analyses demonstrate that this area of burning was later disturbed by the development of the paleosol; bioturbation destroyed the original hearth structure, and organic matter in the soil was mixed with charcoal from the hearth. Therefore radiocarbon samples from this zone could have been rejuvenated by the addition of younger organic matter. To counter this possibility, samples OxA-9508 and OxA-9509 are being processed again (their $\delta^{13}/_{12}C$ values are too high). Likewise the date returned for OxA-9249 should also be interpreted as a minimum age (J. Steele pers. comm. 2000).

As for the other ten samples, no contaminants have been detected by the laboratories that processed them (confirmed by the $\delta^{13}/_{12}C$ values in Table 1). To minimize the risk of possible contamination, the samples were pretreated with acids and alkalis to remove contaminating carbonates and acids (A. Figini pers. comm., 1992; J. Vogel pers. comm., 1998; T. Jull pers. comm., 1999; J. Steele pers. comm., 2000).

The entire cultural sequence is contained in a single buried soil profile. Using these new dates we can discuss the radiocarbon dating of pre-European occupations at the site, the evolution of the environment, and the processes that formed the archaeological record.

Two of the datings from U6, AA-20125 and OxA-8527, seem to be anomalies. They come from different excavation units. Both were taken from similar depths (Table 1 and Figure 1), and both belong to the same stratigraphic unit (U6). Bearing in mind concerns about contamination discussed above, these diachronic differences can be attributed to several possible factors:

a) both samples may have come from a disturbed area;

b) the samples may have been contaminated with acids, alkalis, or carbonates;

c) errors may have been introduced in manipulating the samples;

d) after its deposition, charcoal may have been contaminated with organic matter developed in the soil.

Although there is closer concurrence among the other radiocarbon datings of level 6 in the interval between 11,000 and 10,500 RCYBP, there is no reason to reject the 12,890 RCYBP date as an anomaly; quite to the contrary, an argument can be made to reject the 10,390 RCYBP date for being too young. In any case, the event associated with this date, interpreted as an instance of carcass processing, occurred under existing dry environmental conditions that ca. 11,000 years ago probably became wetter and colder (Borromei in this volume); the sandy matrix and the presence of *Mylodon* sp. sustain this hypothesis. The deposition of Unit 6 or the development of the IIIBT32 horizon (sensu Zárate 1999; Zárate et al. 2000) was the result of a later edaphic process, which began to rework the sediments during the Holocene, about 7500 yr B.P. It is possible that carbonate lixiviation and water mineralization acting on the sample made it appear older. This would be consistent with the development of the soil and the type of substrate, a calcareous bedrock. However, pedogenetic processes could also rejuvenate the sample as discussed above; in this case, all samples from U4/5 and U6 would be imprecise and their radiocarbon dates should be considered minimum ages. The samples taken close to or within the block itself, in squares B and C, and interpreted as a transition between U5 and U6 might have been subjected to similar influences of rejuvenation and aging; in fact, the possibility seems even more likely in this case, owing to the occurrence of a local event of organic matter interposed between the bottom of U5 and the top of U6. Thus it is reasonable to assume that the oldest date of 12,890 RCYBP is reliable and that processes that formed the paleosol perturbed and rejuvenated some of the materials associated with this structure.

The radiocarbon ages for samples from the same unit, although from different excavation units, confirm the internal synchronicity in each of two Pleistocene events. In the case of the second occupational event, which has greater resolution and archaeological integrity, the radiocarbon datings for samples from the block of Units 4/5 or IIB31 and IIB32 Horizons (sensu Zárate 1999; Zárate et al 2000, see Figure 1) range between 10,400 and 9200 RCYBP. Pedogenetic processes are probably the main cause of postdepositional modification; carbonate lixiviation acting on IIBT horizon (Unit 3) affected to a lesser degree organic materials of the lower units. Thus all these radiocarbon datings should be considered minimum ages; all the structures might be older than laboratory results indicate. New samples submitted for radiocarbon dating will be useful in clarifying these issues.

Acknowledgments

We are deeply indebted to Dr. James Steele and Southampton University (UK) for processing and commenting on several radiocarbon datings, as well as Boulder Radiocarbon Laboratory. Other datings were financed through CONICET projects: PEI-1198 and PIP-4305. Nora Flegenheimer read a first draft of this manuscript and made valuable comments.

References Cited

Blasi, A., J. Rabassa, L. Miotti, and G.Cattáneo
1997 Investigación Geoarqueológica en la Localidad Piedra Museo. *Resúmenes XII Congreso Nacional de Arqueología Argentina*: 9. La Plata, Argentina.

Miotti, L.
1992 Paleoindian Occupations at Piedra Museo Locality, Santa Cruz Province, Argentina. *Current Research in the Pleistocene* 9:30–31.

1995 Piedra Museo Locality: A Special Place in the New World. *Current Research in the Pleistocene* 12:37–40.

1996 Piedra Museo (Santa Cruz): Nuevos Datos para el Debate de la Ocupación Pleistocénica en la Argentina. In *Arqueología, Sólo Patagonia,* edited by J. Gómez Otero, pp. 27–38. CENPAT and Secretaría de Cultura de Chubut.

1998 Zooarqueología de la Meseta Central y la Costa de la Provincia de Santa Cruz. Un Enfoque de las Estrategias Adaptativas y los Paleoambientes. Tesis doctoral Facultad de Ciencias Naturales y Museo, Universidad Nacional de La Plata. (1989). Museo de Historia Natural de San Rafael, Mendoza, Argentina.

Miotti, L., and G. R. Cattáneo

1997 Bifacial Technology At 13,000 Years Ago In Southern Patagonia. *Current Research in the Pleistocene* 14:62–65.

Miotti, L., and M. Salemme

1999 Biodiversity, Taxonomic Richness and Specialists-Generalists during Late Pleistocene/Early Holocene in Pampa and Patagonia (Argentina, Southern South America). *Quaternary International* 50:53–68.

2001 Hunting and Butchering Events at the Pleistocene/Holocene Transition in Piedra Museo. An Example of Adaptation Strategies of the First Colonizers of Patagonia. In *Paleoamerican Prehistory: Colonization Models, Biological Populations and Human Adaptations,* edited by R. Gruhn, B. Lepper, and R. Bonnichsen. Center for the Study of the First Americans, Corvallis, OR. In press.

Miotti, L., M. Vázquez, and D. Hermo

1999 Piedra Museo: Un Yamnagoo Pleistocénico en la Colonización de la Meseta de Santa Cruz. El Estudio de la Arqueofauna. In *Soplando en el Viento,* edited by R. Goñi, pp. 113–136. University of Comahue, Neuquén.

Zárate, M.

1999 Geoarqueología de la Localidad Piedra Museo. Unpublished report. Mendoza, Argentina.

Zárate, M., A. Blasi, and J. Rabassa

2000 Geoarqueología de la Localidad Piedra Museo. In *Guía de Campo de la Visita a las Localidades Arqueológicas,* edited by L. Miotti, R. Paunero, M. Salemme, and G. R. Cattáneo, pp. 56–64. Imprenta Servicop, La Plata, Argentina.

Variations in Strategies of Lithic Production and Faunal Exploitation in the Pleistocene/ Holocene Transition at Piedra Museo and Surrounding Region

Laura Miotti[1] and Roxana Cattáneo[2]

This report summarizes technological and functional data of lithic assemblages and archaeofaunal contexts from the Piedra Museo locality. We consider here the two oldest archaeological contexts, U4/5 and U6 (Figure 1 in Miotti et al. this volume), which date to the Pleistocene/Holocene transition. We propose a hypothesis about the use of space and resources during human colonization of the Macizo del Deseado region in the Argentinian Patagonia.

Piedra Museo, like other localities of the Central Plateau, reveals that for the interval 13,000–9200 RCYBP the landscape of the region had abundant rockshelters, faunal resources, vegetation, and minerals (rocks and ocher), with more biodiversity than today, but with a heterogeneous distribution and a pronounced seasonality (Borromei this volume). We believe it would have been significantly useful for occupation by mobile hunter-gatherer societies in ways that changed with time.

During the initial period of colonization, Piedra Museo was a place used for specific activities related to hunting, including trapping, slaughtering, and primary processing of prey. This view is consistent with a colonization stage characterized by occupational redundancy, where the same kinds of activities were carried out in the same places (Miotti 1999;

[1] Departmento de Arqueología, Facultad de Ciencias Naturales y Museo, Universidad Nacional de La Plata–CONICET, Argentina. e-mail: miotti@netverk.com.ar

[2] Departmento Arqueología: Facultad de Ciencias Naturales y Museo, Universidad Nacional de La Plata, and CONICET. Paseo del Bosque s/ n, 1900, La Plata, Argentina. e-mail: androx@infovia.com.ar

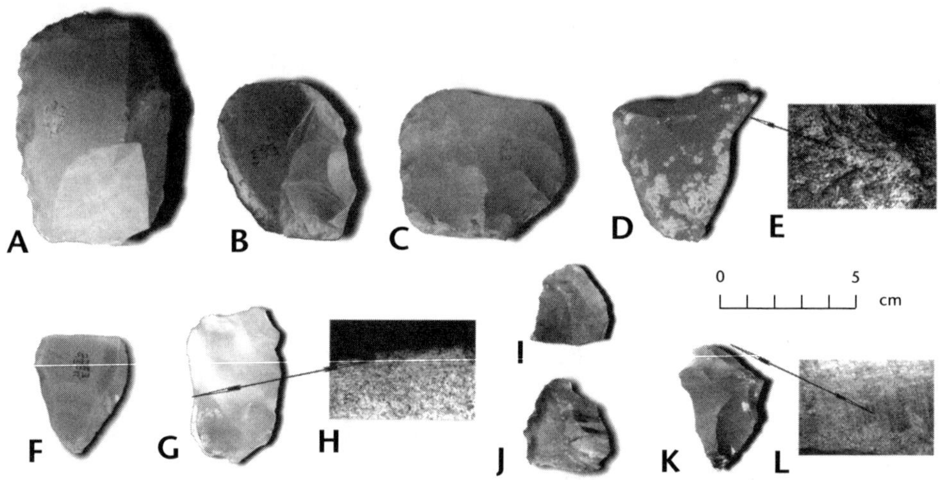

Figure 1. Selected artifacts from PM AEP-1, U4/5: **A,** scraper plane; **B,C,** sidescrapers; **D,** knife; **E,** detail (100X) of microwear polish from butchering. Selected artifacts from PM AEP-1,U6: **F, G,** knives; **H,** detail (200X) of microwear polish and striations from butchering; **I, J,** sidescrapers; **K,** knife; **L,** detail (200X) of microwear polish.

Miotti and Cattáneo 1997), and with the concept of a high-energy landscape in the sense of Wandsnider (2000).

Technological Strategies in Piedra Museo Locality

In each of the two contexts of AEP-1 a different strategy for producing lithic artifacts was used, involving the use of different techniques and different types of rocks.

Technological Aspects

- For U6, knives and sidescrapers were manufactured from bifacial cores. Our microwear use analysis on lithic edges (Cattáneo 2002) concludes that large bifacial thinning flakes from large bifaces were used for butchering: cutting and fleshing bone, sinew, and meat (Figure 1F, G, H, K, L). This generalized type of tool (Andrefsky 1994; Dibble 1988) constitutes 60 percent of the sample; only 3 sidescrapers, corresponding to 40 percent of the sample, were found (Figure 1I, J).
- For U4/5, knives and sidescrapers were manufactured from nodular cores (Figure1A–E). Standardized tools (Andrefsky 1994; Dibble 1991) in U4/5 include 2 broken fishtail projectile points (9 percent), 11 unifacial sidescrapers (48 percent), and 2 limaces, (8.7 percent). Unifacial flaked tools, assumed generalized, were manufactured from nodular cores; they include 4 knives (17.3 percent), 2 limaces (8.7 percent), 2 fragments of hammers (8.7 percent), and a notch (4.3 percent) (Figure 1A, D, E).

Sources of Rocks

Sources in the area were identified by investigating thin sections of artifacts and geologic samples from outcrops and quarries, and by analyzing in situ the characteristics of geologic sources within a radius of approximately 30 km from AEP-1 (Cattáneo 2002). Conclusions about provenience are as follows:

- For U4/5, microlocal raw materials (source within 2 km) predominate, specifically opal (68 percent) for tools and debitage; in second place, vitrified tuff (15 percent) is found in tools (25 percent) and in flakes and debris (5 percent). Two other rocks of local provenience (source within ca. 30 km) are represented, chalcedony and petrified wood. Chalcedony was identified in 14 percent of the artifacts, tools (10 percent), and debitage (18 percent); petrified wood was found in 3.5 percent of the artifacts, tools (5 percent), and flakes (2 percent).
- For U6, local raw material predominates. Silicified wood is found in 46 percent of the artifacts, tools (75 percent), and debitage (17 percent). Chalcedony is found in 43 percent of the artifacts, tools (25 percent), and debitage (61 percent). Of particular interest is opal, which is found only in flakes (11 percent). The presence of opal only in debitage, considered with other characteristics of the archaeological context (Miotti and Cattáneo 1997; Miotti et al. 1999), suggests it represents a single knapping event.

The spatial distribution of sources of raw material and the use of different materials (Cattáneo 2000; 2002) are factors from which we can draw conclusions about the strategy of tool production.

First Occupation of Rockshelter (U6)

1. There is evidence of a tendency to select and use local raw material. Chalcedony and petrified wood, of excellent quality but located at longer distances from the site, are more frequently used.
2. The production and transport of large bifaces to manufacture flaked butchering tools confirms the hypothesis that activities during the first occupational event at AEP-1 were restricted to hunting and processing carcasses (Miotti et al. 1999). The use of bifaces as preforms, which produce tools with large usable edges (Kelly 1988), made efficient use of time that would otherwise be required to transport toolkits of great technical quality.

Second Occupational Event during Pleistocene Times (U4/5)

1. There is evidence of a tendency to select and use microlocal raw materials, opal and vitrified tuff, of good and high quality.
2. Flake tools, made from nodular cores, were used to cut and scrape in hunting and butchering tasks.
3. Practices characteristic of an expedient strategy (minimal manufacturing effort, including low investment in retouches, and inefficient use of lithic resources) were abandoned.

The hypotheses related to toolkit items found in rockshelter AEP-1 of Piedra Museo (Cattáneo 1999; Miotti 1995; Miotti and Cattáneo 1997; Miotti et al. 1999) were formed after contrasting the use of microlocal rocks, which minimizes the time required to procure raw material, with the production and transport of bifacial preforms from longer distances, which produce tools of greater utility and thereby increase the efficiency of hunting and butchering.

Exploiting Faunal Resources

Taxonomic richness and diversity, anatomical and mechanical refitting of bones, and analyses of bone modifications were discussed in previous papers (Miotti et al. 1999). These archaeozoological studies infer from paleoenvironmental data the availability and use of faunal resources during the Pleistocene/Holocene transition, an age of paleoenvironmental stress. Moreover, intrasite analysis of the dispersal and accumulation of archaeofaunal remains reinforces hypotheses formed as the result of lithic studies.

In AEP-1, taxonomic analysis shows evidence of greater biodiversity in U6 than in U4/5; in addition, U6 contains a higher proportion of extinct taxa. Whether U4/5 is considered a single depositional event or repeated depositional events, the mechanical and anatomical refitting of long bones from pedological Units 4 and 5 and the matching of paired bones from the same individual suggest that the remains in U4/5 are evidence of a single hunting episode or a series of episodes that occurred over a short time. As shown by the scatterplot presented in previous papers (Miotti 1999; Miotti et al. 1999), bones are especially concentrated in three different locations in U4/5 and U6.

Camelids and equids are the main taxa in both occupations. *Hippidion saldiasi*, an American extinct horse, is represented by a mandible, lumbar vertebrae, metapodials, and phalanges. Only one of these phalanges belongs to a young individual. A distal humerus from U6 has been radiocarbon dated at 10,925 ± 65 RCYBP (OxA-8528); this specimen shows cutmarks, helical fractures with a point of impact, and hackles on the fracture surface. All these features are indicators of human butchering, evidence that native horses were exploited as a profitable resource (Figure 2A, B).

Lama guanicoe (guanaco), a gregarious mammal, is the most abundant species throughout the sequence at AEP-1 as well as in the rest of sites all over Patagonia (Miotti and Salemme 1999). The different skeletal parts of this extant camelid appear in different proportions in each of the stratigraphic units, occasionally as bone piles. Cutmarks and intentional (helical) fractures appear with moderate frequency on long bones of guanaco, and cutmarks are also found on vertebrae and other skeletal parts (Miotti 1999). On the other hand, whole long bones were found in both contexts. Evidence of guanaco appears in U6 and U4/5; bone modifications by butchering appear with higher frequency in U4/5 than in U6.

We infer that bone piles are the result of hunting activities, representing a locus where prey was procured and dismembered; the piles in U4/5 and U6 are considered toss zones for butchering waste. This theory of human activity is supported by the analysis of fractures, cutmarks, and other pre- and post-depositional and post-burial bone modifications (Miotti 1995). In addition, the low incidence of pits and punctures (evident on less than 1.5 percent of bones) argues against carnivore activity.

Trends in Lithic Production and Faunal Exploitation during the Transition

Detailed archaeozoological and taphonomic analysis of the two occupations of AEP-1 suggests differences between two periods in the early colonization of the area. We note the following contrasts and similarities between the two occupations.

Differences in lithic materials indicate technological variability between the Pleistocene occupations. During the first occupation, ca. 13,000–10,500 yr B.P., the inhabitants exer-

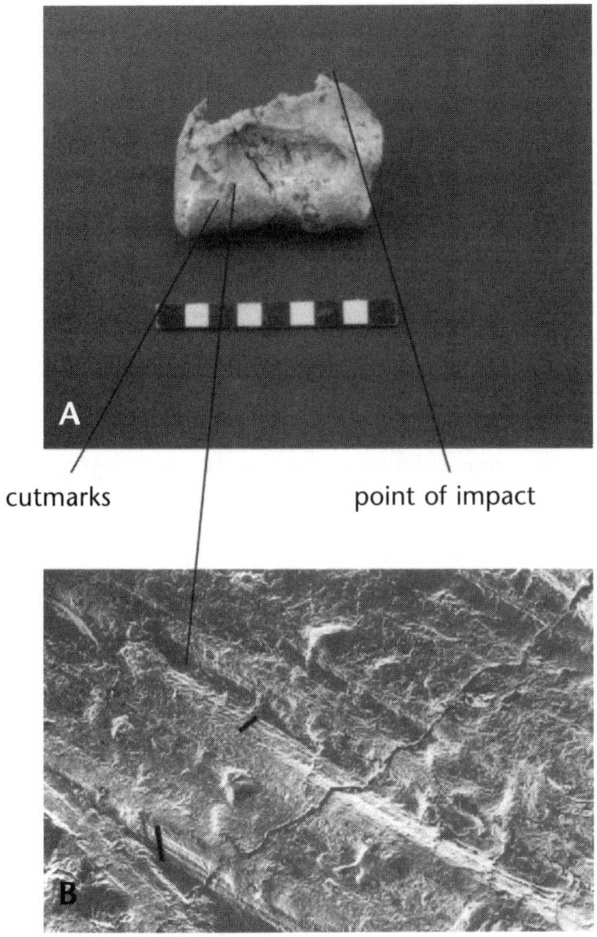

Figure 2. **A,** distal humerus of *Hippidion saldiasi* (American extinct horse) showing location of cutmarks and impact point of helical fracture. This specimen was dated at 10,925 ± 65 RCYBP (OxA8528); **B,** detail (100X) of cutmarks from photo A.

cised a strategy of minimizing the effort in manufacturing tools before undertaking butchering tasks in distant places. During the second occupation, 10,400–9200 yr B.P., the strategy was to minimize the time required to procure lithic resources for manufacturing tools. In both instances the occupants used the rockshelter to process carcasses. Possibly the first occupants had a wider range of mobility than did the second occupants; for hunters in both instances the rockshelter served as a logistical center.

Differences in the kinds of tools and raw materials used in both occupations imply a change in the proportion of time spent in traveling and in manufacturing tools. Most of this variation relates to transported and non-transported toolkit components. This theory has been discussed for other populations of the late Pleistocene (Dincauze 1993); likewise, it was proposed by Borrero and Franco (1997) for the exploratory stage in extra-Andean Patagonia, where good-quality local rocks were used mostly in an expedient manner.

Research carried out in Piedra Museo and neighboring areas of the Central Plateau confirms the theory proposed by Borrero and Franco in the context of the U4/5. However, it appears the theory does not fit all the expectations of the first occupational component of AEP-1, where we found extensive manufacture, use, and transport of bifaces of high technical quality that could only be interpreted as a tendency toward curated technologies. At this moment we do not have evidence of expedient technologies.

The Piedra Museo locality and other areas in extra-Andean Patagonia where excellent rocks for knapping are readily available stand in contrast with areas where isolated outcrops made it necessary to use distant sources of raw materials. Examples of these latter areas are the Andean foothills (Civalero and Aschero, this volume), the Upper Santa Cruz basin (Franco and Borrero in this volume), and the Atlantic coast (currently without studies of availability). The relative abundance or scarcity of toolstone or lack of information may explain the discrepancy in the theory proposed by Franco and Borrero (1997).

Because of the technological considerations discussed above and the marked changes detected in faunal diversity between the first and second occupations, we believe studying other sites would be useful in clarifying the organization of the technology and the use of the landscape and resources during the first events of human occupation in the Central Plateau in the late-Pleistocene/Holocene transition.

Acknowledgments

The research was financed through CONICET project 1198 and FOMEC—University of La Plata projects 734/97 and N244 and 329. Nora Flegenheimer and Mónica Salemme read a first draft of this manuscript and made valuable comments.

References Cited

Andrefsky, W.

1994 Raw Material Availability and the Organization of Technology. *American Antiquity* 59(1):21–34.

Borrero, L., and N. Franco.

1997 Early Patagonian Hunter-gatherers: Subsistence and Technology. *Journal of Anthropological Research* 53:219–239.

Cattáneo, R.

1999 Organización de la Tecnología en la Patagonia Centro Meridional: El Caso de la Localidad Arqueológica Piedra Museo, Provincia de Santa Cruz. In *Actas del XII Congreso Nacional de Arqueología Argentina*, Vol. III, pp. 16–22. La Plata, Argentina.

2000 El Paisaje y la Distribución de los Recursos Líticos en el Nesocratón del Deseado. In *Guía de campo.* Taller Internacional del INQUA, La Colonización del Sur de América durante la Transición Pleistoceno/Holoceno, edited by L. Miotti, R. Paunero, M. Salemme, and R. Cattáneo, pp. 26–35. La Plata, Argentina.

2002 Una Aproximación a la Organización de la Tecnología Lítica entre los Cazadores-Recolectores de Fines del Pleistoceno en la Patagonia Argentina. Doctoral Dissertation. Universidad Nacional de La Plata, Argentina.

Dibble, H.

1988 Typological Aspects of Reduction and Intensity of Utilization of Lithic Resources in the French Mousterian. In *Upper Pleistocene Prehistory of Western Eurasia*, edited by H. Dibble and A. Montet-White, pp. 188–191. Symposium Series 1. University Museum Press, Philadelphia, PA.

1991 Local Raw Material Exploitation and Its Effects on Lower and Middle Paleolithic Assemblage Variability. In *Raw Material Economies among Prehistoric Hunter-Gatherers*, edited by A. Montet White and S. Holen, pp. 33–48. University of Kansas Publications in Anthropology 19, University of Kansas, Lawrence, KS.

Dincauze, D.

1993 Fluted Points in the Eastern Forests. In: *From Kostenki to Clovis. Upper Paleolithic-Paleo-Indian Adaptations*, edited by O. Soffer and N. D. Praslow, pp. 279–292. Plenum Press, New York and London.

Kelly, R.

1988 The Three Sides of a Biface. *American Antiquity* 53(4):717–734.

Miotti, L.,

1995 Piedra Museo Locality: A Special Place in the New World. *Current Research in the Pleistocene* 12:37–40.

1999 Los Primeros Pobladores de la Patagonia Centro-Meridional y su Relación con la Colonización Pleistocénica de América. Chungara, Chile. In press.

Miotti, L., and R. Cattáneo

1997 Lithic Technology at 13,000 Years Ago in Southern Patagonia. *Current Research in the Pleistocene* 14:62–65.

Miotti, L., and M. Salemme

1999 Biodiversity, Taxonomic Richness and Generalist-Specialists Economical Systems in Pampa and Patagonia Regions, Southern South America. *Quaternary International* 50:53–68.

Miotti, L., M. Vázquez, and D. Hermo

1999 Piedra Museo: Un Yamnagoo Pleistocénico en la Colonización de la Meseta de Santa Cruz. El Estudio de la Arqueofauna. *Simposio de Poblamiento*. In *Terceras Jornadas de Arqueología de la Patagonia*, edited by R. Goñi, pp. 113–136. Universidad Nacional del Comahue and Instituto Nacional de Antropologia y Pensamiento Latinoamericano, Neuquén-Buenos Aires, Argentina.

Wandsnider, L. A.

2000 Paisajes Arqueológicos e Historias de Regiones. Posgraduate course, Instituto de Antropología y Pensamiento Latinoamericano (INAPL), Buenos Aires.

Palynology at Piedra Museo Locality, Santa Cruz Province, Argentina

Ana María Borromei

This report documents the change in the paleovegetation community using pollen analysis from a sedimentary deposit at archaeological site Alero El Puesto 1 (AEP-1) at Piedra Museo locality in southernmost extra-Andean Patagonia during the Pleistocene-Holocene transition. Comparison with other pollen records illuminates the paleoclimatic and paleoenvironmental conditions south of latitude 47° S for this interval.

In recent years, various papers have dealt with Quaternary palynological studies of archaeological sites that have advanced our understanding of past climates in the Argentinean Patagonian steppe (Borromei and Nami 2000; D'Antoni 1978; Mancini 1998; Mancini and D'Antoni 1988; Mancini and Trivi 1992; Paez et al. 1999; Prieto et al. 1998). This report discusses paleovegetation and paleoclimatic changes that will improve our understanding of the relationship between humans and their environment in this region.

As described in the report by Miotti et al. (this volume), Piedra Museo locality is situated in the Central Plateau of Santa Cruz Province (Figure 1). The surrounding landscape consists of an endorreic basin belonging to a zone of low plateaus (100–300 m a.s.l.) with shallow erosional channels and ponds. The present vegetation is a grass steppe (*Stipa* sp., "coirón") with thorn shrub, and aquatic plants and grasses in shallow ponds.

The climate of extra-Andean Patagonia is cold-temperate; the mean temperature is 8.5° C, the mean annual precipitation is 180 mm, and westerly winds prevail (Servicio Meteorológico Nacional 1969, 1986). Distribution of the vegetation units (Figure 1) is indicative of the precipitation gradient: *Nothofagus* forests (*Nothofagus antarctica* and *N. pumilio*) in the west (Deciduous Forest District, precipitation more than 400 mm); grass steppe eastward bordering the forests (Sub-Andean District, precipitation 250 mm or more); shrub steppe

CONICET. Laboratorio de Palinología, Departamento de Geología, Universidad Nacional del Sur. San Juan 670. (8000) Bahía Blanca. Argentina. e-mail: borromei@criba.edu.ar

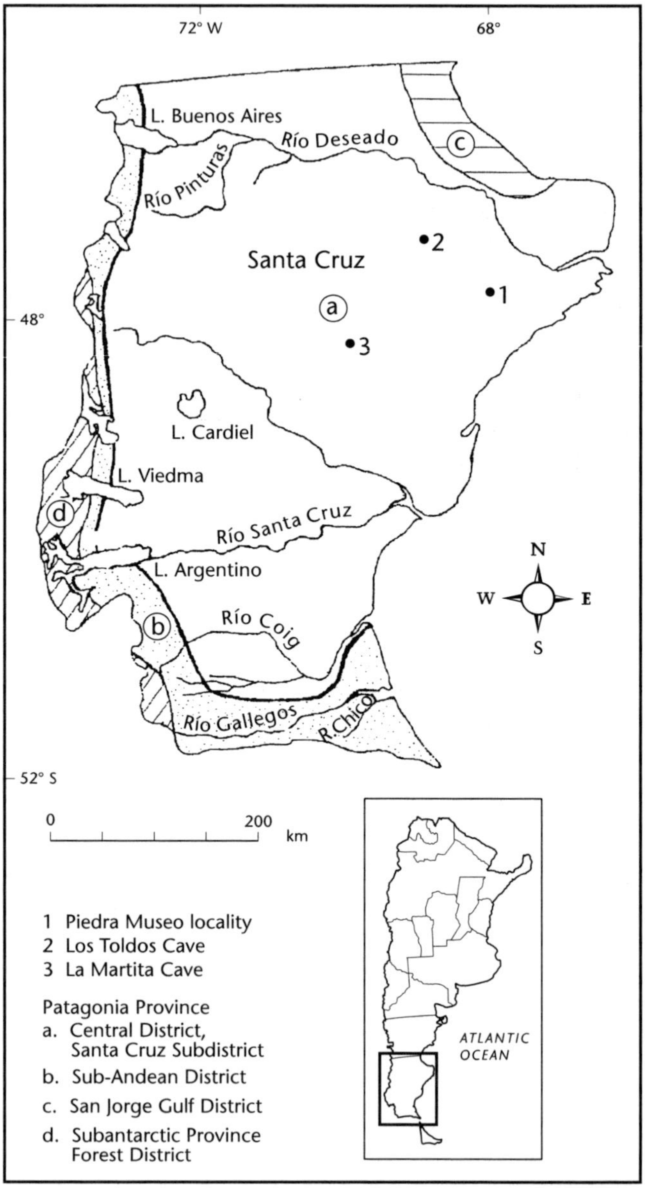

Figure 1. Map of southern Patagonia with vegetation units (Cabrera, 1976; Soriano, 1983) and archaeological sites discussed in the text (after Mancini, 1998).

and semidesert in the middle and eastern sectors (Santa Cruz Subdistrict, precipitation 200 mm or less). Along the ephemeral streams and on salty soils a halophytic steppe is characteristic. Grass and shrub steppes and semidesert are the main vegetation types in this region. The grass steppe of *Festuca* spp. expands to the south and west and into the high plateaus of the semidesert (above 700 m), where the climate is colder and wetter. The shrub steppe vegetation, found in flat areas and valleys or depressed areas on sandy soils, includes *Verbena ligustrina, Senecio filaginoides, Nardophyllum obtusifolium,* and *Berberis cuneata.* Semidesert vegetation is represented by tussock grasses (*Stipa speciosa, S. humilis,* and *S. chrysophylla*), scrubs (*Nassauvia glomerulosa* and *Ephedra frustillata*), cushion plants (*Azorella caespitosa*), and patches of shrubs (*Nardophyllum obtusifolium* and *Verbena tridens*).

All samples were processed following the procedure of Heusser and Stock (1984). Exotic *Lycopodium* spores were added as a check of the accuracy when calculating pollen concentration (grains/gram) (Stockmarr 1971). The pollen diagram was divided into pollen zones according to the "Pollen Zone" concept of Birks and Birks (1980). The fossil pollen spectra were compared with regional pollen spectra from surface soil samples (Mancini 1998) and with present-day vegetation from Santa Cruz Province (Cabrera 1976). Four radiocarbon age determinations establish the chronology for the section: 12,890 ± 90 RCYBP (AA-20125, unit 6), 10,400 ± 80 RCYBP (AA-8428, unit 5), 9710 ± 105 RCYBP (LP-859, unit 4), and 7670 ± 110 RCYBP (LP-450, unit 2) (Miotti 1995). For additional radiocarbon datings from these same units, see Miotti et al. (this volume).

The pollen record at Piedra Museo locality (Figure 2) shows two vegetational changes between 12,890 and 7670 RCYBP; one at ca. 11,000 RCYBP, when the shrub steppe of Asteraceae is replaced by grass steppe; and the second at ca. 9500 RCYBP, when the grass steppe is replaced by shrub steppe of *Ephedra* and Asteraceae.

Between 12,890 and ca. 11,000 RCYBP, the pollen assemblage (**Pollen Zone PM-4,** sample 1 at 1.25 m, unit 6) represents shrub steppe characterized by Asteroideae (54 percent) accompanied by *Nassauvia, Ephedra,* and grasses. Nowadays these xeric shrubs and grasses in regional pollen spectra (Mancini 1998) are associated with annual rainfall of 200 mm or less. Local halophytic vegetation associated with ephemeral stream or salty soils are indicated by Chenopodiaceae. Fluctuations in this taxon throughout the sequence suggest alternating humid and arid periods characteristic of semiarid conditions.

About ca. 11,000 RCYBP, a grass steppe with Poaceae (60 percent) and other herb pollen (20 percent) appeared and lasted until ca. 9500 RCYBP (**Pollen Zone PM-3,** sample 2 at 1 m, unit 5, 10,400 ± 80 RCYBP; and sample 3 at 0.80 m, unit 4, 9710 ± 105 RCYBP). The herb taxa include Cichorioideae, Caryophyllaceae, Brassicaceae, Labiatae, Solanaceae, *Potamogeton, Typha,* and Iridaceae. Shrub pollen is represented by Asteroideae (16 percent) and *Nassauvia* and *Ephedra* (less than 10 percent). This pollen assemblage is distinctive of the grass steppe (Sub-Andean District) in the easternmost lake region and on the high plateaus above 700 m in the semidesert (Mancini 1998). All these plant formations are associated with an annual temperature of 6°–8° C. Precipitation is 250 mm in the grass steppe and 200 mm or less in the semidesert.

Between ca. 9500 and 7500 RCYBP a shrub steppe characterized by *Ephedra* (29 percent) and Asteroideae (22 percent) associated with *Nassauvia* and grasses dominated the spectrum (**Pollen Zone PM-2**, sample 4 at 0.58 m, unit 3; and sample 5 at 0.40 m, unit 2, 7670 ± 110 RCYBP). Nowadays this kind of vegetation is associated with semidesert shrub vegetation with annual rainfall less than 200 mm and mean annual temperature of 8°–10° C (Mancini 1998). Aridity is also indicated by increase of Chenopodiaceae (24 percent).

The past 100 years or so are characterized by a pollen assemblage (**Pollen Zone PM-1**, samples 6 at 0.30 m, 7 at 0.20 m, and 8 at 0.10 m belonging to unit 1) that resembles the modern shrub steppe and halophytic vegetation developed in the eastern sector of the semi-

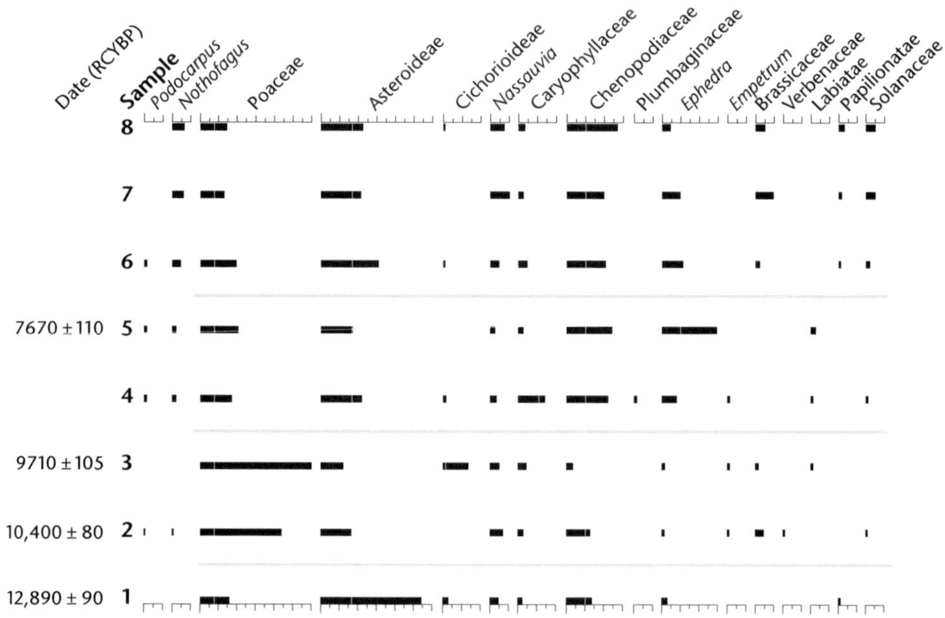

desert (Mancini 1998). The fossil pollen includes Asteroideae (30 percent), Chenopodiaceae (26 percent), and Poaceae (19 percent) associated with *Ephedra*, *Nassauvia,* and minor taxa. Presence of *Prosopis, Schinus,* and *Chuquiraga* may indicate vegetation developed in shallow erosional channels ("cañadones"). According to Zárate et al. (2000), this unit unconformably overlies the sediments of unit 2. The age of this section is recent, based on stratigraphic and sedimentological criteria.

Nothofagus and *Podocarpus* pollen, present in low percentages in the profile, indicate transport by westerly cold air masses from the subantarctic forest region in the Andes.

Pollen concentration is generally very low throughout the sequence. Values imply poor pollen production due to scarce (usually insect-pollinated) vegetation or relatively high sediment accumulation rates due to strong erosional processes (Horowitz 1992). In the latter pollen zone (**Pollen Zone PM-1**), a general increase in pollen concentration in the center of the zone may be the result of pollen percolation (Kelso 1994).

The Pleistocene-Holocene transition was a period of significant paleoenvironmental changes. The pollen analysis at Piedra Museo locality and the fossil pollen evidence from other sequences in the extra-Andean Patagonia show plant communities developed in the main as a consequence of climate changes.

The first climate change, recorded at ca. 11,000 RCYBP, resulted from an increase in effective moisture initiated by an increase in precipitation and a drop in temperature. This change coincides with the replacement of Asteroideae steppe at Piedra Museo and the *Ephedra* steppe at Los Toldos locality (Paez et al. 1999) (Figure 1) by grass steppe. The second climatic change, at ca. 9500 RCYBP, is interpreted as an increase in temperature and precipi-

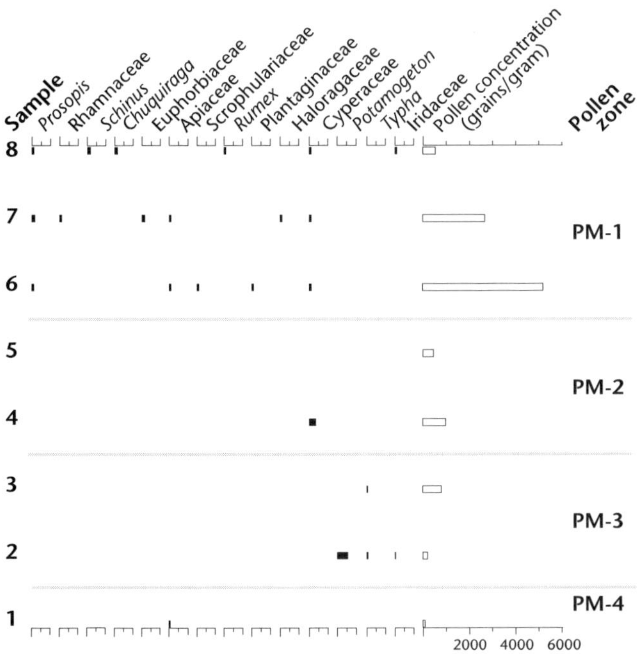

Figure 2. Diagram of pollen frequency, total pollen concentration, and radiocarbon chronology, subdivided by pollen zones, for the 1.5-m section from the AEP-1 site of Piedra Museo locality.

tation within the modern range. At that time the shrub steppe began to dominate, replacing the grass steppe, as recorded in the pollen record from Piedra Museo until ca. 7500 RCYBP, from Los Toldos sequence between 10,000 and 8750 RCYBP, and from La Martita cave between 8000 and 6000 RCYBP (Mancini 1998) (Figure 1).

These environmental changes would result from atmospheric circulation patterns different from the present. According to Heusser (1990) the models favor a central mechanism involving oscillations of the polar front, including variable intensity of zonal circulation in the belt of southern westerly winds. Vegetation modifications resulted from repeated latitudinal displacement or modulation in strength of the Southern Westerlies during the Pleistocene, a process that has apparently continued in the Southern Andes on a smaller scale during the Holocene (Heusser 1995; Heusser et. al 1999).

Acknowledgments

The author thanks Dr. Laura Miotti and Dr. Jorge Rabassa, who provided the palynological samples from Piedra Museo locality. Thanks to Dr. Mirta Quattrocchio for comments on the paper and CONICET for financial support.

References Cited

Birks, H., and H. Birks
1980 *Quaternary Palaeoecology*. Arnold Limited. London.

Borromei, A. M., and H. G. Nami
2000 Contribución a la Paleoecología de la Cuenca del Río Chico en el Extremo Sur de la Provincia de Santa Cruz: El Aporte de la Palinología. In *La Perspectiva Interdisciplinaria en la Arqueología*

Contemporánea, edited by H. G. Nami. *Arqueología Contemporánea* 6:105–122. Buenos Aires, Argentina.

Cabrera, A. L.
1976 Regiones Fitogeográficas Argentinas. In *Enciclopedia Argentina de Agricultura y Jardinería*, edited by Acme, 2nd ed., vol. II, p. 85. Buenos Aires.

D'Antoni, H.
1978 Palinología del Perfil del Alero del Cañadón de las Manos Pintadas. *Relaciones de la Sociedad Argentina de Antropología*, 12:249–262.

Heusser, C. J.
1990 Ice Age Vegetation and Climate of Subtropical Chile. *Palaeogeography, Palaeoclimatology, Palaeoecology* 80:107–127.

1995 Three Late Quaternary Pollen Diagrams from Southern Patagonia and Their Palaeoecological Implications. *Palaeogeography, Palaeoclimatology, Palaeoecology* 118:1–24.

Heusser, C. J., L. E. Heusser, and T. V. Lowell
1999 Paleoecology of the Southern Chilean Lake District-Isla Grande de Chiloé during Middle-late Llanquihue Glaciation and Deglaciation. *Geografiska Annaler* 81 A(2):231–284.

Heusser, L., and C. Stock
1984 Preparation Techniques for Concentrating Pollen from Marine Sediments and Other Sediments with Low Pollen Density. *Palynology* 8:225–227.

Horowitz, A.
1992 *Palynology of Arid Lands*. Elsevier Science Publishers, Amsterdam.

Kelso, G. K.
1994 Pollen Percolation Rates in Euroamerican-Era Cultural Deposits in the Northeastern United States. *Journal of Archaeological Science* 21:481–488.

Mancini, M. V.
1998 Vegetational Changes during the Holocene in Extra-Andean Patagonia, Santa Cruz Province, Argentina. *Palaeogeography, Palaeoclimatology, Palaeoecology* 138:207–219.

Mancini, M. V., and H. D'Antoni
1988 Análisis Polínico de la Cueva 4 de la Martita, Santa Cruz. *Simposio Internacional sobre el Holoceno en América del Sur*. Resúmenes Expandidos 80–83, Paraná.

Mancini, M. V., and M. Trivi
1992 Búsqueda de Análogos Modernos en el Sistema Polen del Alero Cárdenas (Provincia de Santa Cruz). *Asociación Paleontológica Argentina, Publicación Especial* 2:81–84.

Miotti, L.
1995 Piedra Museo Locality: A Special Place in the New World. *Current Research in the Pleistocene* 12:36–38.

Paez, M., A. Prieto, and M. V. Mancini
1999 Fossil Pollen from Los Toldos Locality: A Record of the Late-glacial Transition in Extra-Andean Patagonia. *Quaternary International* 53/54:69–75.

Prieto, A., S. Stutz, and S. Pastorino
1998 Vegetación del Holoceno en la Cueva Las Buitreras, Santa Cruz, Argentina. *Revista Chilena de Historia Natural* 71:277–290.

Servicio Meteorológico Nacional
1969 Estadísticas Climatológicas 1951-1960, Publicación B1 (6). Buenos Aires, Argentina.

1986 Estadísticas Climatológicas 1971-1980, Publicación 36. Buenos Aires.

Soriano, A.
1983 Desert and Semideserts of Patagonia. In *Temperate Deserts and Semi-deserts*, edited by N. E. West, pp. 423–460. Elsevier, New York.

Stockmarr, J.
1971 Tablets with Spores Used in Absolute Pollen Analysis. *Pollen et Spores* 13:615–621.

Zárate, M., A. Blasi, and J. Rabassa
2000 Geoarqueología de la Localidad Piedra Museo. In *Guía de Campo de la Visita a las Localidades Arqueológicas*, edited by L. Miotti, R. Paunero, M. Salemme, and G. R. Cattáneo, pp. 56–64. Taller Internacional La Colonización del Sur de América durante la Transición Pleistoceno/Holoceno. La Plata, Argentina.

Paleoenvironments during the Pleistocene-Holocene Transition in Southern South America, Argentina

Marta M. Paez[1], Marcelo A. Zárate[2], María V. Mancini[3], and Aldo R. Prieto[4]

The hunter-gatherer colonization phase of southern South America occurred during the Pleistocene-Holocene transition (ca. 13,000–8000 RCYBP), an interval of dramatic climatic change. This report discusses the paleoenvironmental records for this period (Table 1) of three archaeological localities, Agua de la Cueva, Cerro La China, and Los Toldos, situated in different environmental settings. Climatic and ecological conditions during human colonization are inferred from sedimentological and palynological analyses performed at the sites.

The Agua de la Cueva Locality

Agua de la Cueva (32° 37′ S, 69° 09′ W, 2,900 m a.s.l.) is a multiactivity rockshelter site in the Andean region of Mendoza (García 1992). Foehn-like winds from the Pacific create a desert environment with a mean annual temperature of 5°–6° C and a mean annual precipitation of 200 mm or less. Above 3,000 m a.s.l. the summit is Andean grassland with cushion plants. Below 3,000 m a.s.l. the vegetation type is shrub steppe mixed with Puna taxa and

[1] Laboratorio de Paleoecología y Palinología, Universidad Nacional de Mar del Plata, Funes 3250, 7600 Mar del Plata, Argentina. e-mail: mmpaez@mdp.edu.ar

[2] CONICET, Facultad de Ciencias Exacias y Naturales. Universidad Nacional de la Pampa, Santa Rosa, La Pampa, Argentina. e-mail: mzarate@exactas.unlpam.edu.ar

[3] Laboratorio de Paleoecología y Palinología, Universidad Nacional de Mar del Plata, Funes 3250, 7600 Mar del Plata, Argentina. e-mail: mvmancin@mdp.edu.ar

[4] CONICET, Laboratorio de Paleoecología y Palinología, Universidad Nacional de Mar del Plata, Funes 3250, 7600 Mar del Plata, Argentina. e-mail: aprieto@mdp.edu.ar

Table 1. Radiocarbon ages corresponding to the different sites discussed in the text.

Site	^{14}C age (B.P.)	Lab. number	References
Agua de la Cueva	9210 ± 70	Beta 64539	García et al. 1999
	10,240 ± 60	Beta 61408	García et al. 1999
	10,950 ± 90	Beta 61409	García et al. 1999
Cerro La China	10,610 ± 180	AA-1328	Zárate and Flegenheimer 1991
Site 3	10,720 ± 150	I-12,741	Flegenheimer 1980
	10,730 ± 150	I-12741	Flegenheimer 1987
Site 1	10,790 ± 120	AA-1327	Flegenheimer 1987
Los Toldos (Cave 3)	8750 ± 480	F.R.A. 97	Cardich et al. 1973
	12,600 ± 600	F.R.A. 98	Cardich et al. 1973

azonal vegetation in springs. The sedimentary record of the site is mostly sandy silts deflated from nearby floodplains and accumulated by wind at the rockshelter. Most of the sediment particles are from local surrounding rocks (metamorphic and volcanic), probably produced by frost action; volcanic ashfalls are a secondary source of particles. Coarse material in the form of slabs and blocks is the result of weathering and collapse of the rockshelter. During the Pleistocene-Holocene transition, sedimentation was continuous (García et al. 1999; Zárate et al. 1997).

The pollen record indicates significant vegetation changes at ca. 12,000 and 9200 RCYBP. Prior to 12,000 RCYBP a grass steppe with herb and hydrophytic taxa dominated, which suggests a much more extreme climate than the present, cooler and wetter with seasonal frosts. Between 12,000 and 9200 RCYBP the grass steppe was replaced by a shrub steppe of Asteroideae with halophytic taxa, which indicates increasing aridity and temperature. The first human groups arrived in the area ca. 11,000 RCYBP. After ca. 9000 RCYBP the pollen record suggests the presence of a shrub steppe with *Larrea*, characteristic of more arid conditions.

The Cerro La China Locality

Cerro La China (37° 57′ S, 58° 37′ W, 150 m a.s.l.) is located in the Tandilia range within the southeastern dry Pampa grasslands. The present climate is subhumid-dry with incipient water deficit, a mean annual temperature of 14° C, and a mean annual precipitation of 800 mm or less. The vegetation is dominated by steppe grasses associated with numerous shrubby edaphic communities in the rocky hill slopes.

The locality includes a rockshelter (Site 1; Flegenheimer 1987) and two open-air sites (Site 2 and Site 3); all show evidence of early human occupations (Zárate and Flegenheimer 1991). Pollen and sedimentological analysis were performed at Site 2 and Site 3. The sedimentary sequences are composed of late-Glacial sandy loess deposits nonconformably overlying a truncated soil profile of late-Pleistocene age (?). Following loess deposition, moderately well developed soil began forming sometime after 10,600 RCYBP and continued during the Holocene marine transgression. Paleoindian occupation of Cerro La China occurred prior to the soil-forming interval (Zárate and Flegenheimer 1991). The relationship between percentages and concentration of long-distance pollen versus local pollen suggests an interval of greater environmental stability during the Pleistocene/Holocene transition; grasses and hydrophytic plant communities indicate more effective moisture (Paez and Prieto 1993; Prieto and Paez 1989).

The Los Toldos Locality

Los Toldos (47° 22′ S, 68° 58′ W, 300 m a.s.l.) consists of numerous caves and rockshelters situated along a "cañadón" (ravine) in the southern Patagonian steppe (Cardich et al. 1973). The climate is cold-temperate with a mean annual temperature of 8.5° C and a mean annual precipitation of 200 mm or less concentrated in winter months. Regional vegetation is characterized by shrub steppe and the Patagonian semidesert. The archaeological record shows Paleoindians and extinct fauna coexisted between 12,600 and ca. 10,000 RCYBP (Cardich 1987; Miotti 1993). Prior to ca. 11,000 RCYBP the pollen record (Paez et al. 1999) is dominated by *Ephedra,* indicating extremely arid conditions with precipitation less than 200 mm. Between ca. 11,000 and 10,000 RCYBP the presence of a grass steppe suggests an effective moisture rise probably related to an increase in precipitation to about 200 mm under cold conditions. Concentrations of gravel and sand intercalated in the sequence indicate a high-energy fluvial deposit (Cardich, et al. 1993–1994; Mazzoni and Spalletti 1974).

Between ca. 10,000 and 8750 RCYBP, when the Toldense industry developed, a shrub steppe of Asteroideae and xeric shrubs began to replace the grass steppe, which suggests semiarid conditions with precipitation of 200 mm or less. Environmental variability is also indicated by sediment layers of fluvial origin related to changes in the stream base level (Cardich and Paunero 1991–1992; Mazzoni and Spalletti 1974).

Although sediment and pollen analysis differ in their sensitivity to environmental changes, the results of both studies on the three localities confirm the Pleistocene-Holocene transition was characterized by significant climatic variability.

Sedimentological records show different sedimentation rates and continuity among the three localities in relation to the different geomorphological responses to climate changes during the Pleistocene-Holocene transition. In the Andean area of Agua de la Cueva, sedimentation started sometime after 13,000 RCYBP and continued without noticeable variation until the mid-Holocene. At Cerro La China in the southern Pampa, the rate of accumulation of late-Glacial loess substantially decreased sometime after 10,600 RCYBP and was followed by a period of relative environmental stability, likely persisting until the mid-Holocene as well. In the southern Patagonian steppe, the alluvial record of Los Toldos reveals fluctuations in fluvial energy, although the environmental significance remains unclear.

Vegetation changes inferred from the pollen records of the three localities indicate regional trends during the Pleistocene-Holocene transition and the existence of paleo-communities not analagous to modern vegetation patterns. At Agua de la Cueva the low vegetation cover is the only feature in common with present-day vegetation. The grass steppes of Los Toldos and Cerro La China bear slight resemblance to patches of grass in semidesert presently restricted (relict?) to some Patagonian topographic or edaphic settings and the humid pampean grassland, respectively.

Records from the localities studied in the Andean and Patagonian environments indicate extreme climatic conditions prior to ca. 11,000 RCYBP without evidence of human occupations. At Cerro La China in the Pampa, no pollen records are available to infer climatic and ecological conditions for this period.

In all three regions colonization by hunter-gatherer groups occurred under a progressive climatic amelioration after ca. 11,000 RCYBP. The Paleoindian occupation at Cerro La China, indicated by numerous lithic artifacts including Fell's cave projectile points associated with a scute of *Eutatus seguini* (Flegenheimer 1987), occurred when loess sedimentation was ongoing and prior to the humid interval documented by the soil profile. The grass steppe of Los Toldos could have sustained isolated individuals of extinct fauna (*Hippidion sp.* and *Lama* (*Vicugna*) *gracilis*). These species might have been a complementary resource for Paleoindians (Miotti 1993). The change from a grass steppe to a shrub steppe of Asteroideae occurred at roughly the same time as the arrival of early groups in the Andean region and the beginning of the Toldense industry. At Agua de la Cueva, a high density of lithic artifacts is associated with abundant remains of *Lama guanicoe* and *Lama* (*Vicugna?*) sp., this latter only present between 11,000 and 9000 RCYBP (Gil et al. 1997). After 9000 RCYBP human occupation of the locality was less intense under increasingly arid conditions (García et al. 1999). In southern Patagonia, the Toldense is associated with modern fauna (mainly *Lama guanicoe* and few fragmented bones of Rheidae and *Eudromia elegans*) and remains of the last Pleistocene fauna (Cardich et al. 1973).

Low values of pollen concentration that characterize the records at the three localities before ca. 10,000 RCYBP might be the result of changes in the rate of sediment accumulation or reduced plant cover.

In conclusion, during the Pleistocene-Holocene transition the type and magnitude of changes in the paleoenvironment and in the structure of paleocommunities caused significant changes in the distribution and availability of natural resources; these effects need to be clearly established. Further studies are needed to calibrate chronological sequences and to resolve other issues. Anomalies in radiocarbon dating during this period and the paucity of high-resolution records are major obstacles that must be overcome.

Acknowledgments

This work has been financed through projects PICT 97/07-01391, PICT 99/07-06477 (Agencia Nacional para la Promoción de la Ciencia y la Tecnología), UNMdP 15/E138 (Universidad Nacional de Mar del Plata), and PIP 98/0418-98 (CONICET).

References Cited

Cardich, A.

1987 Arqueología de Los Toldos y El Ceibo (Provincia Santa Cruz, Argentina). *Estudios Atacameños*, Universidad del Norte: 98–117. Chile.

Cardich, A., L. Cardich, and A. Hajduk

1973 Secuencia Arqueológica y Cronología Radiocarbónica de la Cueva 3 de Los Toldos (Santa Cruz, Argentina). *Relaciones de la Sociedad Argentina de Antropología* 7:85–123.

Cardich, A., and R. Paunero

1991–92 Arqueología de la Cueva 2 de Los Toldos (Santa Cruz, Argentina). *Anales de Arqueología y Etnología* 46/47:49–74. Mendoza.

Cardich, A., R. Paunero, and A. Castro

1993–94 Análisis de los Conjuntos Líticos de la Cueva 2 de Los Toldos (Santa Cruz, Argentina). *Anales Instituto de la Patagonia* 22:149–173. Chile.

Flegenheimer, N.

1980 Hallazgos de Puntas "Cola de Pescado" en la Provincia de Buenos Aires. *Relaciones, Sociedad Argentina Antropología* (N.S.) 14(1):169–176.

1987 Recent Research at Localities Cerro La China and Cerro El Sombrero, Argentina. *Current Research in the Pleistocene* 6:12–13.

García, A.

1992 Early Occupations at Agua de la Cueva-sector sur. Province of Mendoza. *Current Research in the Pleistocene* 9:13–14.

García, A., M. A. Zárate, and M. M. Paez

1999 The Pleistocene/Holocene Transition and Human Occupation in the Central Andes of Argentina: Agua de la Cueva Locality. *Quaternary International* 53/54:43–52.

Gil, A., G. Neme, and A. García

1997 Preliminary Zooarchaeological Results at Agua de la Cueva- Sector Sur Rockshelter. *Current Research in the Pleistocene* 14:139–140.

Mazzoni, M. M., and L. A. Spalletti

1974 Sedimentología de la Cueva de Los Toldos, Provincia de Santa Cruz. *Revista de la Asociación Argentina de Mineralogía, Petrología y Sedimentología* 5:15–34.

Miotti, L. L.

1993 La Ocupación Humana en la Patagonia Austral durante el Holoceno. In *El Holoceno en la Argentina,* edited by M. Iriondo, pp. 94–130. CADINQUA.

Paez, M. M., and A. R. Prieto

1993 Paleoenvironmental Reconstruction by Pollen Analysis from Loess Sequences of the Southeast of Buenos Aires (Argentina). *Quaternary International* 17:21–26.

Paez, M. M., A. R. Prieto, and M. V. Mancini

1999 Fossil Pollen from Los Toldos Locality: A Record of the Late-glacial Transition in Extra-Andean Patagonia. *Quaternary Internationa*l 53/54:69–75.

Prieto, A. R., and M. M. Paez

1989 Pollen Analysis of Discontinuous Stratigraphical Sequences: Holocene at Cerro La China Locality (Buenos Aires, Argentina). *Quaternary of South America and Antarctic Peninsula* 7:219–236.

Zárate, M., and N. Flegenheimer

1991 Geoarchaeology of the Cerro La China Locality (Buenos Aires, Argentina): Site 2 and Site 3. *Geoarchaeology* 6(3):273–294.

Zárate, M. A., M. M. Paez, A. García, and A. Blasi

1997 Condiciones Ambientales entre los 14.000 y los 5.000 Años ^{14}C a.P. en la Precordillera de Mendoza, Argentina: Localidad Agua de la Cueva. *ABEQUA Abstracts* :517–521. Brazil.

The Presence of a Pleistocene Colonizing Culture in La María Archaeological Locality, Casa del Minero 1

Rafael S. Paunero

La María archaeological locality lies 150 km northwest of Puerto San Julián in the department of Magallanes (48° 25′ S, 68° 55′ W), 150–450 m. a.s.l. La María is remarkable because of its rock art, which is extraordinarily rich in variety and quality. The polychromy used in diverse motifs constitutes an important example of parietal art. Four and sometimes even five colors appear in a single composition, and images are painted in natural holes or on the prominences of walls, achieving an outstanding degree of abstraction and symbology (Cardich and Paunero 1994; Paunero 2000).

Different aspects of rock art, including overlapping by sector and panel, motifs, and groups of motifs, have been studied (Franchomme 1991; Paunero 2001); techniques, raw materials, pigments, and clays and gypsum have been analyzed (Aschero 1988; Paunero 1992); and various symmetries related to location and different uses of space have been identified. Present efforts are directed at integrating research from archaeology, ethnography, present social perception, and experimentation to discover the probable sequence and chronology of different stylistic expressions (Gradin 1987, 1988; Miotti 1991; Onetto 1991; Paunero 2001).

Since 1993, when we researched Estancias San Rafael, Los Granaderos, and other sites, we have systematically registered and surveyed the 22,000 hectares that compose the region. By using the GPS system to locate archaeological variables within its limits, we have plotted the location of microenvironments, plateaus, canyons, lagoons, creeks, quarries, and open campsites. Twelve sectors are defined, based on environmental, archaeological, and landscape features (Criado Boado 1991; Miotti et al. 1997; Paunero 2000, 2001)in La María locality.

Departamento Científico de Arqueología. Facultad de Ciencias Naturales y Museo. UNLP, La Plata, Argentina.. e-mail: rpaunero@museo.fcnym.unlp.edu.ar

During the summer of 1996 we started excavating with the aim to identify the earliest human occupation in the locality. We also planned to fit our discoveries within the context of the natural and cultural stratigraphy of other localities of the Central Plateau of Santa Cruz.

We set up initial grids in four sectors: La María Bajo, La María Quebrada, Cañadón de la Ventana, and Cañadón de la Mina. In an excavation at Cueva de la Mesada of La María Quebrada, we identified a component from the early Holocene, dated to 9090 ± 40 RCYBP (Beta–135963). Two samples from Cueva de la Ventana yielded ages of 7970 ± 40 RCYBP (Beta–135965) and 7665 ± 75 RCYBP (AA–35237).

In 2000 we started the first excavation at the Casa del Minero 1 site, in Cañadón de la Mina, the subject of this report. Cañadón de la Mina is located at 48° 34′ 33″ S, 68° 54′ 45″ W, 1,360 m northeast of Laguna Grande. At the bottom of the canyon we identified a spring that feeds a basin, producing a course of water that ends in the lagoon. There are two outstanding caves in this sector, named Casa del Minero 1 and 2. In the latter we found evidence of naturalistic rock art.

The stratigraphy in the excavated sector is sealed by roof fall, which separates two archaeological components. The lower one contains remains of Pleistocene fauna.

Stratigraphic Units (Figure 1)

C: Volcanic ash from the Hudson volcano (1991); thickness 1–2 cm.

1. Light gray loose sediment with medium sands, without guano, and with historical cultural remains from miners' occupation during last century; thickness 6–8 cm.
2. Compact sand with faded lines of charcoal in the base and Holocene archaeological remains; thickness 5–10 cm.
3. Silt-sand compacted layer with medium-size stones contains lithic artifacts and fragments of bone in the two levels of Holocene occupation. It overlies the fallen rocks or unit 4; thickness 10–14 cm.

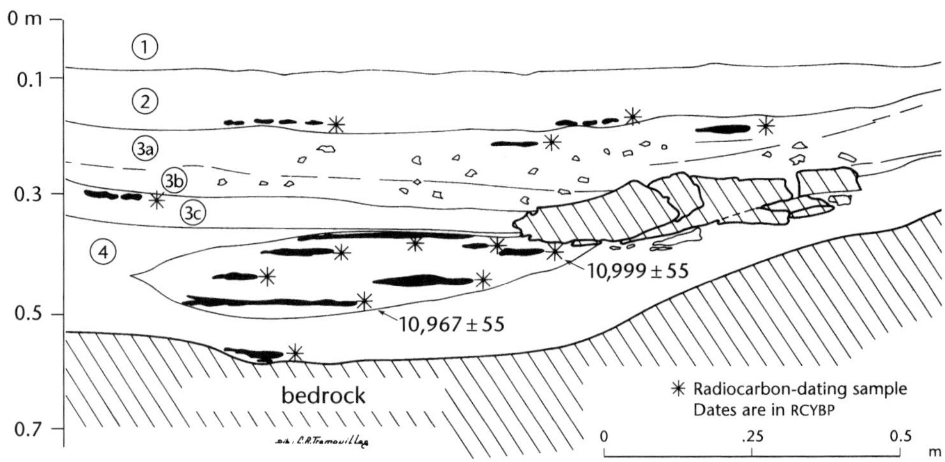

Figure 1. Stratigraphic profile, square A, Estancia La María, Cañadón de la Mina, Casa del Minero site 1.

RD: Roof fall

4. Compact light ocher sediment of sand and silt with an important cultural content and a lenticulate hearth structure; thickness 10–20 cm. The following datings were obtained: 10,999 ± 55 RCYBP, -24.6 $\delta^{13}/_{12}C$ (‰) (AA 37207); 10,967 ± 55 RCYBP, -25.9 $\delta^{13}/_{12}C$ (‰) (AA 37208).
5. Light-colored sediment of sand and silt that overlies the bedrock, without archaeological content; thickness 8–14 cm.

The archaeological context dating to the Pleistocene contains lithic tools and remains of fauna, both extant and extinct species.

Lithic Assemblage

Tools

- A knife with an inverse-extended retouch and a bifacial distal retouch made of a red flint (*silex*) blade (Figure 2A).
- A sidescraper with unifacial and bifacial retouches made of a wide flake of petrified wood (Figure 2B).

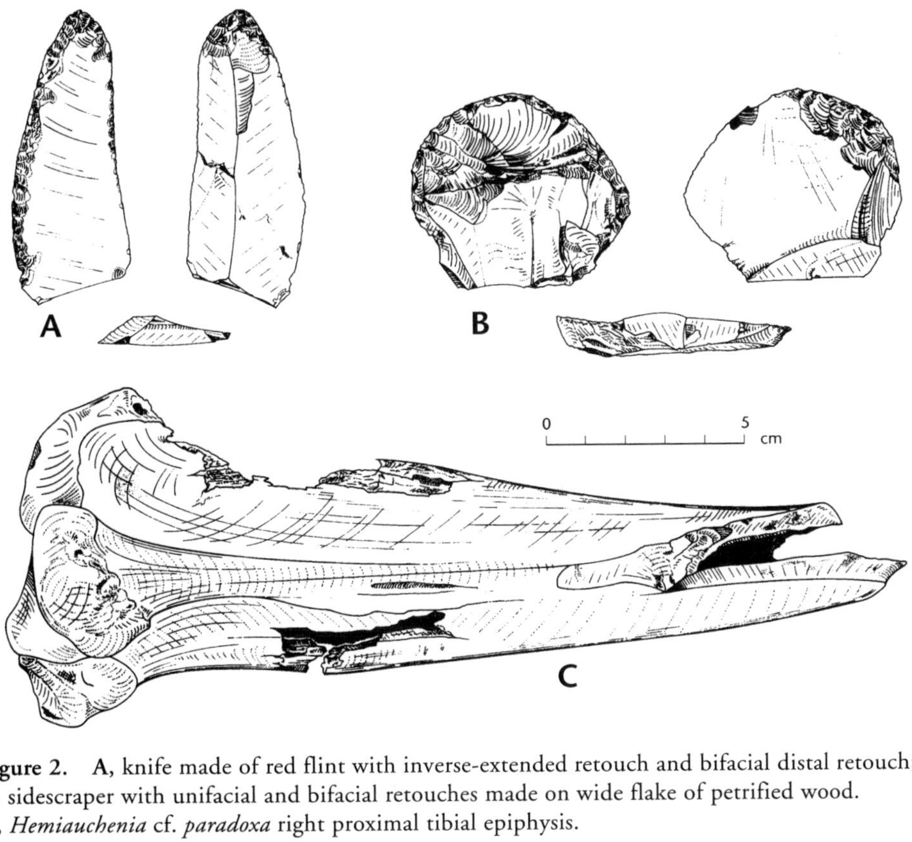

Figure 2. **A,** knife made of red flint with inverse-extended retouch and bifacial distal retouch; **B,** sidescraper with unifacial and bifacial retouches made on wide flake of petrified wood. **C,** *Hemiauchenia* cf. *paradoxa* right proximal tibial epiphysis.

Debitage

- 130 flakes, 6 wide flakes, 2 long flakes, a blade, and a triangular flake; materials are red flint (60.76 percent), chalcedony (32.30 percent), and other kinds of flint (6.92 percent).
- 129 small flakes; materials are red flint (69.76 percent), chalcedony (22.48 percent), and other flint (7.75 percent).
- 310 microflakes; materials are red flint (89.35 percent), chalcedony (3.22 percent), and other flint (7.42 percent).

Small flakes of secondary flaking and bifacial retouch are almost exclusively red flint. No cores are recorded.

The raw material consists of only two kinds of stone, red flint and chalcedony. We located a quarry of red flint 400 m from the cave in the direction of the lagoon. This quarry has an approximate diameter of 550 m; lithic material is concentrated in a central area 400 m across.

Faunal Evidence

The bone assemblage contains remains of *Lama guanicoe* and extinct camelids: *Hemiauchenia* cf. *paradoxa* (right proximal tibial epiphysis (Figure 2C) and complete right cuboid, both from adult animals); and *Lama (Vicugna) gracilis* (left distal humerus epiphysis and right proximal metacarpals, both from adult animals). We also recorded remains of Canidae (eight metapodials, a scapula, three phalanges, and three molars, all from adult animals) and *Rhea* sp. (a second phalanx of finger 3) (M. Bond pers. comm.; L. Miotti pers. comm.). In this component we found bone tools, three awls made of diaphysis flakes from an undetermined large mammal.

The presence of the extinct camelid *Hemiauchenia* cf. *paradoxa* (Menegaz et al. 1989) in southern Patagonia is noteworthy, especially since we found evidence of human modifications (distinct blow marks and an anthropogenic fracture in the analyzed right proximal tibia). The same Pleistocene genus has been recorded in such North American sites as Rancho La Brea (Webb 1965), Natural Trap Cave (KU), and Bergner Gravel Pit (SDSM 5181) (Breyer 1974). Extinct camelids have also been recorded in some South American sites: *Hemiauchenia* sp. in Paso Otero 5 (Martínez 1997); *Paleolama* sp. in Arroyo Seco (Fidalgo et al. 1986); and *Lama owenii* in Cueva del Medio (Nami and Menegaz 1991). However, up to the moment Casa del Minero 1 is the only site in the Central Plateau of Santa Cruz with a record of this genus. Note that the smaller camelid *Lama (Vicugna) gracilis* was recorded in the lower components of Los Toldos, El Ceibo, and Piedra Museo (Cardich 1987; Cardich and Miotti 1983; Miotti et al. 1999).

Conclusions

From the evidence obtained we can draw the following inferences:

1. The lower component was clearly sealed by a roof fall in the interior sectors that kept it undisturbed.
2. A high-resolution lithic assemblage shows low diversity of raw materials and a technology using unifacial and bifacial knapping.
3. The remains of extinct and extant camelids with evidence of butchering and consumption (helical fractures, cutmarks, and spatial distribution close to a hearth) rein-

forces the hypothesis of late-Pleistocene occupations in the region by hunter-gatherer societies and their exploitation of megamammals.

4. During the Pleistocene the lagoon probably had a larger diameter than at present and therefore would have been closer to the excavated site. The Cañadón de la Mina sector thus constituted a favorable environment, with shelter close to critical resources (water, fauna, and good-quality firewood) and sources of excellent minerals for knapping and making pigments.
5. The proximity to a large lagoon supports the theory that preferred hunting and primary processing sites during the late Pleistocene were places near water. By the time of the early Holocene, climatic oscillations in the region resulted in a shrub-like steppe replacing a herbaceous steppe; the environment was becoming drier and windier and probably more stressful for Pleistocene mammals.

In sum, we have identified an early occupation dating to the late Pleistocene at Casa del Minero Cave in the La María locality. Work will continue at the site and in the area in search of new evidence to discover cultural patterns in the late Pleistocene.

References Cited

Aschero, C.
1988 Pinturas Rupestres, Actividades y Recursos Naturales: Un Encuadre Arqueológico. In *Arqueología Contemporánea Argentina*, edited by H. D. Yacobaccio, L. A. Borrero, and L. C. Garcia, pp. 109–146. Ediciones Búsqueda. Buenos Aires, Argentina.

Breyer, J.
1974 Examination of Selected Postcranial Elements in Pleistocene Camelids. *Contributions to Geology* 13:75–85.

Cardich, A.
1987 Arqueología de Los Toldos y El Ceibo (Provincia de Santa Cruz, Argentina). *Investigaciones Paleoindias al Sur de la Línea Ecuatorial*, edited by L. Núñez and B. Meggers, pp. 98–117. *Estudios Atacameños*. 8. Chile.

Cardich, A., and L. Miotti
1983 Recursos Faunísticos en la Economía de los Cazadores-recolectores de Los Toldos (Provincia. de Santa Cruz, Argentina). *Relaciones Sociedad Argentina de Antropología XV (n.s.)*:145–157.

Cardich, A., and R. S. Paunero
1994 *Localidad arqueológica "La María". Santa Cruz.* Argentina. Informe para Honorable Cámara de Diputados de Santa Cruz. Facultad de Ciencias Naturales y Museo, Universidad Nacional de La Plata. MS.

Criado Boado, F.
1991 Construcción Social del Espacio y Reconstrucción Arqueológica del Paisaje. *Boletín de Antropología Americana* 24:5–29, México.

Fidalgo, F., L. Meo Guzman, G. Politis, M. Salemme, and E. Tonni.
1986 Investigaciones Arqueológicas en el Sitio 2 de Arroyo Seco (Partido de Tres Arroyos, Provincia de Buenos Aires, Rep. Argentina). In *New Evidence for the Pleistocene Peopling of the Americas,* edited by A. Bryan, pp. 221–269, Center for the Study of the First Americans, Oregon State University, Corvallis, OR.

Franchomme, J. M.
1991 *L'art Rupestre Prehistorique de Patagonie.* Doctoral dissertation, Université de Paris.

Gradin, C.
1987 Tendencias Estilísticas del Arte Rupestre de Patagonia Central y Meridional. *Comunicaciones de Primeras Jornadas de Arqueología de la Patagonia.* Serie Humanidades 2:139–152. Chubut, Argentina.

Gradin, C.
1988 Caracterización de las Tendencias Estilísticas del Arte Rupestre de la Patagonia (Provincias de Río Negro, Chubut y Santa Cruz). *Contribución al Estudio del Arte Rupestre Sudamericano (Boletín)* 2:54–67. La Paz, Argentina.

Martinez, G.
1997 A Preliminary Report on Paso Otero 5, a Late Pleistocene Site in the Pampean Region of Argentina. *Current Research in the Pleistocene* 14:53–55.

Menegaz, A., F. Goin, and E. Ortiz Jaureguizar
1989 Análisis Morfológico y Morfométrico Multivariado de los Representantes Fósiles y Vivientes del Género *Lama* (Artiodactyla, Camelidae). Sus Implicancias Sistemáticas, Biogeográficas, Ecológicas y Biocronológicas. *Ameghiniana* 26(3-4):153–172. Buenos Aires, Argentina.

Miotti, L.
1991 Manifestaciones Rupestres de Santa Cruz: La Localidad Piedra Museo. In *El Arte Rupestre en la Arqueología Contemporánea Argentina,* edited by M. M. Podestá, M. I. Hernández Llosas, and S. F. Renard de Coquet. pp. 132–138.

Miotti, L., N. Carden, and M. J. Canosa
1997 Paisajes Arqueológicos de Cazadores-recolectores, Arte Rupestre y Lagunas: Los Nuevos Hallazgos de Petroglifos en la Meseta Central de Santa Cruz. *XII Congreso Nacional de Arqueología Argentina, Actas* III, edited by C. Diez Marin, pp. 54–61, Facultad de Ciencias Naturales y Museo, UNLP, La Plata, Argentina.

Miotti, L., M. Vázquez, and D. Hermo
1999 Piedra Museo: Un Yamnagoo Pleistocénico en la Colonización de la Meseta de Santa Cruz. El Estudio de la Arqueofauna. In *Soplando en el Viento, 3ras. Jornadas de Arqueología de la Patagonia,* pp. 113–136. Universidad Nacional del Comahue and Instituto Nacional de Antropologia y Pensamiento Latinoamericano, Neuquen-Buenos Aires, Argentina.

Nami, H, and A. Menegaz
1991 Cueva del Medio: Aportes para el Conocimiento de la Diversidad Faunística hacia el Pleistoceno-Holoceno en Patagonia Austral. *Anales del Instituto de la Patagonia* 20:117–132. Punta Arenas, Chile.

Onetto, M.
1991 Propuesta para la Integración del Arte Rupestre dentro del Sistema de Comportamiento de los Cazadores–Recolectores del Valle de Piedra Parada. In *El Arte Rupestre en la Arqueología Contemporánea Argentina,* edited by M. M. Podestá, M. I. Hernandez Llosas, and S. F. Renard de Coquet, pp. 123–131.

Paunero, R. S.
1992 Manos Pintadas en Negativo: Un Ensayo de Experimentación. *Revista de Estudios Regionales CEIDER* 9:47–68. Universidad Nacional de Cuyo. Mendoza, Argentina.

2000 Relevamiento, Arte Rupestre y Sectorización de la Localidad Arqueológica La Mara. In *Guia de Campo de la Visita a las Localidades Arqueológicas,* edited by L. Miotti, R. Paunero, M. Salemme, and G. C. Cattáneo, pp. 104-120. Taller Internacional sobre La Colonización del Sur de América Durante la Transición Pleistoceno/Holoceno. La Plata, Argentina.

2001 *Investigaciones Arqueológicas en Estancia La María, Provincia de Santa Cruz, Argentina.* M.S.

Webb, S. D.
1965 The Osteology of Camelops. *Bulletin of the Los Angeles County Museum* 1:1–54.

The Cerro Tres Tetas (C3T) Locality in the Central Plateau of Santa Cruz, Argentina

Rafael S. Paunero

For several years we have been carrying on research in the Central Plateau of Santa Cruz province at estancias La María, San Rafael, Los Granaderos, La Asturiana, El Ceibo, La Evelina, and Santa Catalina with the aim of reconstructing the past of the region (Paunero 1994, 1996, 2000a, 2000b; Paunero and Castro submitted).

The Cerro Tres Tetas (C3T) archaeological locality, previously unknown in scientific publications, was found in 1993. It is located at 48° 08′ 58″ S, 68° 56′ W, 450–480 m a.s.l., 55 km north of the La María and El Ceibo localities (Cardich 1987; Paunero 2000b) and approximately 75 km southwest of the Piedra Museo locality (Miotti 1995; Miotti et al. 1999).

One of the most important missions in American archaeology is establishing the time of arrival of the first colonizing human groups in the Southern Cone. This report, based on the datings of Pleistocene archaeological sites, discusses different theories regarding the technology, settlement patterns, diet, and origin of these hunter-gatherer colonizers.

Cueva 1, C3T is a multicomponent site whose stratigraphy and archaeological contexts date to the colonization phase of the Central Plateau of Santa Cruz in the late Pleistocene. It therefore constitutes an ideal subject for testing regional hypotheses, especially those proposed for the Los Toldos, El Ceibo, La María, and Piedra Museo localities (Cardich et al. 1973, 1982; Cardich and Paunero 1991, 1994; Miotti 1995; Paunero 2000b).

Stratigraphy of Cueva 1, C3T

The mouth of Cueva 1 is oriented towards the west. The cave lies 110 m from a present spring and 9.13 m above it. It is dark; soot covers the roof, and there are paintings on the

Departamento Científico de Arqueología. Facultad de Ciencias Naturales y Museo. UNLP, La Plata, Argentina. e-mail: rpaunero@museo.fcnym.unlp.edu.ar

walls. A systematic excavation was done in 1994 and 1995. Nine grids divided in sectors were excavated, covering a total area of 12.25 m^2 .

Identified Units (Figure 1)

0: Hudson volcanic ash (from August, 1991); thickness 2–6 cm.

1: Gray sand layer containing sheep dung; thickness 3–8 cm.

2: Sand layer, much darker, without dung, containing small and very small stemmed projectile points, hearth remains, and glass; thickness 6–12 cm.

3a: Light gray sand layer with a hearth in grid B, with small points similar to those of layer 2, but without glass or European material. Bone and lithic remains were found; thickness 8–12 cm.

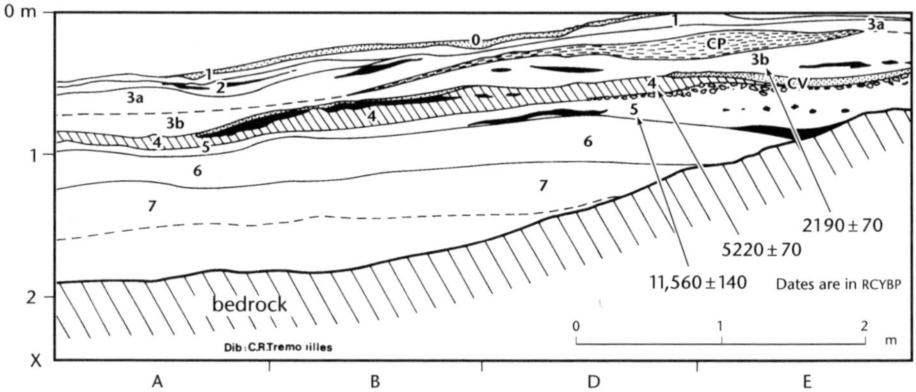

Figure 1. Stratigraphic profile, Cerro Tres Tetas.

CP: Layer of hay placed as a lens; thickness 2–16 cm.

E: Fine-grained light-colored sand layer, archaeologically sterile; thickness 11–20 cm.

3b: Fine-grained dark gray sand unit, with hearths; thickness 12–16 cm.

CV: Lens of volcanic ash. It overlies layer 4 except in the interior, where it lies directly over the roof of Unit 5; thickness 2–5 cm.

4: Sand and lime-brown-colored layer, with archaeological content; thickness 10–14 cm. An erosive nonconformity separates unit 4 from unit 5. Rocks of medium and small size fallen from the roof of the cave constitute an excellent natural seal over layer 5. They were found in the interior grids. The latest hearth from the initial component is directly covered by this depositional unit.

5: Light-ocher-colored slime-sandy layer, separated from layer 4 by a clear nonconformity. In the outer grids this layer is very thin (6 cm), but in the interior it is thicker, reaching 38 cm. In this layer the earliest occupation of the site was found, represented by four important hearths with a lenticulate structure and ranging in size from 80 to 120 cm. Lithic material and some bone remains were associated.

6: Clay and sandy layer, archaeologically sterile.

Lithic Analysis

The technical and morphological classification below should also be optimal for a functional analysis using the high-augmentation technique. A total of 523 pieces were recovered in the lower cultural component. This assemblage was divided into four technological groups: instruments, cores, debris, and unmodified rocks (Figure 2A, B, D, E).

Tools 31.

Scrapers 8: sidescrapers, 7; retouched flakes, 9; knives, 3.

Bifacial tools 2, a chopper and a hammer.

Cores 2 of flakes; also 3 fragments.

Debris 474 pieces.

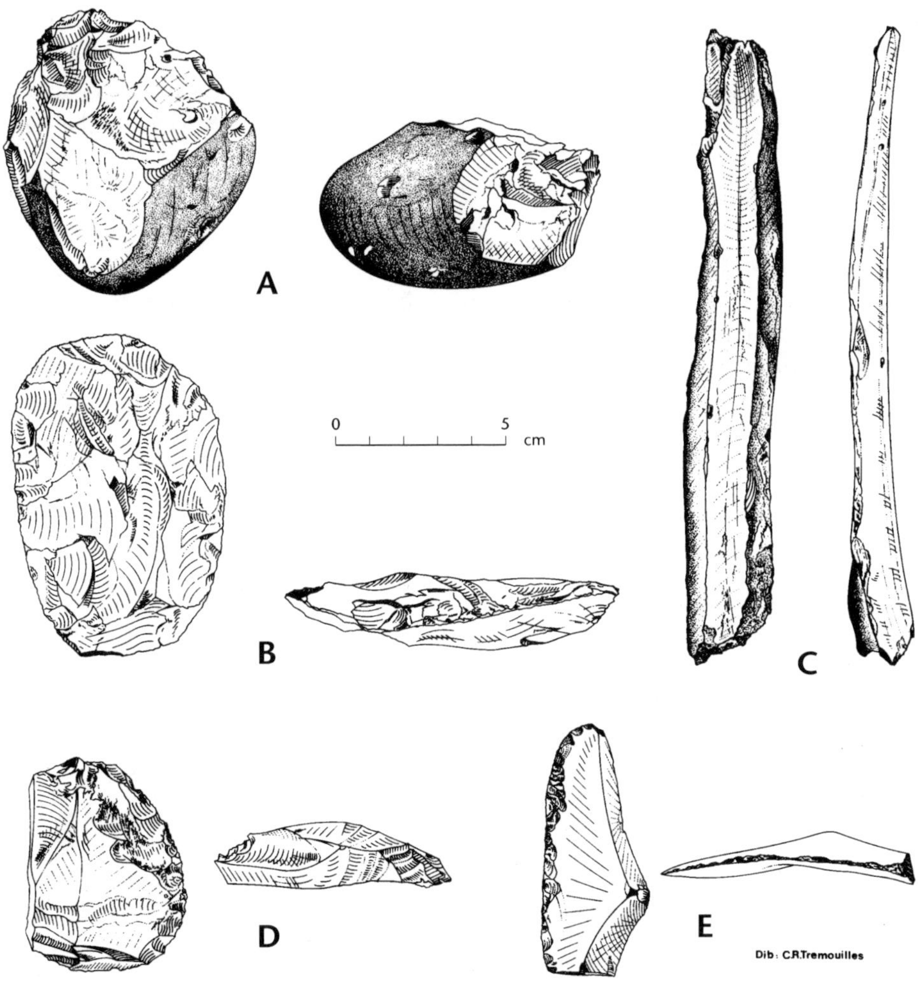

Figure 2. **A,** core; **B,** double lateral sidescraper; **C,** tool made from *Lama guanicoe* diaphysis; **D,** lateral scraper; **E,** knife with extended unifacial retouch.

Complete flakes and identified fragments 174.
Unidentified chipping fragments 71.
Microflakes 229.
Unmodified rocks 14.

Size of Tools
Length 3.6–10.3 cm.
Width 3–8 cm.
Thickness 0.4–5.7 cm.

Blanks
Thirteen instruments were made from flakes, eight from wide flakes, four from long flakes, one from a blade, one from a very wide flake, two from cobbles, and two from unidentified blanks.

Retouch
Tools are unifacial except for a notch and a preform with bifacial retouch. The marginal retouch on the dorsal face (short and long) is the most common; it is rarely on the ventral face.

Platforms
Among the complete tools, the most abundant platforms are natural (8), plain (7), and finally faceted (3), worn out (2) and dihedral (1). Among the debris, the types of platforms are 38 faceted (30.1 percent), 33 plain (26.2 percent), 17 natural (13.5 percent), 14 dihedral (11.1 percent), 8 prepared (6.3 percent), and 6 "punctiformes" (4.7 percent). Among the complete debris (and among the identified fragmented products) are 95 flakes (57.2 percent), 33 wide flakes (19.8 percent), 24 very wide flakes (14.4 percent), 12 long flakes (7.2 percent), and 2 blades (1.2 percent).

Raw Materials
There is a great diversity of materials from the flint (*silex*) family, with different colors and different degrees of homogeneity and fracture conditions. We have located several sources of raw material. In one instance, pebbles were taken from the creek that flows through the locality; in another, rock exposures of different concentrations located in the highest places near the site show evidence of quarrying. Among the instruments, 18 are made of flint, 8 of petrified wood, one of silicified tuff, 3 of chalcedony, and none of obsidian. Among the identified debris, 106 pieces are flint, 60 are petrified wood, 29 are chalcedony, 27 are silicified tuff, and 5 are obsidian.

Functional Analysis
A sample was selected from the complete lithic assemblage for the functional analysis of microwear (Keeley 1977, 1980; Semenov 1964; Vaughan 1981); based on a stratified criterion of sampling, the sample of 57 lithic pieces included 23 instruments, 32 pieces of debris, and 2 cores (Paunero and Castro submitted). The study determined that 10 pieces were used for working hides and 3 for working bones. A tool defined as a scraper had been used to work on hide and bone. Analysis of the spatial distribution of cultural materials in the cave identified two activity areas; in one the main activity was scraping hide, and in the other it was mainly working hide and scarcely any bone.

Heat Treating

The use of thermal treatment techniques to prepare tool blanks can be recognized by changes in the structure and color of the mineral, by a shiny surface (Nami et al. 2000), and by diagnostic thermal fractures. Of the sample artifacts selected for functional analysis, 13 showed evidence of heat treatment; moreover, 11 of these were found within 75 cm of the hearths (Paunero 1994, 1996; Paunero and Castro submitted).

Faunal Remains

In the cultural level, unlike the middle and upper components, there are few bone remains. It seems unlikely that this situation is due to postdepositional transformations, since the recovered bone fragments and flakes are very well preserved.

Bones and associated artifacts found consist of *Lama guanicoe* (a proximal right femur fragment, a distal fragment of metapodial, two fragments of diaphysis, a tool made of diaphysis with evidence of thermal treatment and marginal retouches forming a blade (Figure 2C), a fragment of proximal metapodial and a diaphysis with cut marks, a distal end of phalanx, a right upper molar and two vertebrae); and unidentified mammal (a small mammal vertebra, 30 flakes with evidence of heat treatment, 46 fragments, a light-colored awl made of a fragment without evidence of heat treatment, and two fragments of long bones).

In six units no bone remains were recovered. It is remarkable that the lithic artifacts and bone fragments were not found within the hearths; instead, they were found surrounding the structures or distributed in some sectors of the sedimentary light-ocher matrix, typical of unit 5.

It is also noteworthy that a botanical analysis made of one of the radiocarbon-dating samples detected the *Schinus* genus (J. Steele pers. comm.). In accordance with bibliographic research and recognition of present flora, it could be assigned to the local "Molle": *Schinus (duwana) polygamus patagonicus* (Cabrera 1938, 1971).

Conclusions

Unit 5 contains the Pleistocene cultural component. This unit overlies the bedrock in the interior of the cave and layer 6 in the rest of the excavated surface. In its upper part it is separated from unit 4 by a nonconformity, and in the interior grids of layer 5 it is sealed by medium-size fallen rocks. This initial cultural level (Table 1), referring to the colonization phase of the Central Plateau of Santa Cruz, spans the period from 11,560 RCYBP (LP-525), based on evidence from the three hearths at the bottom, until 10,260 RCYBP (LP-800), based on evidence from the hearth at the top of this layer, which is sealed by fallen rock.

Analysis of the lithic assemblage concludes that the chipping technique was direct percussion with hard hammers, rarely soft, with pressure retouch on a small scale. Two strategies were used to obtain blanks for tools. One was the direct method, selecting rocks of optimal quality and nodules with natural structural possibilities to obtain normal or wide flakes. In the other strategy, percussion platforms were prepared to create cores from which predetermined forms could be made (Tixier 1980), yielding products with faceted or dihedral blanks (Mansur 1987; Paunero 1994). In all these cases, the chosen forms were almost exclusively normal and wide flakes, resulting in tools intended to be gripped by hand. The tools would have been designed for specific functions.

Table 1. Radiocarbon chronology for components and units of C1 C3T.

Cultural component	Stratigraphy		Standard radiocarbon age (RCYBP)	Lab no.
	O	volcanic ash		
	1			
Historic Tehuelche	2			
Late Tehuelchense	3a	upper	830 ± 60	LP-770
	3a	lower	1340 ± 50	LP-1180
	CP	hay layer	1740 ± 60	LP-1187
	E			
Tehuelchense	3b		2190 ± 70	LP-541
	CV	volcanic ash		
Casapedrense	4		5220 ± 70	LP-538
		roof fall		
Initial component	5	upper	10,260 ± 110	LP-800
	5	lower	10,850 ± 150	LP-781
			10,853 ± 70	AA-39366
			10,915 ± 65	OxA-9244
			11,015 ± 66	AA-39368
			11,100 ± 150	AA-22233
			11,560 ± 140	LP-525
	6			
		bedrock		

The evidence reveals hearths, thermal treatment techniques, and scarce faunal remains. These findings suggest controlled cultural management of fire and a site compartmentalized into specific working areas, resulting in a highly efficient system for preparing tool blanks and refining the finished products.

It appears likely that the practice of fracturing long bones to obtain edible bone marrow was rarely used. Although it is possible that meat without bone was consumed, primary processing and consumption must have been done in some other site near the cave. Near the cave there is a depression crossed by the creek that traverses the locality; the depression crosses the locality in a southeast direction and constitutes an ideal locale for hunting and processing prey.

The context of Cerro Tres Tetas is an example of the functional variability of early sites of the region. The spatial distribution of artifacts and structures suggests space was divided into areas intended for specific activities. In this way the site contributes to the evolving theory about the role of caves in different activity patterns of societies of the late Pleistocene.

References Cited

Cabrera, A. L.

1938 Revisión de las Anacardiáceas Austroamericanas. *Revista del Museo de La Plata,* N.S. II, Sección Botánica: 3–64. La Plata, Argentina.

1971 Fitogeografía de la República Argentina. *Boletín de la Sociedad de Botánica,* XIV(1-3):25–36. Buenos Aires, Argentina.

Cardich, A.

1987 Arqueología de Los Toldos y El Ceibo (Provincia de Santa Cruz, Argentina). In *Investigaciones Paleoindias al sur de la línea ecuatorial,* edited by L. Núñez and B. Meggers, pp. 98–117. Estudios Atacameños 8, Universidad del Norte, Antofagasta, Chile.

Cardich, A., L. Cardich, and A. Hajduk

1973 Secuencia Arqueológica y Cronología Radiocarbónica de la Cueva 3 de Los Toldos (Santa Cruz, Argentina). *Revista Relaciones* 7:87–122 Sociedad Argentina de Antropología.

Cardich, A., M. E. Mansur-Franchomme, M. Giesso, and V. A. Durán

1982 Arqueología de las Cuevas de El Ceibo (Provincia de Santa Cruz, Argentina). *Relaciones* 14(2):173–209 Sociedad Argentina de Antropología.

Cardich, A., and R. S. Paunero

1991 Arqueología de la Cueva 2 de Los Toldos (Santa Cruz, Argentina). *Anales de Arqueología y Etnología* 46/47:49–97.

1994 Mid-Holocene Herding in Central Patagonia. *Research and Exploration* 10(3):368–369.

Keeley, L. H.

1977 *An Experimental Study of Microwear Traces on Selected British Paleolithic Implements*. Ph. D. Dissertation, Oxford University.

1980 Experimental Determination of Stone Tool Uses: A Microwear Analysis. In *Prehistoric Archaeology and Ecology Series,* edited by K. Butzer and L. G. Freeman, pp. 1–212. The University of Chicago Press, Chicago and London.

Mansur, M. E.

1987 Características Tecno-tipológicas y Análisis Funcional de la Industria "Nivel 11". *Comunicaciones de Primeras Jornadas de Arqueología de la Patagonia.* Serie Humanidades 2:153–159. Chubut, Argentina.

Miotti, L.

1995 Piedra Museo Locality: A Special Place in the New World. *Current Research in the Pleistocene* 12:37–40.

Miotti, L., M. Vázquez, and D. Hermo

1999 Piedra Museo: Un Yamnagoo Pleistocénico en la Colonización de la Meseta de Santa Cruz. El Estudio de la Arqueofauna. *Simposio de Poblamiento en Terceras Jornadas de Arqueología de la Patagonia.* In *Soplando en el Viento,* edited by R. Goñi, pp. 113–136. Universidad Nacional del Comahue and Instituto Nacional de Antropologia y Pensamiento Latinoamericano, Neuquén–Buenos Aires, Argentina.

Nami, H., R. Cattáneo, and M. Pupio

2000 Investigaciones experimentales sobre el tratamiento térmico en algunas materias primas de Pampa y Patagonia. *Anales del Instituto de la Patagonia* (Serie Ciencias Sociales) 28:315–331, Punta Arenas, Chile.

Paunero, R. S.

1994 El Sitio Cueva 1 de la Localidad Arqueológica Cerro Tres Tetas (Estancia San Rafael, Provincia de Santa Cruz, Argentina). *Anales de Arqueología y Etnología.* 48/49:73–90.

1996 Noticia sobre Nuevas Fechas Radiocarbónicas del Sitio Cueva 1, C3T, Santa Cruz, Argentina. *Anales de Arqueología y Etnología* 50-51:189–199.

2000a Localidad Arqueológica Cerro Tres Tetas. In *Guía de Campo de la Visita a las Localidades Arqueológicas,* edited by L. Miotti, R. Paunero, M. Salemme, and G. C. Cattáneo. pp. 89–100. Taller Internacional sobre La Colonización del Sur de América Durante la Transición Pleistoceno/Holoceno. La Plata, Argentina.

2000b Relevamiento, Arte Rupestre y Sectorización de la Localidad Arqueológica La María. In *Guía de Campo de la Visita a las Localidades Arqueológicas,* edited by L. Miotti, R. Paunero, M. Salemme, and G. C. Cattáneo. pp. 104–120. Taller Internacional sobre La Colonización del Sur de América Durante la Transición Pleistoceno/Holoceno. La Plata, Argentina.

Paunero, R., and A. Castro

2001 Análisis Lítico y Funcionalidad del Componente Inferior de Sitio Cueva 1, Localidad

Arqueológica Cerro Tres Tetas, Provincia de Santa Cruz, Argentina. *Anales del Instituto de la Patagonia*. Punta Arenas, Chile.

Semenov, S. A.
1964 *Prehistoric Technology.* Cory, Adams and MacKay, London.

Tixier, J., M. L. Inizan, and H. Roche
1980 *Prehistorie de la Pierre Taille.* Circle de Recherches et d'Etudes Prehistoriques, Antibes, France.

Vaughan, P.
1981 Microwear Analysis of Experimental Flint and Obsidian Tools. Third International Symposium on Flint, *Staringia* 6:90–91.

Early Occupations at Cerro Casa de Piedra 7, Santa Cruz Province, Patagonia, Argentina

María Teresa Civalero[1] and Carlos Alberto Aschero[2]

This report provides information about recent advances in research project PIP/CONICET 4628 at the Cerro Casa de Piedra locality in Perito Moreno National Park, Andean foothills, Santa Cruz province. The latest results about this site have been discussed in several publications and in conferences held in Argentina (Aschero 1996a, 1996b; Aschero et al. 1992; Aschero et al. in press; Civalero 1995,1999; Civalero in press).

The main research issues addressed here are:

a) the characteristics of occupation populations in the forest-steppe ecotone of the Andean foothills compared with those in extra-Andean Patagonia (e.g., the Central Plateau and foregoing Cordillera, Alto Río Pinturas zone);
b) exploited resources in the ecotone and in the Central Plateau, inferred from cultural remains;
c) information about group interactions, such as communication between nearby and distant areas, inferred from lithic and bone artifacts, rock art, and the organization of the rockshelter or other site structure.

The results of research in Alto Río Pinturas and the Central Plateau (Aguerre 1981/82, 1987, 1997; Cardich and Flegenheimer 1978; Cardich et al. 1981/82; Gradin et al. 1976, 1979; Miotti 1996; Miotti et al. 1999) can help us discover the effect of the forest-steppe ecotone on hunter-gatherer mobility during the Pleistocene/Holocene transition.

Environmental Aspects

Cerro Casa de Piedra 7 (47° 57.322′ S, 72° 05.680′ W) lies 6 km east-southeast of Lago

[1] CONICET–INAPL 3 de Febrero 1378 (1426) Buenos Aires, Argentina. e-mail: mtcivalero@fibertel.com.ar

[2] CONICET–Instituto de Arqueologia. San Martín 1545 (4000) Tucumán, Argentina. e-mail: aschero@unt.edu.ar

Burmeister (Figure 1). According to Cabrera and Willink (1973), the area belongs to the Antarctic phytogeographical region, subantarctic domain and province, characterized by the presence of *Nothofagus* forest called "lengas." Nowadays the site is in transition between *Nothofagus* forest (*N. pumilio)* and shrub steppe. This ecotone is composed of shrub steppe and scattered spots of *Nothofagus* forest. Isolated patches of this species scattered on the foothills are generally medium size and usually have a shrub-like shape on hilltops. Perito Moreno National Park (PNPM), at ca. 900 m a.s.l. is one of the highest glacial basins in Santa Cruz province.

Climatic information for the region is available for the last 7000 years. Mancini et al.

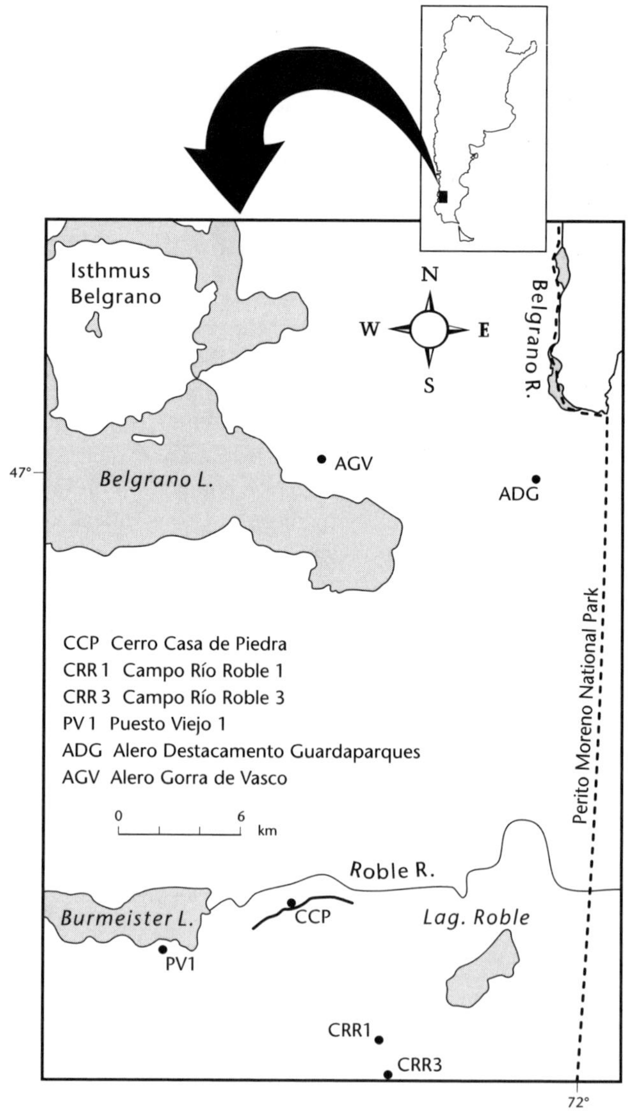

Figure 1. The study area in Burmeister Valley showing the position of CCP and other sites.

(1997) suggest the development of floral/vegetational scatters of *Nothofagus* forest, grass, and shrub steppe before 6500 yr B.P. Further studies of fossil pollen are needed to reconstruct the vegetation history before 7000 yr B.P. Mancini (1998) believes humidity levels reached their maximum in the early Holocene. A wet and cold climate is indicated by the expansion of *Nothofagus* forest in latitudes 50°–55° S and by increased levels in Cardiel Lake, about 150 km southeast of PNPM (Stine and Stine 1990), between 9800 and 7700 yr B.P. We can assume from this record that by 10,000 yr B.P. climatic conditions were wetter and colder than today.

Geomorphological studies suggest that Belgrano and Burmeister Lakes may be relict stages of a deep lake basin. According to González (1992), this paleolake would have reached a level 100 m higher than that of modern Belgrano Lake (800 m a.s.l.). Successive transgression pulses in this paleolake defined three different beach crests. The latest of these was dated ca. 2200 yr B.P. from carbonate (M. González pers. comm.). This date is regarded as the minimum chronological limit for the coastal transgressions; presently there is no way to determine the maximum limit for these events. González (1992) argues that the paleobasin was probably shaped by an increase in glacial activity in the eastern Andean foothills. The most significant transgression episodes probably did not last for long. From an archaeological point of view, however, resulting changes in the vegetation could have affected available space and access to resources.

Early Component in Cerro Casa de Piedra

Cerro Casa de Piedra is mainly a volcanic rhyolithic hill. There are several caves and rockshelters looking northwards, but only one of them, cave number 7 (CCP7), has yielded evidence dating to the Pleistocene/Holocene transition. During an early occupation, the rocky roof sheltered ca. 223 m^2 of space. However, rockfall episodes ca. 3400 yr B.P. sealed the west wing of the site and no later evidence could be recovered.

Studies of the west wing indicate the cave was inhabited during the early Holocene in recurrent extensive occupations. A stratigraphic sequence of 19 units has been defined (Figure 2). Radiocarbon dates indicate that between 9730 ± 100 yr B.P. (BETA 59925) and 3480 ± 70 yr B.P. (LP300) this cave was used by humans. Earlier occupations may be confirmed when materials from the top of stratigraphic unit 18 are dated. An area of 12.75 m^2 has been excavated, but only an area of 5.75 m^2 has reached down to level 18.

In this report we discuss the earliest levels of occupation, which span levels 15 to 18. They were chosen for their close chronological agreement and the uniformity of recovered materials and technological features.

Four radiocarbon dates were obtained (Figure 2): level 15, from wood, 9730 ± 100 yr B.P. (BETA 59925); level 16, from wood, 8920 ± 200 yr B.P. (UGA 7383); level 17, one from wood, 9640 ± 190 yr B.P. (UGA 7384), the other from charcoal, 9100 ± 150 yr B.P. (LP364). There is only one date with no human association, that of extinct herbivorous dung (S.Vizcaíno pers. comm.), 10,530 ± 620 yr B.P. (UGA 7385).

The cold and dry conditions in the cave favored the preservation of guanaco (*Lama guanicoe)* skin/hide, vegetable fiber, bones with periosteum, vein thread, and wooden artifacts. Faunal evidence includes guanaco bones with and without cut marks (M. De Nigris pers. comm.) and huemul bones (*Hippocamelus bisulcus).*

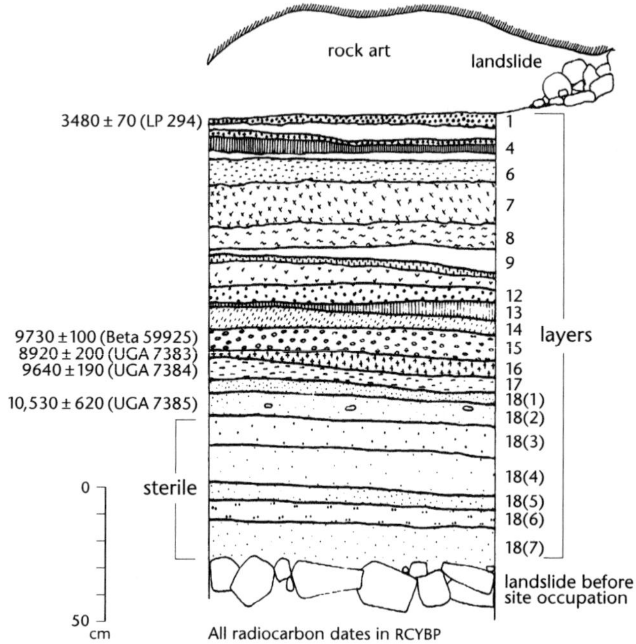

Figure 2. Stratigraphy of Cerro Casa de Piedra 7, with radiocarbon dates.

Lithic materials include retouched artifacts, unretouched flakes and cores made of obsidian, rhyolite, siliceous rocks, and basalt.

The assemblages show evidence of different raw materials collected from widely scattered sources at varying distances. For example, sources of obsidian and some siliceous rocks are found 35–40 km from the site. Stern (1999) points out that black obsidian artifacts were made from raw material from an area called "Pampa del Asador," 40 km to the east. Basalt sources are 25 km to the northeast; rhyolite sources are no farther than 5 km. Siliceous rocks come from the Alto Río Pinturas zone; they are readily available, but in general they were not used to make artifacts.

Obsidian and siliceous rocks were the most profitable raw materials for making retouched artifacts, called *versatile* design by Nelson (1991).

The lithic evidence includes only a few types of artifacts, most of them large endscrapers, scrapers, projectile points, and knives. Cores are also present, most of them exhausted.

In summary, lithic analysis indicates an assemblage representative of a broad manufacture technology. Tools are made of thick flakes: flake tools with unifacial marginally retouched edges such as endscrapers and scrapers; and flakes with natural edges with continuous damage (natural knives?) and exhausted cores. The bifacial technique is restricted to triangular projectile points and bifaces made of obsidian. Resharpening is evident in the points; some were resharpened when being shafted, indicated by the remaining mastic position.

We detected evidence of tendencies in lithic technology:

- *Versatile* designs, those that can be used for a variety of purposes and do not change in form (after Nelson 1991), are typified by retouched obsidian and siliceous rock artifacts. The sources of these raw materials are the most distant from the site.

- Artifacts of reliable design, those characterized by redundant functions that can perform different tasks and always work when needed (Nelson 1991), typified by the projectile points, are made of obsidian.
- Cores made of rocks from distant sources, rather than from nearby sources, are more abundant.
- Recycling is most evident on artifacts made of rocks from sources farthest from the site (implying highest gathering costs). This could be interpreted as a strategy for maximizing the life-use of tools made of rocks not available in the near vicinity. The recycled artifacts are endscrapers made of obsidian cores and siliceous rocks, as well as a big endscraper made from a siliceous core.
- Raw materials from the closest sources were worked expediently.
- Some of the initial occupations may be associated with paintings of guanaco and female huemul. This rock art, colored in red, shows dynamic scenes. The paintings are found in the most lighted sector of the rockshelter, belonging to group "A" (red series) from Cueva de Las Manos, Alto Río Pinturas (Gradín et al. 1976).

Our hypothesis is that exploring groups of highly mobile hunters were trying to find new resources in unknown territories (Borrero, 1989).

The chronology here obtained bears a close relationship with early levels from Cueva de Las Manos, which produced dates of 9320 ± 90 RCYBP (CSIC-138) and 9300 ± 90 RCYBP (CSIC-385) (Gradín et al. 1979), and Cueva Grande de Arroyo Feo, which dated to 9410 ± 70 RCYBP (CSIC-514) (Alonso et al. 1984–85). Both caves are located in Alto Río Pinturas.

We believe it is important to point out that early-Holocene hunter-gatherers were using the same obsidian source. Stern et al. (1995a, 1995b) and Stern (1999) verify the presence of one specific source area around Pampa del Asador, 40 km east of CCP7. Several artifacts made of black obsidian recovered at the earliest levels of archaeological sites located in central-south and southern Patagonia and dated ca. 10,000 yr B.P. show the same chemical composition as the Pampa del Asador source. This fact suggests that black obsidian has been circulating since early times in south Patagonia within a range of 500 km (Stern 1999). Taking into account the low population density (Borrero 1999) suggested for these early times, it is unlikely any group exercised control over the source. It is important to note the wide range of circulation these hunter-gatherers could have had exploring different environments during the Pleistocene-Holocene transition.

We believe this evidence attests to different *pulses* of exploration from the Central Plateau—the area yielding the most ancient dates in southern Patagonia—by groups that shared material cultural practices. New excavations and radiocarbon dates and a more precise comparison of our record with that recovered from Alto Río Pinturas and Central Plateau will fuel a rich discussion in these alternatives.

Acknowledgments

We are grateful to all students who helped in the Project, specially Antonella Divruno, Damián Bozzuto and Paula Limbrunner, for the technic supply. We also thank to Marcelo Torres, Gabriela Lublin, Vanina Dolce, Karen Borrazo and Natalia Revestido and the above mentioned for their help in the excavations at the CCP7 site. Leonardo Paulides help us in the translation of this paper. We thank Administración de Parques Nacionales

(Argentina). These works were supported by Consejo Nacional de Investigaciones Científicas y Tecnológicas (CONICET) projects "Variabilidad Temporal y Espacial en Sociedades Cazadoras-recolectoras del Ámbito Cordillerano Patagónico" and "Arqueología del Area Río Belgrano-Lago Posadas, Provincia de Santa Cruz " and to the Secretaría de Cultura de la Nación, through the Instituto Nacional de Antropología y Pensamiento Latinoamericano.

References Cited

Aguerre, A. M.

1981-82 Los Niveles Inferiores de la Cueva Grande (Arroyo Feo), Area Río Pinturas, Provincia de Santa Cruz. *Relaciones de la Sociedad Argentina de Antropología* XIV(2):211–239.

1987 Investigaciones Arqueológicas en el Area de La Martita, Dto. Magallanes, Provincia de Santa Cruz. *Comunicaciones de las Primeras Jornadas de Arqueología de la Patagonia, Serie Humanidades* 2:11–16. Gobierno de la Provincia de Santa Cruz. Dirección de Impresiones Oficiales, Rawson, Argentina.

1997 *Replanteo de la Industria Toldense, Arqueología de Patagonia Centro-Meridional.* Ph.D. Dissertation, Facultad de Filosofía y Letras, Universidad de Buenos Aires.

Alonso, F., C. Gradín, C. A. Aschero and A. M. Aguerre

1984–85 Algunas consideraciones sobre recientes dataciones radiocarbónicas para el área Río Pinturas, Provincia de Santa Cruz. *Relaciones de la Sociedad Argentina de Antropología* XVI NS, Buenos Aires.

Aschero, C. A.

1996a El Area Río Belgrano-Lago Posadas (Santa Cruz): Problemas y Estado de Problemas. In *Arqueología, Sólo Patagonia,* edited by Julieta Gómez Otero, pp. 17–26. Puerto Madryn, Argentina.

1996b ¿Dónde Van Esos Guanacos? In *Arqueología, Sólo Patagonia,* edited by Julieta Gómez Otero, pp. 153–162. Puerto Madryn, Argentina.

Aschero, C. A., C. Bellelli, M. T. Civalero de Biset, R. Goñi, G. Guráieb, and R. Molinari

1992 Cronología y Tecnología en el Parque Nacional Perito Moreno (PNPM): Continuidad o Reemplazos? *Arqueología* 2:89–106. Universidad de Buenos Aires.

Aschero, C. A., R. A. Goñi, M. T. Civalero, R. L. Molinari, S. Espinosa, A. G. Guráieb, and C. T. Bellelli

1998 Holocenic Park: Arqueología del Parque Nacional Perito Moreno. *Anales de Parques Nacionales No. XVII.* In press.

Borrero, L. A.

1989 Replanteo de la Arqueología Patagónica. *Interciencia* 14(3):107–135.

1999 The Prehistoric Exploration and Colonization of Fuego-Patagonia. *Journal of World Prehistory* 13(3):321–355.

Cabrera, A. L., and A. Willink

1973 *Biogeografía de América Latina.* Washington, Secretaría General de la Organización de los Estados Americanos. Monografía 13, Serie de Biología.

Cardich, A., and N. Flegenheimer

1978 Descripción y Tipología de las Industrias líticas más Antiguas de los Toldos. *Relaciones de la Sociedad Argentina de Antropología* XII:225–242. Buenos Aires.

Cardich, A., M. E. Mansur-Franchomme, M. Giesso, and V. Durán

1981-82 Arqueología de las Cuevas de El Ceibo. *Relaciones de la Sociedad Argentina de Antropología,* XIV(2):173–210. Buenos Aires.

Civalero, M. T.

1995 El Sitio Casa de Piedra 7: Algunos Aspectos de la Tecnología Lítica y las Estrategias de Movilidad. *Cuadernos del Instituto Nacional de Antropología,* 16:283–296. Buenos Aires. Argentina.

1999 Obsidiana en Santa Cruz, una Problemática a Resolver. In *Soplando en el Viento. Actas de las III Jornadas de Arqueología de la Patagonia*, pp. 155–164. Neuquén-Buenos Aires.

1999 Circulación, Aprovechamiento de Recursos Líticos y Estrategias de Diseño en el Sur Patagónico. *Arqueología* 10. Buenos Aires. in press.

González, M. A.
1992 Paleoambientes del Pleistoceno Tardío/Holoceno Temprano en la Cuenca de los Lagos Belgrano y Burmeister (47° 40'/48' Sur, 72° 30'Oeste), Santa Cruz. *Fundación Carl C:zon Caldenius. Informes Técnicos* 9:1–7. Buenos Aires.

Gradín, C. J., C. Aschero, and A. Aguerre
1976 Investigaciones Arqueológicas en la Cueva de las Manos, Estancia Alto Río Pinturas, Provincia. de Santa Cruz. *Relaciones de la Sociedad Argentina de Antropología* X:201–270. Buenos Aires.

1979 Arqueología del Area Río Pinturas (Provincia de Santa Cruz). *Relaciones de la Sociedad Argentina de Antropología* XIII:183–221. Buenos Aires.

Mancini, M. V.
1998 Vegetational Changes During the Holocene in Extra-Andean Patagonia, Santa Cruz Province, Argentina. *Palaeogeography, Palaeoclimatology, Palaeoecology* 138:207–219.

Mancini, M. V., M. M. Paez, and A. R. Prieto
1997 Vegetational History During the Last 7000 Years in the Steppe-forest Ecotone, Santa Cruz, Argentina. In *Southern Hemisphere Paleo and Neoclimates. Methods and Concepts*, edited by W. Volkheimer and Smolka. Cambridge University Press.

Miotti, L.
1996 Piedra Museo, Nuevos Datos para la Ocupación Pleistocénica en Patagonia. In *Arqueología, Sólo Patagonia*, edited by Julieta Gómez Otero, pp. 93–101. Puerto Madryn, Argentina.

Miotti, L., M. Vázquez, and D. Hermo
1999 Piedra Museo, un Yamnagoo Pleistocénico. In *Soplando en el Viento. Actas de las III Jornadas de Arqueología de la Patagonia*, pp. 113–136. Neuquén-Buenos Aires.

Nelson. M. C.
1991 The Study of Technological Organization. *Archaeological Method and Theory* 13:57–100.

Stern, C. R.
1999 Black Obsidian from Central-South Patagonia: Chemical Characteristics, Sources and Regional Distribution of Artifacts. In *Soplando en el Viento. Actas de las III Jornadas de Arqueología de la Patagonia*, pp. 221–234. Neuquén-Buenos Aires.

Stern, C., F. Mena, A. Aschero, and R. Goñi
1995a Obsidiana Negra de los Sitios Arqueológicos en la Precordillera Andina de Patagonia Central. In *Anales del Instituto de la Patagonia (Serie Ciencias Sociales)* 23:111–118. Punta Arenas, Chile.

Stern, Ch., A. Prieto, and N. V. Franco
1995b Obsidiana Negra en los Sitios Cazadores-recolectores Terrestres en Patagonia Austral. *Anales del Instituto de la Patagonia (Serie Ciencias Sociales)* 23:105–109. Punta Arenas, Chile.

Stine, G., and M. Stine
1990 A Record from Lake Cardiel of Climate Change in Southern South America. *Nature* 345:705–708.

Chorrillo Malo 2: Initial Peopling of the Upper Santa Cruz Basin, Argentina

Nora Viviana Franco[1] and Luis Alberto Borrero[2]

Chorrillo Malo 2 is a rockshelter located near Lago Roca, south of Lago Argentino (50° 30′ S, 72° 40′ W), ca. 200 m a.s.l., in southern Patagonia (Figure 1). The site is close to the Andean range at the foot of the Baguales Massif.

The climate of the area is continental, under strong influence of the Pacific anticyclone. It is cold and wet in the west, with transition to the arid climate of the steppe (Furque 1973). The vegetation is forest in the west, grass steppe with isolated shrubs at lower altitudes in the east, and Altoandean desert above 1000 m a.s.l. (Mancini 1998 and pers. comm. 2002; Pisano 1974).

A radiocarbon date of ca. 10,000 yr B.P. on the basal peat close to Brazo Rico (Stern 1990) suggests the area was already deglaciated and available for human occupation at that time. The Moreno glacier was basically at the same location that it is today (Mercer 1968).

The rockshelter is oriented southward and quite exposed to the wind. A test pit with an area of 2 x 1 m was excavated, reaching almost 1.7 m deep, where the presence of glacial till was recorded (Belardi et al. 1995; Favier Dubois 1995). The sedimentary sequence is composed of both autochthonous material from the weathering of the rockshelter, and allochthonous material deposited by wind and water circulation (Favier Dubois 1995). Fragments of rock, common in the stratigraphic sequence, are especially abundant at depths between 105 and 120 cm. Because their size makes it very difficult to work, the excavation area was reduced to 1 x 1 m.

A series of radiocarbon dates were obtained (Figure 2).

[1] Departamento de Investigaciones Prehistóricas y Arqueológicas (IMHICIHU) y Universidad de Buenos Aires. Saavedra 15, 5to. Piso, Buenos Aires (C.P.1039), Argentina. e-mail: nvfranco@ciudad.com.ar

[2] Departamento de Investigaciones Prehistóricas y Arqueológicas (IMHICIHU) y Universidad de Buenos Aires. Saavedra 15, 5to. Piso, Buenos Aires (C.P.1039), Argentina. e-mail: laborrero@hotmail.com

Figure 1. View of Chorrillo Malo 2 rockshelter.

- The lowest level that could be dated (150–155 cm below surface) has two radiocarbon dates: 9740 ± 50 RCYBP (GX-25279, AMS) on a splinter of guanaco (*Lama guanicoe*) humerus with evidence of cutmarks and a lateral blow, and 9690 ± 80 RCYBP (CAMS 71152, AMS) on a fragment of guanaco scapula with evidence of cutmarks and a lateral blow.
- A mixture of several guanaco bones found only 10 cm above these (i.e., 140–145 cm below surface) yielded a date of 4520 ± 70 RCYBP (Beta 82292). Considering the abundance of rocks along the sequence, the mixing of sediments, including bones, was likely. Under these conditions it was a mistake to submit this sample, consisting of several bones, that may represent multiple ages.
- A guanaco proximal radius-ulna with evidence of cutmarks found 115–120 cm below surface was dated at 6170 ± 50 RCYBP (CAMS 71153, AMS). Within this level, as we already mentioned, there are abundant rocks.

Above them, two dates were obtained, one of 3790 ± 80 RCYBP (Beta 148743, AMS) for a splinter of guanaco humerus with evidence of cutmarks and a lateral blow (85–90 cm below surface), and another of 1950 ± 60 RCYBP (LP-502) for flecks of vegetable charcoal obtained 75–85 cm below surface. The laboratory advises regarding the latter date with caution owing to the small sample size.

Taking these results into account, we focus here on the lowest part of the sequence, with dates between ca. 9700 and 6100 RCYBP. Palynological analysis shows the presence of a gramineous steppe with Poaceae, Cyperaceae and Fabaceae, changing to Asteraceae, Tubuliflorae, *Mulinum,* and Solanaceae shrubs above a depth of 140–145 cm (Mancini 1999).

Lithic artifacts and faunal remains are present all along the sequence. The only artifact recovered below the depth dated ca. 9700 RCYBP was black obsidian debitage. XRF and

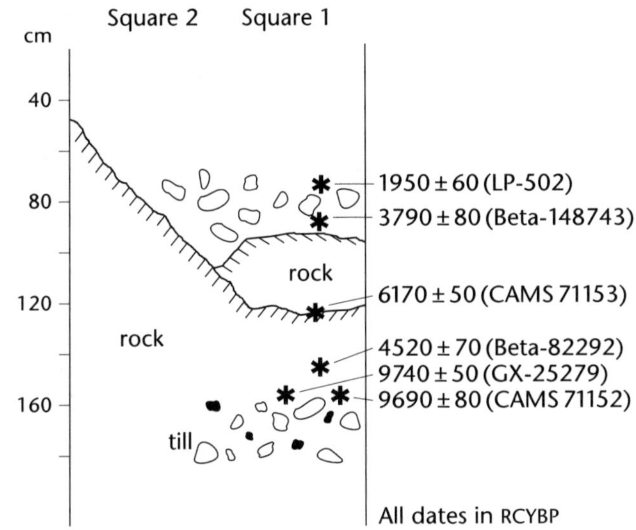

Figure 2. Stratigraphy of Chorrillo Malo 2.

neutron activation analysis identify its provenience as Pampa del Asador, more than 260 km to the north (Stern 1999; Stern pers. comm. 1999). We believe this obsidian was part of the toolkit transported by early populations. Its presence at other sites of the region is dated ca. 3000 yr B.P. (Carballo Marina et al. 1999).

Only one tool was recovered from the lower part of the sequence dated 9700–6100 yr B.P. It is a short, thick bifacially retouched point made of immediately available green dacite with macroscopic traces of damage. Flakes and debitage of immediately available and local rocks (sensu Meltzer 1989) were also recovered. Immediately available dacite and porphyry are present in the oldest deposits. Among the local raw materials we note the presence of chalcedony, basalt, and dacite of very good quality, trydimite, and banded gray-green obsidian, the latter probably coming from the Baguales range (Stern and Franco 2000). Most of the artifacts are very small. Flakes from multidirectional cores are the most common ones. There are also flakes from bifacial reduction, resharpening, and core rejuvenation. Ocher is also present.

No remains of extinct fauna were found at the site. Guanaco is the only recorded food resource. Fragments, splinters, and basically appendicular parts were recovered at these deposits. Many of them display evidence of cutmarks and lateral blows. Flecks of charcoal as well as small fragments of burned bones are also present. Rodent bones have also been recovered at the lower levels.

The importance of this site is that, owing to its location near the Andean range, it probably records the initial occupations of the Upper Santa Cruz Basin. We plan to continue work at the site, extending the surface of the excavation, while pursuing the radiocarbon-dating program together with technological and faunal analysis.

Acknowledgments

We wish to thank Dr. Tom Brown, from the Center for Accelerator Mass Spectrometry, Lawrence Livermore National Laboratory, and Dr. Scott Stine for dates CAMS 71152 and 71153. This work was financed by

CONICET (project "Magallania"), Agencia Nacional de Promoción Científica y Técnica (PICT 97 No. 04-00000-00807), and Universidad de Buenos Aires (UBACyT Fi 141 and F133).

References Cited

Belardi, J. B., N. V. Franco, and L. A. Borrero

1995 Informe de las Tareas Realizadas en el Sitio Chorrillo Malo 2 (área de Lago Roca, Lago Argentino). Unpublished report for Administración de Parques Nacionales.

Carballo Marina, F., L. A. Borrero, N. V. Franco, J. B. Belardi, V. D. Horwitz, A. S. Muñoz, P. Campan, F. M. Martin, F. Borella, M. F. García, F. Muñoz, F. Savanti, and J. L. Lanata

1999 Arqueología de la Costa del Lago Argentino, Río La Leona y Pampas Altas Intermedias (Provincia de Santa Cruz, Argentina). *Praehistoria* 3:13–33. Buenos Aires, Argentina.

Favier Dubois, C.

1995 Aproximación Geoarqueológica a los Estudios de Formación de Sitio. Análisis de Casos en Fuego-Patagonia. Tesis de Licenciatura. Universidad de Buenos Aires.

Furque, G.

1973 Descripción Geológica de la Hoja 58b, Lago Argentino. Provincia de Santa Cruz. Carta Geológica de la Hoja 58b, Lago Argentino. *Boletín* 140, *Servicio Nacional Minero Geológico*. Buenos Aires, Argentina.

Mancini, M. V.

1998 Vegetational Changes during the Holocene in Extra-Andean Patagonia, Santa Cruz Province, Argentina. *Palaeogeography, Palaeoclimatology, Palaeoecology* 138:207–219.

1999 Cambios de la Vegetación y del Clima durante los Últimos 5000 Años en el Área del Lago Argentino, Santa Cruz. X Simposio Argentino de Paleobotánica y Palinología. *Asociación Paleontológica Argentina, Publicación Especial* 6, pp. 49–53. Buenos Aires, Argentina.

Meltzer, D.

1989 Was Stone Exchanged among Eastern North American Paleoindians? In *Eastern Paleoindian Lithic Resource Use*, edited by C. J. Ellis and J. Lothrop, pp. 11–39. Westview Press, Boulder, CO.

Mercer, J.

1968 Variations of Some Patagonian Glaciers since the Late-Glacial: I. *American Journal of Science* 266:91–109.

Pisano, E.

1974 Estudio Ecológico de la Región Continental Sur del Área Andino-Patagónica. II Contribución a la Fitogeografía de la Zona del Parque Nacional Torres del Paine. *Anales del Instituto de la Patagonia* 5(1-2):59–104. Punta Arenas, Chile.

Stern, C. R.

1990 Tephrochronology of Southernmost Patagonia. *National Geographic Research* 6:110–126.

1999 Black Obsidian from Central-south Patagonia; Chemical Characteristics, Sources and Regional Distribution of Artifacts. In *Soplando en el Viento. Actas de las III Jornadas de Arqueología de la Patagonia*, pp. 221–234. Instituto Nacional de Antropología y Pensamiento Latinoamericano and Facultad de Humanidades de la Universidad Nacional del Comahue. Neuquén–Buenos Aires, Argentina.

Stern, C. R., and N. V. Franco

2000 Obsidiana Gris Verdosa Veteada de la Cuenca Superior del Río Santa Cruz, Extremo Sur de Patagonia. *Anales del Instituto de la Patagonia* (Serie Cs. Hs.) 28:265–273. Punta Arenas, Chile.

Fell 1 Hunters' Hearths in the Magallanes Region by the End of the Pleistocene

Mauricio Massone

Background

Five archaeological sites in the Magallanes region of uttermost Chile have yielded evidence of human hunters of extinct and modern fauna. Radiocarbon datings range from ca. 8600 to 12,400 RCYBP. The sites are Fell Cave and Pali Aike Cave, both located in the Pali Aike volcanic area; the Tres Arroyos cave in Tierra del Fuego; and the Cueva del Medio and Lago Sofía caves in the Última Esperanza area (Figure 1). Research at these sites has been pursued by scientists over the decades (Bate 1982; Bird 1938, 1946, 1951, 1988; Emperaire et al. 1963; Massone 1981, 1983, 1987, 1996, 1999; Massone et al. 1998; Nami 1985–86, 1987, 1994; Nami and Menegaz 1991; Nami and Nakamura 1995; Prieto 1991).

These early cultural contexts associated with Fell 1 hunter-gatherers demonstrate a relationship among cultural remains, extinct Pleistocene fauna, basin hearths, and the manufacture of certain lithic artifacts, such as distinctive "fishtail" projectile points, large discoidal stones, huge endscrapers, sidescrapers, and stone pieces for polishing artifacts. The use of red pigments and the development of a bone-based technology using bird bone epiphyses and diaphyses can also be considered part of the assemblages. These bird bones have been cross-cut to create end-sided bony ornaments and pressure flakers for working lithic artifacts.

The diet was mainly based on American native horse and guanaco, complemented with other animals such as extinct Camelidae, Canidae, birds, and sometimes ground sloth (*Mylodon* sp.), and possibly various vegetables (Massone and Prieto, in press).

Research has focused on such site archaeological contexts as lithic and bone technology, raw materials, faunal remains, *chaînes opératoires,* chronological considerations, and the relationship between contexts and the local or regional paleoenvironment. However, research on hearths

Museo de Historia Natural de Concepción, casilla 1054, Concepción, Chile. e-mail: mmassone@surnet.cl

Figure 1. Fell 1 sites in the Magallanes region.

used by early hunters at campsites in southern Patagonia, where household activities were carried out, is still pending. This report presents a comparative analysis of fire preparation patterns, the organization of burning spaces with respect to nearby areas, and activities associated with artifacts and ecofacts. It discusses the sites assigned to Magallanes Fell 1 groups.

Fire Hearth Analysis

A total of 19 hearths at 5 sites in the Magallanes region were studied, all related to Fell 1 contexts: 7 hearths at Fell Cave, 2 at Pali Aike cave, 5 at Tres Arroyos, 4 at Cueva del Medio, and one at Lago Sofía. Our study analyzed the size and shape of hearths, the cultural and ecofact content of internal and external hearths, and radiocarbon dates on charcoal and bone from hearths. In addition, taxon dates from bone pieces have been selected in order to state ages for different species.

Size

The maximum diameter of hearths ranges from 94 to 31 cm. Of 19 hearths, 11 (57.9 percent) have a maximum diameter of 31–55 cm; one hearth (5.3 percent) has a diameter greater than 55 cm; no information is available on the diameter of the other 7 hearths (36.8 percent).

Depth ranges from 5 to 12.7 cm, measured from the ground surface at that time. Of 19 hearths, 8 (42.1 percent) have a depth of 10–12.7 cm; 5 (26.3 percent) have a depth of 5–7 cm; no information is available on the depth of the other 6 hearths (31.6 percent).

Shape

The shape of the hearths studied in all sites varies from deep circular or semicircular vats to enlarged and shallow vats. A large and uneven coal stain, larger than the vats found at Fell Cave, is the single exception (Bird 1988).

Content

Of 19 hearths studied, 17 (89.5 percent) contained remains of extinct fauna; 12 (63.2 percent) contained remains of modern fauna; 16 (84.2 percent) contained lithic material. Regarding faunal remains found inside and near the hearths, the American native horse was present in 12 hearths (63.2 percent), *Mylodon* sp. in 10 (52.6 percent); *Lama* sp. in 9 (47.4 percent); and Canidae in 4 (21.1 percent).

The horse-*Mylodon* sp. association was found in 10 hearths (52.6 percent), the horse-*Lama* sp. association in 6 (31.6 percent), and the horse-Canidae association in 3 (15.8 percent).

Lithic raw materials

Using data compiled from hearths 3, 4, and 5 of the Tres Arroyos cave in Tierra del Fuego, we can compare the raw materials and distribution of lithic artifacts found within and near the hearths.

Hearth 3 contained 20 artifacts of dacitoid tuff (43.5 percent), 14 of rhyolitic tuff (30.4 percent), 9 of petrified wood (19.6 percent), one of flint (2.2 percent), and 2 of unidentified material. Hearth 3 was dated at 10,580 ± 50 RCYBP (Beta 113171) by a charcoal sample dated by the AMS method.

Hearth 4 contained 54 pieces of dacitoid tuff (42.5 percent), 36 pieces of flint (28.3 percent), 18 pieces each of rhyolitic tuff and petrified wood (14.2 percent each), and one piece of unidentified material (0.8 percent). Hearth 4 was dated at 10,130 ± 210 RCYBP (OxA-9666) by a charcoal sample dated by the standard ^{14}C method.

Hearth 5 contained 17 artifacts of petrified wood (42.5 percent), 15 of dacitoid tuff (37.5 percent), 4 of flint (10 percent), 3 of rhyolitic tuff (7.5 percent) and one of unidentified material (2.5 percent). No dating has been obtained for this fire hearth yet.

Chronology

Of 36 radiocarbon dates compiled for the five sites in Fell 1 context (Table 1), 30 of these dates (83.3 percent) fall between 10,080 ± 160 RCYBP (I 5146) and 11,120 ± 130 RCYBP (NUTA 1737); 3 dates (8.3 percent) fall between 11,570 ± 60 RCYBP (PITT-0684) and 12,390 ± 180 RCYBP (PITT-0343); 3 dates (8.3 percent) fall between 8639 ± 450 RCYBP (C 485) and 9770 ± 70 RCYBP (Beta 40281) (Massone and Prieto in press). A total of 19 radiocarbon dates were obtained either directly from hearth charcoal or from bone remains (taxon dates by the AMS method) found inside or around the hearths; 15 of these dates (78.9 percent) fall between 10,130 ± 210 RCYBP (OxA-9666) and 11,040 ± 250 RCYBP (NUTA-2197).

Conclusions

Our analysis of 19 hearths in 5 sites, which yielded evidence of Fell 1 hunter activities in the Magallanes region during the late Pleistocene and the Pleistocene/Holocene transition, suggests recognizable patterns in preparing hearths and in contextual relationships.

Hearths of Fell 1 groups were prepared by digging a circular or semicircular cavity in the

Table 1. Radiocarbon dates of Fell 1 occupation sites (Massone and Prieto, in press).

Site	Material	^{14}C age (RCYBP)	Lab no.	Reference
Fell's Cave				Bird 1988
	charcoal	10,720 ± 300	W 915	
	charcoal	11,000 ± 170	I 988	
	charcoal, end of Period I (beginning of Period II?)	10,080 ± 160	I 5146	
Pali Aike				Bird 1951
	bones	8639 ± 450	C 485	
Tres Arroyos 1				Massone 1983, 1987; Massone et al. 1998; Massone and Prieto in press)
	bones	10,280 ± 110	Dic. 2732	
	bones	10,420 ± 100	Dic. 2733	
	bones, hearth 1	11,880 ± 250	Beta 20219	
	charcoal (AMS), hearth 2	10,600 ± 90	Beta 101023	
	charcoal (AMS), hearth 3	10,580 ± 50	Beta 113171	
	Dusicyon avus (AMS)	10,575 ± 65	OxA-9245	
	Vicugna sp. (AMS)	10,630 ± 70	OxA-9246	
	Hippidion sp. (AMS)	10,685 ± 70	OxA-9247	
	Panthera onca (AMS)	11,085 ± 70	OxA-9248	
	charcoal, hearth 4	10,130 ± 210	OxA-9666	
Cueva del Medio				Nami 1987; Nami and Nakamura 1995
	charcoal, hearth 3	9595 ± 115	PITT-0344	
	bone	9770 ± 70	Beta 40281	
	charcoal, hearth 2	10,310 ± 70	Gr-N 14913	
	burned bone, hearth 1	10,350 ± 130	Beta 58105	
	charcoal	10,430 ± 80	Beta 52522	
	burned bone, hearth 1	10,550 ± 120	Gr-N 14911	
	Hippidion saldiasi (AMS)	10,710 ± 100	NUTA-1811	
	charcoal	10,930 ± 230	Beta 39081	
	burned bone, hearth 1	12,390 ± 180	PITT-0343	
	Hippidion saldiasi (AMS), hearth 1	10,860 ± 160	NUTA-2331	
	Lama cf. *owenii* (AMS), hearth 1	11,040 ± 250	NUTA-2197	
	Lama cf. *owenii* (AMS), hearth 1	10,430 ± 100	NUTA-1734	
	Lama cf. owenii (AMS)	11,120 ± 130	NUTA-1737	
	Lama cf. owenii (AMS)	10,960 ± 150	NUTA-2330	
	Lama guanicoe (AMS)	10,450 ± 100	NUTA-1735	
	Lama guanicoe (AMS)	10,710 ± 190	NUTA-2332	
	Lama guanicoe (AMS)	10,850 ± 130	NUTA-1812	
Lago Sofía 1				Prieto 1991; Massone and Prieto in press
	charcoal, hearth	11,570 ± 60	PITT-0684	
	Lama guanicoe (AMS), hearth	10,710 ± 70	OxA-8635	
	Onohippidion saldiasi (AMS)	10,780 ± 60	OxA-9319	
	Onohippidion saldiasi (AMS)	10,310 ± 160	OxA-9504	
	Pseudalopex culpaeus (AMS)	10,140 ± 120	OxA-9505	

ground. Size generally ranged from 55 to 31 cm in diameter and from 5 to 13 cm deep, measured from the existing surface. Rocks were rarely used to construct hearths, although an instance of basalt blocks surrounding a fire hearth has been mentioned for Fell Cave (Emperaire et al. 1963); next to the edge of hearth 3 at Tres Arroyos cave, a sandstone block was found with one smoked and soot-covered surface (Massone et al. 1998).

Extinct and modern fauna, lithic artifacts, and bone objects are materials usually found with hearths.

Extinct fauna species most frequently found associated with hearths are the American native horse (*Hippidion* sp./ *Onohippidium* sp.) and ground sloth (*Mylodon* sp); remains of modern and extinct camelids (*Lama guanicoe* and *Lama* sp.) and canids are also significant. *Mylodon* sp. remains, sometimes partially burned, were found in the context of 10 hearths (52.6 percent). This is quite surprising, and perhaps the evidence argues against Saxon's statement (1976) that *Mylodon* sp. would not have been hunted in southern Patagonia. However, the association between horse and *Mylodon* sp. remains in 10 hearths (52.6 percent) is interesting, as well as the association between Camelidae, mainly guanaco (*Lama guanicoe*), and *Mylodon* sp. in 6 hearths (31.6 percent). These associations are especially significant, since all scientists who have dealt with this issue agree that the American native horse and the Camelidae were regularly hunted by Fell 1 groups, as indicated by evidence of cutmarks and burned areas on some bones.

It has been stated that flintknapping for tool manufacturing was often done close to hearths. Our study found lithic materials inside or close to 16 hearths (84.2 percent). Various flakes found at Tres Arroyos cave also bore traces of soot.

Analysis of lithic artifacts at Tres Arroyos cave makes it possible to determine which raw materials were chosen when tools were made close to hearths. Dacitoid and rhyolitic tuff are the principal materials flaked by hearth 3; dacitoid tuff and flint were mostly used by hearth 4; and petrified wood and dacitoid tuff were mostly used by hearth 5. Such differences may signify either different activity events or different preferences during the same activity; at present we do not have enough dates for the various hearths or other evidence to defend either hypothesis. The choice of raw material varied in the case of the remaining sites. The use of basalt and siliceous materials stands out at a Fell cave; basalt is also found at Pali Aike; tuffs and vulcanite prevail at Cueva del Medio; and tuff and shale are found at the Lago Sofía site (Bird 1988; Nami 1987; Prieto 1991). All these cases show us that the priority of Fell 1 groups was the use of local lithic resources.

Finally, it is important to note the use and discard of bone objects close to the hearths. Both Tres Arroyos and Cueva del Medio show evidence of the use of bird bone pieces cross-cut to produce ornaments (Massone 1988; Nami 1987); end and side pressure flakers made from the diaphyses of guanaco *(Lama guanicoe)* bones have been found in Cueva del Medio and Lago Sofía (Jackson 1989–90).

This study was based on data from research carried out over the years on early hunters in the Magallanes region. These data, obtained by using various on-site methodologies and referring to different records, have proved useful in launching a program of comparative research whose purpose is to learn more about the relationship between fire and Fell 1 hunters in far southern Patagonia and Tierra del Fuego. After all, an important part of their lives took place around fires burning in their homes.

References Cited

Bate, L.

1982 *Orígenes de la Comunidad Primitiva en Patagonia.* Escuela Nacional de Antropología e Historia, México DF.

Bird, J.

1938 Antiquity and Migrations of the Early Inhabitants of Patagonia. *The Geographical Review* 28(2):250–275.

1946 The Archaeology of Patagonia. *Handbook of South American Indians, Bureau of American Ethnology Bulletin* 143(1):17–29, Washington, D.C.

1951 South American Radiocarbon Dates. *Memoirs* 8:37–49 Society for American Archaeology, Salt Lake City, UT.

1988 *Travels and Archaeology in South Chile,* J. Hyslop, editor. University of Iowa Press, Iowa City, IA.

Emperaire J., A. Laming-Emperaire, and H. Reichlen

1963 La Grotte Fell et Autres Sites de la Region Volcanique de la Patagonie Chilienne. *Journal de la Societé des Americanistes* 52:167–254.

Jackson, D.

1989–90 Retocadores Extremo-laterales en Contextos Paleo-indios. *Anales del Instituto de la Patagonia* 19:121–124, Serie Ciencias Sociales, Punta Arenas, Chile.

Massone, M.

1981 Arqueología de la Región Volcánica de Pali Aike (Patagonia Meridional Chilena). *Anales del Instituto de la Patagonia* 12:95–124. Punta Arenas, Chile.

1983 10,400 Años de Colonización Humana en Tierra del Fuego. *Infórmese* III(14):24–32. Punta Arenas, Chile.

1987 Los Cazadores Paleoindios de Tres Arroyos (Tierra del Fuego). *Anales del Instituto de la Patagonia* 17:47–60. Punta Arenas, Chile.

1988 Artefactos Óseos del Yacimiento Arqueológico Tres Arroyos (Tierra del Fuego). *Anales del Instituto de la Patagonia* 18:107–112. Punta Arenas, Chile.

1996 Hombre Temprano y Paleoambiente en la Región de Magallanes: Evaluación Crítica y Perspectivas. *Anales del Instituto de la Patagonia* 24:81–98. Punta Arenas, Chile.

1999 Aproximación Metodológica al Estudio de las Ocupaciones Tempranas de Cazadores Terrestres en la Región de Magallanes. *Soplando en el Viento. Actas de las III Jornadas de Arqueología de la Patagonia,* pp. 99–112. Universidad Nacional del Comahue and Instituto Nacional de Antropologia y Pensamiento Latinoamericano, Neuquén-Buenos Aires, Argentina.

Massone, M., and A. Prieto

2003 Evaluación de la Modalidad Cultural Fell 1 en Magallanes. *Actas del XV Congreso Nacional de Arqueología Chilena*, Arica, Chile. In press.

Massone, M., A. Prieto, D. Jackson, G. Cárdenas, M. Arroyo, and P. Cárdenas

1998 Los Cazadores Tempranos y Sus Fogatas: Una Nueva Historia para la Cueva Tres Arroyos 1, Tierra del Fuego. *Boletín de la Sociedad Chilena de Arqueología* 26:11–18. Santiago, Chile.

Nami, H.

1985–86 Excavación Arqueológica y Hallazgo de una Punta de Proyectil Fell I en la Cueva del Medio. Seno de Última Esperanza, Chile. *Anales del Instituto de la Patagonia* 16:103–109, Punta Arenas, Chile.

1987 Cueva del Medio: Perspectivas Arqueológicas para la Patagonia Austral. *Anales del Instituto de la Patagonia* 17:73–106. Punta Arenas, Chile.

1994 Reseña sobre los Avances de la Arqueología Finipleistocénica del Extremo Sur de Sudamérica. *Chungara* 26-2:145–163. Arica, Chile.

Nami, H., and A. Menegaz
1991 Cueva del Medio: Aportes para el Conocimiento de la Diversidad Faunística hacia el Pleistoceno-Holoceno en Patagonia Austral. *Anales del Instituto de la Patagonia* 20:117–132. Punta Arenas, Chile.

Nami, H., and T. Nakamura
1995 Cronología Radiocarbónica con AMS sobre Muestras de Huesos Procedentes del Sitio Cueva del Medio (Última Esperanza, Chile). *Anales del Instituto de la Patagonia* 23:125–133. Punta Arenas, Chile.

Prieto, A.
1991 Cazadores Tempranos y Tardíos en cueva del Lago Sofía 1. *Anales del Instituto de la Patagonia* 20:75–99. Punta Arenas, Chile.

Saxon, E.
1976 La Prehistoria de Fuego-Patagonia: Colonización de un Hábitat Marginal. *Anales del Instituto de la Patagonia* 7:63–73. Punta Arenas, Chile.

Index